CASHING IN
ON CRIME

CASHING IN
ON CRIME

The Drive to Privatize California State Prisons

Karyl Kicenski

FIRST**FORUM**PRESS

A DIVISION OF LYNNE RIENNER PUBLISHERS, INC. • BOULDER & LONDON

Published in the United States of America in 2014 by
FirstForumPress
A division of Lynne Rienner Publishers, Inc.
1800 30th Street, Boulder, Colorado 80301
www.firstforumpress.com
www.rienner.com

and in the United Kingdom by
FirstForumPress
A division of Lynne Rienner Publishers, Inc.
3 Henrietta Street, Covent Garden, London WC2E 8LU

Library of Congress Cataloging-in-Publication Data
Kicenski, Karyl.
 Cashing in on crime: the drive to privatize California state prisons /
Karyl Kicenski.
 Includes bibliographical references and index.
 ISBN 978-1-935049-61-6 (hc : alk. paper)
 1. Prison-industrial complex—California. 2. Prison industries—California.
3. Prisons—California. 4. Corrections—California. 5. Privatization—California. I. Title.
HV9475.C2K53 2014
365'.9794—dc23   2013029730

British Cataloguing in Publication Data
A Cataloguing in Publication record for this book
is available from the British Library.

This book was produced from digital files prepared by the author
using the FirstForumComposer.

Printed and bound in the United States of America

∞   The paper used in this publication meets the requirements
    of the American National Standard for Permanence of
    Paper for Printed Library Materials Z39.48-1992.

5 4 3 2 1

To a world that works for everyone
and
To the consciousness that might bring it forth

Contents

Acknowledgments

The idea for this book came from an article I read in the 1990s in *Covert Action Quarterly*. From that inspiration, I worked for years to construct an insightful analysis of the ramifications of prison privatization by playing with the intersections of the work of Karl Marx, Michel Foucault, and the Centre for Contemporary Cultural Studies, Birmingham. I am thankful not only to those visionary thinkers, but also to those who have helped me through the process of evaluating and teasing out the arguments made within this book.

I am grateful to the University of California, Los Angeles, for its excellent and accessible Charles E. Young Research Library, as well as the Hugh and Hazel Darling Law Library. Both resources helped improve the quality of data and depth of this book. Jane Bitar, Christie Bliss, and Pia Svenson provided me with invaluable administrative support and make joining the Department of Communication Studies a pure joy. I must also thank my dedicated student research assistants—Lotus Fung, Samantha Taylor, and Monica de Leon—who helped to locate obscure statistics, check criminal justice facts, and substantiate claims advanced in the work. In addition, I am indebted to the rich support from friends and colleagues at my beloved College of the Canyons (COC). Victoria Leonard, Patricia Robinson, David Stevenson, and Michael Leach provided encouragement throughout the researching and writing of the book. I am so lucky to call COC my home.

I owe a huge debt of gratitude to my dear friend Peter Martson, who inspired me to turn my research into a book manuscript. He helped shape the original book proposal and talked me through countless issues, from the publishing process to questions about how to construct better arguments. Every page of this work is marked with his support, concern, and kindness.

I wish to thank Floyd Moos, whose copyediting skills curbed my tendencies to be at times overly ambiguous and grammatically chaotic. His guidance and feedback on early versions of the text have been invaluable. If the writing is at all compelling, it is due in large part to his careful and loving attention to detail.

I am grateful to one of my longtime mentors, Christie Logan, who provided feedback on chapters and encouragement to stay focused. Her love and belief in me means more than I can articulate here.

I am so blessed to have had the counsel and critical eye of several amazing friends who graciously offered feedback on chapter ideas, writing, and arguments in the work: Marc Chambers, Russell Richardson, and Jessica Baty. Also, Ben Attias was a savior to me on so many levels in the midst of writing the manuscript. He was there when the idea for this work was born back in 1996 and has been a "go-to" person for more challenges than I can list here. GiGi Hessamian devoted tireless help with formatting issues and editing, and she talked me off the ledge when I simply wanted to quit. Her friendship keeps me sane and is such a precious gift. Randi Picarelli's questions and comments on several chapters of the manuscript offered insightful ideas to substantiate claims I advanced, and her care for this book project has inspired me over several years. Each of these people has nourished me with deep love, laughter, and support—I could never thank you in the way my heart feels your brilliance.

My editor at FirstForumPress, Andrew Berzanskis, has been kind, helpful, and always willing to assist me over the course of the publishing process. In fact, I am thankful to Andrew for originally contacting me and offering the manuscript a home. It was his curiosity and diligence that ignited the flame for the final product you hold in your hands.

It wouldn't make sense if I did not acknowledge the Agape International Spiritual Center, Reverend Coco Stewart, and members of the Joel S. Goldsmith cohort. I have changed by virtue of their influence—and the aim of this book has come forward through our interaction. The writing of the manuscript was a process of recognizing the oneness of all things. The very heart, the purpose of this book, has been fed by the wisdom-presence that motivates that Truth. I can never fully express my gratitude for that awareness—one fueled in part by the people at Agape.

Finally, I must thank my family—especially my mother and brother—who give me the unconditional love and gentle patience that anchors my strength. They enable my belief that I can make contributions to this world that matter. I love them so.

1

The Emergence of Private Prisons

A few years ago in a small county in Pennsylvania, fourteen-year-old Phillip Swartley attended a slumber party where he was getting into mischief, engaging in a bit of petty crime. Caught by the police rifling through unlocked cars for change and incidentals, he was arrested and eventually appeared before Judge Mark Ciavarella. Swartley was charged with a misdemeanor that his mother guessed would be punished with a modest fine or perhaps some type of community service. She could then discipline him later on her own terms. But what Swartley and his mother could not have known then was that Judge Ciavarella was receiving kick-backs from a private prison facility of approximately $2.6 million in exchange for rulings that favored detention for juveniles at that facility. In all, the boy stole some change and a prepaid cell phone that night, but in the end he was led out of the courtroom in shackles and deposited into a youth detention center and later a boarding school for at-risk youth for almost a year. After the crimes of Ciavarella were uncovered, it was discovered Swartley was one of at least 5,000 juveniles who appeared before the judge in a five-year period.

The story of Judge Ciavarella and Phillip Swartley goes to the heart of questions surrounding the privatization of public prisons, the growth and entrenchment of markets that center around incarceration, and the manner in which these markets become profitable.[1]

Since the 1980s, private corporations have increasingly assumed the responsibility for housing exploding numbers of state and federal inmates across the United States. Part of the reason for this phenomenon is the expansion of the country's prison institutions, which have experienced the most rapid and sustained increase in prisoners ever recorded since their birth in the nineteenth century. Between 1973 and 1997, the number of people behind bars rose more than 500 percent and today, state and federal prisons along with local jails house more than 2.2 million inmates—approximately one in every 131 U.S. residents.[2]

As a result of this increase, one of the most significant current trends in American criminology is the continuing growth and expansion of what has been called the "prison market," "the corrections commercial complex,"[3] or the "prison industrial-complex" (PIC).

The PIC has been defined as the diverse set of interest groups who do business with correctional facilities. But it has also referred to the larger confluence of government interests and private companies that have a vested interest in the capital produced by the punishment "industry," over and above the rehabilitation for inmates or the reduction of crime.[4] In simple terms, the prison market consists of a burgeoning set of businesses that profit not only on contracts to provide for the provision of goods and services needed by penal institutions (e.g. food, education, healthcare), but also on building new prison facilities, managing prison operations and selling inmate labor. Making large-scale profits from incarcerated inmates, however, is a relatively new enterprise.

Historically, most state and federal prisons were self-sufficient until the mid-1930s when prison inmates produced the food and goods they needed to survive for themselves.[5] While they did sell off a portion of what they produced and were often put to work to produce industrial goods that generated a profit, the notion of imprisonment as a purely "for-profit" industry in itself simply has no modern precedence. Today, the profits made by employing inmate labor are often touted as a prudent side-effect of offering the prisoner vocational training or even rehabilitation; however, there is little, if any, compelling evidence supporting this claim. When one examines the types of jobs inmates take—typically low-skill, labor intensive, repetitive tasks—the closest comparison to actual work available in the American job market might be positions being exported overseas to our global neighbors.

But profits for this prison industrial complex are not just made on inmate labor. Selling products and services to corrections departments that cater to prison populations is also a lucrative investment. Today, businesses offer everything from biometric identification systems, suicide resistant toilets, prison management teams to even the simple pay phone—which can generate up to $15,000 per year.[6] Many times these products or services are chosen on the basis of the company "kick-backs" made available to corrections departments, as opposed to what is economically prudent or most appropriate for inmates. In other words, contracts are awarded to certain companies depending upon the volume of "benefits" allotted back to the department itself. Phone service companies, for example, have often agreed to give a portion of profits back to corrections facilities for exclusive rights to provide lines for inmates. Here then corrections departments, not just private, for-profit companies, become implicated in the commodification of prisoners. When state corrections departments are allotted in excess of 10 billion dollars a year, corporate interests, small-time entrepreneurs, union officials and others take notice. Evidently, not since the convict-leasing program of the post-slavery era has there been such a developed system of mining wealth from those legally sentenced to prison.[7]

But as we saw above, the profitability of the prison market becomes not only complicated but also particularly disturbing when viewed as a symbiotic relationship between government officials and/or their appointees and private enterprise.

Public Versus Private?

Whether profits are produced by selling products that cater to inmate populations or privatizing whole prisons, we are pressed to ask whether partnerships between private firms and government bodies undermine the capacity for the state to fairly and adequately protect the general welfare—particularly in the face of seductive opportunities to gain financially from the miscarriage of such a duty. There are plenty of situations where such a question might be relevant. For instance, how do decisions about who should care for inmates (unionized guards or simple unregulated wage labor), what legal sentences inmates should serve (indeterminate sentences or fixed time for particular crimes), or what should count as a prior infraction for determining penalty alter the population of offenders or the cost to care for those offenders? Analyzing the relations within and between the public and private spheres is in many ways examining the modes through which the "prison market" becomes lucrative—in other words, how it becomes a market at all. It urges us to consider for whom it becomes lucrative when it succeeds in making profits, and upon whose backs that wealth is produced.

Such questions are not just limited to private businesses within the prison market either. Privatization of public provisions beyond the prison institution is becoming a larger trend in American culture. For instance, in 2009 California began to consider allowing 51 new schools in Los Angeles as well as 200 existing schools across the state to be open to bids by privately-controlled "charters," private organizations that deliver the "product" of education. As this process has unfolded, questions about the effects of transferring public institutions to private control emerge. How, for example, might this transfer alter labor contracts and the longtime predominance of the California Teachers unions in the state given that private schools are not required to be unionized? Or, how does the nature of the K-12 curriculum change if charters are overseen by individuals whose salaries are paid by particular special interests?[8] As we see the private sector enter into previously restricted "publicly sponsored" territory, old equations between state and citizen are being recast.[9]

These tensions are not just found at the city or state level, however: they can be traced in federal business dealings as well. Burgeoning relationships between private military firms and government officials have developed during the Iraq and Afghanistan wars. Reports of former CIA personnel taking high-level positions in military contracting companies like Blackwater (now known as Xe Services LLC) fuel suspicion and distrust in the context of these firms being awarded lucrative contracts by the U.S. government. And perhaps more disturbing are Blackwater's own contract disclosures suggesting that the CIA has out-sourced work as sensitive as interrogating prisoners. In the case of private prison companies, it is no secret that many seem to be a virtual turnstile for former government employees.

A look at one of the largest private prison companies, Corrections Corporation of America (CCA), and its "management team" reveals that over a dozen of those on its Executive Management staff, its senior officers list and Board of Directors have held top-level positions for the federal government. Donna M. Alvarado, a member of the Board of Directors for CCA, for example, has served as deputy assistant secretary of defense for the U.S. Department of Defense; counsel for the U.S. Senate Committee on the Judiciary subcommittee on Immigration and Refugee Policy, and staff member of the U.S. House of Representatives Select Committee on Narcotics Abuse and Control. Another Board member is Thurgood Marshall, (the son of the historic Supreme Court Justice, Thurgood Marshall). He has held appointments in each branch of the federal government, including Cabinet Secretary to President Clinton, Director of Legislative Affairs, and Deputy Counsel to Vice President Al Gore.

One more example of the revolving door that seems to exchange government officials with private corporate leaders is Stacia Hylton. Hylton was appointed as the director of the United States Marshals Service by President Obama in his first term. Hylton first worked for the U.S. Marshals Service 30 years ago. She went on to manage the detention of prisoners slated for deportation as a federal detention trustee. During this time the private prison contracting firm, the GEO Group secured several lucrative contracts with the federal government to run its detention centers, amounting to about $85 million annually.

Later, Hylton opened the consulting firm Hylton Kirk & Associates LLC, a firm whose only reported client was the same GEO Group. The work for GEO was referred to as "federal relations" and paid a salary over $100,000 a year. Coming full-circle, Hylton returned to the federal government as the head of the Marshals Service, a position for which she is charged with overseeing federal contracts that in recent years have increased for private prison operators—particularly those that provide care for undocumented immigrants.

While there might be countless differences between school systems, military operations and prisons, it's fair to ask how educating, defending, and indeed, punishing Americans (or foreigners for that matter) might be affected by their transfer into private hands—and how private hands are so easily remade into public hands, especially when the amount tax-payers are paying into state budgets for corrections continues to grow—in fact 660 percent since 1982—and the volatility of economic markets since at least 2008 have been so unstable.

Within this consideration, the lucrative private contracting for goods and services—or whole state prisons in some cases—unfolds and marks the tensions alive in questions about what roles are inherently governmental and which may be appropriately auctioned off to the highest bidder. Are there some jobs that are simply too critical to outsource? How do capitalist social relations aid or compliment certain roles, and, is it even feasible to draw a line between the two spheres (public/private) in some cases? These questions are particularly interesting as they emerge in the rise and fall of prison privatization within the prison system in California—a network that competes with a handful of other states for the title of largest corrections system in the nation. In many ways, the state of California has been a harbinger of nationwide trends, not only within incarceration but also within the crime control field generally.[10] Its historical entry into privatization offers an interesting portrait of socio-political tensions existing in state governments nation-wide since so many of the same structural dynamics exist across multiple states such as large budget deficits, high prison populations and demand for efficient inmate care. To address these questions it's useful to trace the start of private contracting of prisons both nationally and within the state of California.

The Start of Privatization

The roots of prison privatization can be traced to Kentucky, in 1825, but its contemporary start seems to be in 1979. According to criminologist Douglas McDonald, the renewed interest in contracting prison service started principally with the network of detention centers controlled by the U.S. Immigration and Naturalization Service (INS). Private contractors were desirable primarily because they could construct new centers more rapidly than the federal government, notes McDonald, due to the lengthily lead times required for approval of new sites. By 1988, private companies held approximately 30 percent of all aliens under INS authority.[11] Once firms were successfully contracted by federal agencies to hold illegal immigrants waiting for either hearings or deportation, their use at the state level became more feasible. Accordingly, these detention centers served as seedbeds for the current drive to privatize across the nation. This development enabled two of today's largest private firms, Nashville-based Corrections Corporation of America (CCA) and the GEO Group (formerly Wackenhut Inc.), a foothold into the market. The real growth of the movement, however, lay in the birth of CCA in 1983. The firm was distinct in that "It had been able. . . to obtain substantial working capital, to persuade a number of experienced and highly regarded correctional administrators to move' from the public to the private sector [and] to establish a division of labor within its corporate structure which called for senior business and senior corrections executives to exercise decision-making powers in their respective areas of expertise."[12] Using local jails as building blocks to gain experience and credibility, CCA and the GEO Group became positioned to benefit from the 1988 decision of the Texas Department of Criminal Justice to contract out four facilities to the private sector. It was at this point, criminological researcher Charles Thomas writes, that private prisons moved from being an "interesting experiment" to a mature project.[13] In eight years, the initial four Texas prisons grew to 118 either operational or commissioned facilities across the US. The rated capacity for these facilities was approximately 78,000 or 5 percent of the total prison and jail population in the nation.[14] Today, the numbers of privately-owned beds has grown to over 99,000 located in approximately 264 facilities, mostly located in Florida, Tennessee, Kentucky, New Mexico, Arizona, Virginia, District of Columbia, and Louisiana.

In California, private contracting did not become popular until the 1980s, when the California Department of Corrections (or the CDC until it added the term "rehabilitation" in 2006 to become the CDCR) needed additional space to house those who had short-term sentences and an increasing number of parole violators. Harsher sentencing mandates meant incarcerated folks were returning to prison at a faster rate due to technical violations of their parole. As in many jurisdictions across the country, the *golden state* began to consider the possibility of using private contractors to manage a small number of prison beds to meet these outstanding needs. Cornell Corrections (formerly Eclectic Communications) became one of the first companies to contract with the state to operate what were termed community correctional facilities (CCFs), bridging the gap between community treatment centers and something similar to a halfway house. Many of these developed as a function of the passage of Proposition 13 in 1978 that mandated fifty new expenditure controls and revenue restrictions which put a damper on easy funding sources for new prison projects. The Cornell facility, called Hidden Valley Ranch, was located in La Honda in the northern part of the state. The deal allowed the CDC to focus on those inmates deemed to be the greatest threat to public safety and leave the lower risk inmates to the contractor. Private contracts expanded over the next decade but remained at modest numbers into the late 1990s. Between 1992 and 2007, sixteen community correctional Facilities (CCF) opened housing over 4,000 inmates, but these facilities ran with little public attention.

In the late 1990s, a bill was introduced to the state legislature, SB 2156, the "California Correctional Facilities Privatization Commission Act of 1996." The law proposed to create a panel of nine officials who would be charged with contracting with private prison companies and overseeing those agreements. The idea was attractive. Other states, such as Florida, had created such panels successfully and the number of inmates within the California hadn't dipped significantly in decades— making over-crowding a growing issue. In addition, the cost to house these increasing numbers had expanded faster than public expenditures. This was true particularly after 1980 when federal aid began to shrink and the state was without direct assistance for the first time since the early 1970s.[15]

The bill was narrowly defeated—by just two votes in the Senate in fact— but it caught the attention of one of the largest private contractors of prison beds around the globe CCA, which had a solid reputation by then, owning half of all private beds worldwide. Its expanding share of the world market sent its stock shares soaring in 1998, placing the company's performance among the top five on the New York Stock exchange that year. Taking note of the possibilities in the state given its skyrocketing prison growth (and the initiation of a debate for a greater presence of private contracting in California), the firm appointed a West Coast Regional President to cultivate opportunities within the southwest. One of the first projects that needed overseeing came in mid-1998 when CCA broke ground on California's first major maximum-security commercial penal institution in the desert location of California City—

just two hours from Los Angeles. The $100 million facility was built on speculation—that is, constructed before there was a contract to house prisoners. Subsequently, Chairman and CEO of CCA, Doctor R. Crantz, declared California to be one of his firm's most promising markets, and he made it abundantly clear that he looked forward to a long and successful partnership with leaders of the "golden state."[16] At the time, it appeared that the practice of privately contracting prisons was poised to expand—as CCA official David Myers put it, "If we build it, they will come."[17] But in fact, this expansion never occurred. The potential partnership between CCA and the department of corrections failed even though legally, economically, and logistically it seemed like a fitting solution to an enduring problem. According to the *Sacramento Bee*, the 500-bed prison was dismissed because the state had a "lower than expected inmate population."[18] And therefore CCA, unable to secure a contract with the state, turned to another more cooperative client, the Federal Bureau of Prisons.

Privatization Stalls in California

Oddly, the original private facilities built in California (the CCFs) for low-level offenders ultimately marked the end of the state's increased use of private contracting within state borders. Three of the facilities were closed in June of 2010[19] as others seem to be barely hanging on to stable and consistent state contracts. Today, there are eight CCFs operated by private companies and seven of these are slated for closure. Each time the state closed a private facility or rejected a new contract, the "decreased prison population" was cited as the cause.[20]

Upon review of the records over the past nine years, far from becoming less crowded, the California system has become more and more populated. According to the CDCR's own records, the inmate population has only increased over the last decade, with the exception of a dip between 2001 and 2003 of approximately .044 percent of the average total number of state inmates over the last ten years.[21] Even during the years the prison population did not increase, the state facilities continued to operate at an average of 188 percent of their original design capacity. These overcrowded conditions caused the CDCR to declare a "state of emergency" in May 2004.[22] By January 2006, the department reported it needed seven new prisons (housing a population of at least five-thousand each) for the projected inmate increase over the next ten years. In addition, by the time this report was published, lawsuits brought by inmates caused the state's prison healthcare network to go into receivership. Judges decried the overcrowding at prison reception centers in California—which had approached three times their original design capacity—arguing that such increased numbers in inmates made it virtually impossible to identify incoming prisoners with medical or mental health problems.[23] Because of this overcrowding, federal courts finally ruled in August, 2009, that the state had no choice but to reduce the inmate population by nearly 43,000. This decrease would mean the CDCR would house no more than 137 percent of the system's original design capacity.[24] Claiming that its prison system was its own business, California appealed the case to the Supreme Court. However, in May, 2011, the appeal lost: the court argued that conditions were so substandard inside the facilities, they violated the U.S. Constitution's ban on cruel and unusual punishment.

In light of such serious overcrowding, it makes little sense to claim that a decrease in inmate population was the cause for the closures of the CCFs or the rejection of a contract with the CCA California City facility. There has not been a fall-off in the numbers of incoming inmates into the system, and in fact, as the years have passed, the CDCR has become more severely plagued with problems due to overcrowding. It is perplexing, then, that California officials did not take advantage of the CCA facility at that time and have almost completely abandoned privatization as a means to solve the state's expanding penal problems.

Or have they?

Upon closer inspection, the state has not only *not* abandoned the option, but rather embraced the practice with a bounding, if quiet, enthusiasm. The single most important detail, however, is that these private prisons now being used by the CDCR are all located across state lines. The large-scale transfer of inmates to private prisons began as a legislative decree in October of 2006 to relieve overcrowding in the form of "The Public Safety and Offender Rehabilitation Services Act of 2007." And since the decree was made to relieve a "state of emergency" declared by then Governor Schwarzenegger, it circumvented any deliberation within the legislature and certainly a prolonged political debate which might have forestalled the transfer. In fact, it allowed corrections officials to immediately contract with out-of-state correctional facilities to "temporarily" house California inmates. Within a month of the mandate, the state was transferring 2,260 inmates to Arizona, and Oklahoma to facilities owned by The GEO Group as well Corrections Corporation of America. As of June 2010, approximately 10,000 California inmates had been shipped off to private hands to be housed in facilities in Arizona, Mississippi, Oklahoma and Michigan. Contracts with CCA as of December 2010 were worth over $600 million.[25]

It makes sense to ask what has justified the fluctuating adoption of private contracting by California officials. How can we understand the contradictory rationales for closures of functioning private prison facilities or outright rejection of new contracts, particularly given the potential to fix some penological and economic issues faced by the state's corrections department? How did the CDC originally open the small privately run facilities early on and what has driven the state to begin the process shipping inmates into private care today?

This book offers some answers to these questions by presenting the history of the embrace, rejection, and now renewed adoption of the private contracting for California state prisoners. It's an account that is noteworthy not only for revealing a series of curious events—penological, sociological, and cultural—but also to understand and predict other similar developments in states across the nation that continue to adopt private contracting of prisons and other various traditionally publicly owned and managed services.

Theoretical Approaches

In the course of detailing this history, I want to argue that forces giving rise to the prison market illustrate the more deeply-rooted and complex relations between three dimensions of the state. The first dimension is the economic structures and practices within California. Second, state politics and public policy, including political discourse and actions in state government and public campaigns. And, thirdly the ideological representations of fear, crime and delinquency circulated in both state and popular rhetoric. I make the claim that the drive to privatize prisons is the story of the formation of social relationships that function to produce and reproduce the very structure and nature of the state itself. From this perspective, both the adoption of privatization and its demise is far from some dead practice of containment or punishment, or even of simply turning a profit. It becomes a rich and generative project that defines political platforms and candidacy, gives impulse to public policy, promotes particular union interests, and builds in no small way our very understanding of race and class in this country. Approaching the phenomenon of privatization from this angle gives us tools to conceptualize it as a *social phenomenon* that integrates state structures of economy and politics with ideological predilections of popular opinion and the media. We see its appearance on the penological stage not in isolation, as some autonomous object of correctional history, but as a sociological event, a set of relations containing contradictions shaped by a wider historical juncture that has certain conditions of existence.[26]

Losing sight of this notion is a common error in some analyses of criminal justice trends. Many treatments of criminal justice issues often ignore the fact that practices in the crime control field stand at an intersection of institutional processes, sociological structures and historical conditions. I would argue that part of what disables our ability to understand these trends is ignoring the tenuous links between these contradictory forces—links between economics, political and legal pressures within a given jurisdiction and rhetorical discourse that induces social actors to behave in particular ways. In reality, the phenomenon of privatization—and the prison industrial complex within which it exists—occurs at the center of a complicated nexus of these relations and is best framed as an active social practice linking together culture and politics.

Given this perspective, a guiding ethos for the questions I ask within this analysis is a claim made by Michel Foucault in his classic text, *Discipline and Punish*, written over thirty-five years ago. It was here that he suggested we look not at the "failure" of the prison to understand it fully—given that the prison as an institution has faltered as it purports to decrease crime and/or rehabilitate inmates—but rather at what that failure *allows* for *productively*. His work argued that the history of discipline and social control in sixteenth century France was in fact a look inside a functioning power to distribute both people and illegalities into a general economy. That is, by confining, policing, and separating criminals, a very particular system of power was initiated and carried out. But rather than stop delinquency, or significantly decrease crime, prisons—at the very least—have only continued to expand and accumulate more people in them. Incarceration has not been able to eradicate crime and still constitutes a rather failing enterprise on a number of levels as Foucault made plain. Today, illegality is simply an expected feature of society and laws merely distribute and order this condition in meaningful and manageable ways. As Foucault put it, "Punishment in general is not intended to eliminate offenses, but rather to distinguish them, to distribute them, to use them. . ."[27]

Critiques of Foucault have suggested that power or social control cannot be the only aims of everything that occurs inside a prison institution. David Garland, for example, claims that not all elements of penal sanctions operate effectively as forms of control or social regulation and some aspects of the prison are simply not constructed as "control measures" to begin with.[28] He is correct. My argument certainly does not assume that penal policy or corrections more specifically is by any means soley motivated by the central aims of social control or the failure of any penal mechanism—any system of punishment is not that facile. Indeed, my reading underlines the argument that I articulate above: we cannot look at the prison or private prisons in isolation from a myriad of other socio-political factors such as the economy, political forces or popular criminal justice rhetoric. Foucault's value to this analysis is not in the absolute calculation of whether or not California's prison system is or is not failing, or whether or not its sole purpose is caught up in wielding power. His value is rather in his insistence that we consider the ways that forms of punishment and institutional structures which deliver that punishment produce unintended consequences. And further if privatizing prisons capitalizes upon the flaws—purposeful or unintended—of the prison institution in California more generally.

The contemporary context of the prison in the twenty-first century both within California and beyond adds one more dimension to Foucault's observations. Among the effects of crime control is the production of a systematic power, it's true. But today, the punishment of offenders also produces profits that increase as that punishment fails to decrease crime. For example, a cursory glance at California's ever-increasing rates of incarceration and recidivism suggest that imprisonment is a substantial miscarriage of public funds. As of this writing, the state prison population is at a record high of 171,000. Indeed, between 1980 and 2000—a period roughly coinciding with the emergence of the prison market—the inmate population increased six-fold, a singular event in American correctional history. Within two years of releasing any one inmate, there has consistently been a seven in ten chance that he or she will return back into the hands of the California criminal justice system once again. What has been "productively" accomplished in maintaining such an ailing system is an expanding budget for the CDCR, exponential growth of businesses selling products and services to maintain high rates of imprisonment, and entire corporations—whose stock is publicly traded—devoted to building and managing prison facilities. An important question to be raised is how the prison market is poised to complement—or perhaps exacerbate—this productivity. If successful, an examination of this dynamic offers insight into the ways private contracting is a force in shaping the crime control field and a significant influence on social and political policy more generally. It may in fact reveal how a culture of crime is produced by way of the very mechanisms put in place to stop its expansion. And it certainly prompts us to examine how private enterprise and public responsibility for punishing "criminality," as I suggest above, coexist within the boundaries of the state.

The links that form the necessary conditions for both the rise and fall of private contracting—not as some linear history per se, but as a series of dynamic forces exerting pressure on one another—distinguishes my reading. It is not meant to be a comprehensive historical narrative of the development of private contracting, but a history of the conditions that allowed it to emerge, be productive and eventually fail *within the state lines* of California. Accounting for this history leads to a focus on particular shifts in corrections in particular, as well as changes in the American crime control field more generally.

My analysis is organized into three different sets of questions that address the dimensions of the state I identify above: the economic, socio-political, and rhetorical conditions within California. Before I address those questions, I lay a foundation for each to be effectively examined in Chapter 2. This second chapter focuses on a history of the present state of economic, political and cultural conditions influencing transformations in the penological landscape of the U.S. more generally. I argue that one cannot possibly hope to understand how we arrived at a shift in current crime control sensibilities, including the trend to privatize prisons, without recognizing the tumultuous changes the country went through over the course of the end of the twentieth century. In describing these historical shifts, I underscore the point that they are best understood as new pressures upon the previous culture of penal-welfarism, a penological framework preceding our current crime control philosophies and practices. Reactions to the shifts during this time set the stage for a number of new obstacles to appear for the social and political actors in the criminal justice field. I use the 1966 California gubernatorial campaign as a means to parse out particular public concerns over lawlessness and crime as well as responses to these issues by government officials. The chapter ends by suggesting the altered terrain established by way of this uncertain time in American history.

Chapter 3 begins my examination of the first component of the tripart system of the state of California: the economic system and its relation to the rise of the privatization of prison goods, services and management. The series of questions posed to understand the economic field of California examines social, demographic, and historical developments that offer insight into relationships between capital and labor as well as state budgets and public expenditures. Central to this analysis are the questions: what forces within the state economy enabled the conditions of existence for public contracting of public prisons to take hold? And, how has the prison market generally become viable given these contexts?

Chapter 4 focuses upon questions that help analyze the social and political field of California and investigate how historical developments of penology are deeply connected to institutional shifts in the processes of passing public policy, running for and holding public office, the trends toward penal populism and a relatively new focus on victims' rights. My prime interest is to establish the ways in which privatization has worked—and continues to work—in tandem with new political and legal conventions developed by Californians over the last forty years.

Chapter 5 contains inquiry into rhetorical discourses that have animated public images of crime and criminality. I focus upon what has been named the *culture of fear*, how it developed in California, and ways it exacerbated inflammatory perspectives of crime within the state. I also examine the rhetoric of capitalism as a market solution to a problem of dashed faith in "big government." It becomes clear that private contracting took hold in part simply because it was not controlled and executed by government hands. I explore a network of tropes and socially-constructed narratives that have become normalized through criminological scholarship, media representations, and the discourses of crime control workers themselves. My purpose is to reveal how these influence perceptions of and practices toward prisoners (or those who might be potential prisoners) and suggest the ways that race and class have become marked anew by the processes of incarceration.

Chapter 6 explains exactly why privatization has seemingly failed inside the state given the opportunities it had to flourish. I describe how the economic, political and discursive features have worked to allow for the present state of contracting in California in light of the monolithic resistance of the California prison guards' union. I recount the story of union efforts to end private contracts in California for good and the means by which these efforts were (in part) thwarted. I bring the history of private contracting within California up to date and suggest what the future might hold given its current correctional predicaments.

Chapter 7 presents what I term the *mythology of privatization*. This mythology represents a logic, a sensibility, or an economy that organizes the arguments for private contracting of California's state prisons. In the course of detailing the mythology of privatization, I explain how the mystification of current socio-political and rhetorical conditions in California enable private contracting to appear both logical and prudent. I argue that that the state's penal systems do not just dispose of offenders as they imprison them—whether they end up in a private prison or a state managed facility. The incarcerated are used and useful even as we assign to them the status of reject—both literally and metaphorically. "The carceral network," as Foucault notes, "does not cast the unassimilable into a confused hell; there is no outside. It takes back with one hand, what it seems to exclude with the other. . . It is unwilling to waste even what it has decided to disqualify."[29] Foucault's point is perhaps even more insightful as applied to the trend of the PIC in California. For, as I conclude, the state has not only simply refused to pay close attention to what its penal institutions disqualify, but also who profits from that process.

---

[1] See: Stephanie Chen, "Pennsylvania Rocked by 'Jailing Kids for Cash' Scandal," CNN Justice Page. 23 Feb. 2009 Web. 2 Aug. 2011; Terrie Morgan-Besecker, "Crime of Punishment?" *The Times Leader* 1 March 2009 Web. 2 August 2011.

[2] Isis N. Walton, "The Prison Industrial Complex: Contributing Mechanisms and Collateral Consequences of Disproportionality on African American Communities," ed. Nicolle Parsons-Pollard *Disproportionate Minority Contact: Current Issues and Policies* (Durham, NC: Carolina Academic Press, 2011) 223.

[3] J. R. Lilly & P. Knepper, "The Corrections-Commercial Complex," *Crime and Delinquency* 39 (1993): 150-66.

[4] Walton "The Prison Industrial Complex," 216.

[5] Paul Wright, "Slaves of the State," eds. Daniel Burton-Rose, Dan Pens & Paul Wright *The Celling of America: An Inside look at the U.S. Prison Industry.* Monroe, Maine: Common Courage Press, 1998) 102.

[6] Eric Schlosser, "The Prison Industrial Complex," *The Atlantic Monthly* Dec. 1998.

[7] According to Angela Davis "[I]n the immediate aftermath of slavery, the southern states hastened to develop a criminal justice system that could legally restrict the possibilities of freedom for newly released slaves. Black people became the prime targets of a developing convict lease system, referred to by many names as a reincarnation of slavery. Angela Davis, *Are Prisons Obsolete?* (New York: Seven Stories Press, 2003) 29.

[8] Howard, Blume, "Charters Get a Chance to Grow, But How Big," *Los Angeles Times* 2 Sept. 2009 A1/A10.

[9] In 2010, for example, the Los Angeles Unified School district floated an idea to sell naming rights to school auditoriums or athletic fields. One estimate of potential revenues to the city was $18 million, quite an attractive sum. Something so minor couldn't possibly impact the process of education. Or could it? It is unclear how grade school experience would be different if classrooms were named: Sony Hall or Sit-n-Sleep learning annex. But naming is important in this culture if only in the sheer ubiquity of corporate messaging that inspires us to experience advertising and marketing as if it were normative or "natural."

[10] I borrow the term *crime control field* from David Garland. I am using it here to refer to the myriad of agencies employed to police, sentence, judge, research, legislate, and of course, oversee the population we send to prison. This field also contains laws that define illegality, proper treatments for offenders, and official rationales for delinquent behavior. David Garland, *The Culture of Control: Crime and Social Order in Contemporary Society.* (Chicago: University of Chicago Press, 2001).

[11] Douglas C. McDonald, "Public Imprisonment By Private Means: The Re-emergence of Private Prisons and Jails in the United States, The United Kingdom, and Australia," *British Journal of Criminology* 34 (1994): 30. See also: Douglas C. McDonald, "The Costs of Operating Public and Private Correctional Facilities," ed. D. C. McDonald *Private Prisons and the Public Interest* (New Brunswick, NJ: Rutgers University Press, 1990) 92.

[12] Charles Thomas & Charles Logan, "The Development, Present Status and Future Potential of Correctional Privatization in America," ed. Gary Bowman, Simon Hakim, and Paul Seidenstat *Privatizing Correctional Institutions* (N.J.: Transaction, 1993) 219-21.

[13] Charles Thomas "Correctional Privatization: The Issues and the Evidence," Paper presented at the Privatization of Correctional Services Conference, Toronto Canada, July 1996.

[14] Richard Harding, "Private Prisons," ed. Michael Tonry *The Handbook of Crime and Punishment* (New York: Oxford University Press, 1998) 632.

[15] Douglas, McDonald, "Private Penal Institutions," *Crime & Justice* 16 (1992): 393.

[16] Marc Lifsher, "Busting Into the Prison Business—Corrections Corp. of America Casts Longing Eyes on California," *The Wall Street Journal* 27 May 1998: 1.

[17] Robert Gunnison, "Privately Run Prison Planned for Mojave," *San Francisco Chronicle* 1 August 1997: A22.

[18] Andy Furillo, "Prison Budget Shifts Strategy; Governor Looks to Rely on County Jails, Private Prisons to Ease Overcrowding," *Sacramento Bee* 15 Jan. 2006: A-3.

[19] California Department of Corrections and Rehabilitation. "CDCR to Close Three Community Correctional Facilities Due to Downward Trend in Low-Security Inmates." CDCR Homepage. 2009 Web. 11 Nov. 2011.

[20] Governor Gray Davis, for example, claimed that the decreased numbers of inmates made a need for private contracting obsolete. Staff, "Davis Proposes to Cut Five Prisons in State Budget," *The Associated Press State & Local Wire* 15 March 2002. The California Department of Corrections and Rehabilitation, as well, asserted the inmate population was becoming ever smaller, terminating a need for private beds. Dan Morain, "Private Prison Deal Voided," *Los Angeles Times* 4 Feb. 2005: B-3.

[21] California Department of Corrections & Rehabilitation Office of Public and Employee Communications. "Corrections: Moving Forward." Fall 2009. Web. 14 April 2010. "Spring 2006 Adult Population Projections"; "Total Population" *The California Department of Corrections & Rehabilitation Homepage*. 27 February 2006. State of California. Web. 6 May 2006.

[22] Staff, "Pound Foolish: Prison System in State of Emergency," *The San Diego Union Tribune* 3 May 2004, B-6.

[23] Carol J. Williams, "State Gets Two Years to Cut 43,000 From Prisons," *Los Angeles Times* 5 Aug. 2009 A-1, A-19.

[24] Williams, State Gets Two Years.

[25] Dan Morain, "Private Prisons? A Sweet Deal For Some," *The Sacramento Bee* 7 Jan. 2010 Web. 26 Jan. 2010.

[26] I am indebted to the work of Stuart Hall and his colleagues for this insight made so poingnently in *Policing the Crisis.* Stuart Hall, Chas Critcher, Tony Jefferson, John Clarke, and Brian Roberts, *Policing the Crisis: Mugging,*

the State, and Law & Order, (New York: Holmes & Meier Publishers, Inc. 1978) viii-ix.

[27] Foucault, *Discipline* 272.

[28] David Garland, *Punishment and Modern Society: A Study in Social Theory* (Oxford: Clarendon Press) 162-6.

[29] Foucault, *Discipline* 301.

2

Transformations of the Prison Landscape

To begin an analysis of private contracting in California, it must be understood that its present-day crime control field has not been formed in a vacuum. The conditions framing penal policy, the values and beliefs undergirding the proper modes of punishment, indeed, the concept of criminality itself, have been shaped directly by the history of penological modernism. Therefore, framing the developments that lead to privatization necessitates a clear view of changes that occurred in the state's penological practice and theory. In this chapter, I will first detail the ethos of penological modernism. Next, I will explain how political-economic disruptions both nation-wide and inside California between the mid-1960s through the end of the 1980s created changes to that project. Finally, I will examine how these disturbances initiated new rationales for punishment that set the stage for the blossoming of the prison market in California. In describing that period within the U.S., my aim is certainly not a full accounting of social, political or economic history of the time in question, but rather an examination of particular changes *forming the conditions* for penal policy and practice at the end of the twentieth century.

Penal Welfarism: The Progressive Era of Criminal Justice

Penological modernism, a designation sometimes interchanged with the term, "penal welfarism," has been used to denote the philosophy, reasoning, and practices of crime control roughly between 1890 and 1970.[1] David Rothman has called this age a progressive era where a modernist penal project became distinct in terms of theory, practice and desire.[2] Penal welfarism crystallizes a consensus in approach, interpretation, and response to crime and criminality. When we look at political platforms, official reports, and public policy in this era, a set of assumptions guides widespread views of crime and its eradication. Under the auspices of penal welfarism, attitudes held by official crime control workers—as well as the public—regarding illegality shifted from understanding the offender as a moral failure to be "reconditioned" by work, to a social science project to be rehabilitated.

Methods for treating delinquents changed to reflect the growing belief that prisoners could be cured of the psychological sicknesses causing them to commit crime. The image of the condemned man was not animated by juridical concerns of accusation, judgment, or condemnation, but rather by reform, treatment and rehabilitation. Combating crime during this period was akin to ameliorating the deficiencies of particular *people* as opposed to our present model that typically has no concern for the ailments of any single individual. The penal-welfarist ethos recognized individuals who broke the law as somehow "broken" or compromised by infirmity themselves. As Cesare Lombroso argued in his text on the causes of crime, "The extinction of the criminal class and the ultimate abolition of prisons are ideals to be kept in view, just as the elimination of disease must be the perpetual aim of medical sciences."[3]

According to this analogy, offenders were not criminal because they were naturally immoral, hostile, from some particular culture or predisposed to feel disdain for the law, but because they had not been properly socialized or adjusted to mainstream society. Indeed, those who chose lawlessness were "sick" on some level and must be treated, reformed and re-adjusted so that they could take their rightful place among law-abiding citizens. An anonymous inmate demonstrated just such a sentiment when he wrote in 1911 that he was better served behind bars "until cured, just as a person suffering from a physical disease or infection is sent to a hospital or asylum to remain for such period as may be necessary for his restoration to health."[4] In contrast to our own twenty-first century common sense, this perspective dictates that criminals do not choose illegality, but are rather debilitated by an infirm mind and rationality, thus unable to be clear decision makers. Once an individual was brought back to normative mental/psychological health, heeding the rule of law was a natural choice that brought the advantages of well-being and social progress. To accomplish this task, penal measures were seen to be effective to the extent they could identify the problem in a convict that created delinquency to begin with and eradicate it.

Unlike a century before, retribution against the incarcerated was sharply dismissed. It was an unenlightened and ineffective goal and its practice marked a state institution as crude and backward. Repression was replaced with therapeutics within this approach and American criminologists rallied around Tannenbaum's argument that, "There is not a shred of evidence that punishment—severe or mild, with good intentions or bad ones—has beneficial effects on the future lives of men punished."[5] In fact, according to Dr. Karl Menninger, the act of punishing criminals, rather than treating them, was a sign of our own pathology.[6] Indeed, we were the ones who were maladjusted and ignorant when we opted to treat criminals as punitive objects. Criminals were to be nurtured and rehabilitated. Otherwise, "The inescapable conclusion is that society secretly wants crime, needs crime, and gains definite satisfaction from the present mishandling of it!"[7]

In this way, simple imprisonment was not a popular answer to crime since it was merely a coercive instrument that stifled men and women and ignored the unique nature of the offender. Progressives guiding inmate treatment did not completely discard the traditional morality so important to discipline in the penitentiaries and reformatories of the past, but they recognized it in a new form: that which emerged under degenerate social and economic conditions. The causes of crime lay in social and economic environments where "conditions of employment in the sweat shops and loft manufactories (as well as) the seasonal fluctuations of labor (create) unrest and lawlessness." Slums bred poverty that created delinquency that in turn produced criminals.[8] If crime was to be obliterated, so too would "wretched living conditions," "child labor," "the wrong kind of education," and "unsupervised street life." It was poverty that generated crime—or at least conditioned its existence. However, it was not just, as Miller wrote, that lower class values and middle-class values were different, and thus created a clash in the moment of the criminal act, or, that some people just happened to be poor. It was, according to one of the most significant works on the causes of criminality in the first half of the twentieth century, that criminality graduated out of a certain "social location." For, "[I]f, in a given social location, illegal or criminal means are not readily available, then we should not expect a criminal subculture to develop." A person's *place*, directed what tools s/he might have at his or her disposal, what behaviors he or she might engage. And those tools determined the available choice of solutions for everyday problems. In short, the general wisdom among crime control scholars was that responses to life—and indices of crime—were driven by social conditions, whether those conditions be environmental or relational.[9]

From the purview of contemporary perspectives of crime, it is interesting that penal welfarism held that delinquent behavior could be permanently corrected. It was believed that as the work of social hygiene continued, we would ultimately remove "the epidemic forms of criminality" so that "nine-tenths of the crimes [would] disappear."[10] Today, this kind of optimism would be folly. Current mainstream views of criminality hold that either *individuals* are primarily responsible for criminal behavior—versus the environments they exist within—or specific *cultural systems*. And completely removing crime from our streets is not seen as possible. Our logic for addressing crime and/or criminality generally eclipses conditions existing inside the state and certainly denies that wrongdoing is a creation of a state's institutional structure or environment. Nevertheless, treatment properly performed under the penal-welfarist approach had to address the causes driving *each individual offender*; that is, a person's whole psychology. It wasn't enough to take stock of the crime committed and devise punishment that fit that indiscretion. Indeed, the punishment should *not* fit the crime, against our own popular adage. Instead, the punishment should fit the man or woman who committed the crime. According to Charlton Lewis, "the method of apportioning penalties according to degrees of guilt. . .is as completely discredited and as incapable. . .as is the practice of astrology or. . . witchcraft."[11] Accordingly, approaches to treating offenders not only had to be unique but applied with a good deal of discretion.

Penal Welfarist Policies

As penal welfarist philosophy developed, institutional approaches to its forms of knowledge followed. If an offender's rehabilitation had to be suited to his or her unique person, then conventions of sentencing had to allow for individual flexibility. One approach to this flexibility was accomplished through indeterminate sentencing, probation and parole. Adopting such practices enabled the U.S. to use the court system and the prison to practice what academics and theoreticians preached.[12] Arguing for increased flexibility and discretion on the part of penal experts, Frederick Wines explained that prisoner reform had to be directed by the character of the actor we were attempting to reform. And given this, it was impossible to predict how long a sentence ought be for any particular offender. Indeed, he wrote, the time "required to alter (him) cannot be estimated in advance any more than we can tell how long it will take for a lunatic to recover from an act of insanity."[13] Clearly, if inmates were ill and in need of care, it was completely illogical to assign sentences—or rehabilitative programs—before a complete therapeutic assessment of each individual could be made. In California, indeterminate sentencing officially entered into law for a number of criminal convictions in 1917; by 1944, the *entire* sentencing framework was wholly indeterminate. In support of the measure, the California Supreme Court argued the "modern" penal expert was obliged to create opportunities for reform of which indeterminate sentences were a prime example: "It is generally recognized by the courts and by modern penologists that the purpose of indeterminate sentencing law is to mitigate the punishment which would otherwise be imposed upon the offender. These laws place emphasis upon the reformation of the offender. They seek to make the punishment fit the criminal rather than the crime. They endeavor to put before the prisoner great incentive to well-doing in order that his will to do well should be strengthened and confirmed by the habit of well-doing."[14]

The beauty of indeterminate sentencing was that it gave courts the freedom to assign prison terms on the basis of each inmate's case and further heightened the level of autonomy enjoyed by judges, prison officials and crime control workers generally. Typically, a judge set minimum and maximum terms and bowed out of the process to allow parole boards to decide the actual number of years served. This discretion enabled early release for good time served and created a flexibility to monitor and assess the inmate's progress during "treatment." If a prisoner amassed enough "good marks" or "credits," it signaled that reform had been achieved and she should go free. Probation was an additional route to increased correctional discretion. When probation was given to a convicted criminal, it allowed that individual to avoid prison altogether and simply maintain contact with an official charged with ensuring the convict's lawfulness. But perhaps parole was the most complementary program to indeterminate sentencing since it essentially "tried the inmate out" in public to see if he could fly right without the restrictive walls of the prison. Parole consisted of release from the prison structure under the legal supervision of a parole board. In this way, offenders were granted freedom from living inside the prison, but could be summoned back anytime they were deemed incapable of being law abiding. Boards granted parole by examining variables such as the seriousness of the offender's crime, the offender's behavior in prison, and how successful s/he might be if released. Many believed that parole would make up for inconsistencies in sentencing by judges and provide yet another route to identify the good apples from the bad.[15]

Ideology and Penal Welfarism

In the literature on penological modernism, it was recognized that the American criminal justice system was imperfect, to be sure. But the starkest departure from our own current views of criminology, as I suggest above, was the notion that the (near) eradication of crime was certainly possible, even probable, given the wonders of modernism in general. In this sense, penal-welfarism marked an unquestioned faith of the criminal justice field to unlock the possibilities and potentialities of social engineering. Progressives believed in the knowledge produced by state experts, modern research, science, and technology. In short, these were the tools to achieve the full flowering of the social contract. James Scott frames this cumulative logic "high-modernist ideology": a form of thinking invested in "scientific and technical progress, the expansion of production, the growing satisfaction of human needs, the mastery of nature (including human nature), and, above all, the rational design of social order commensurate with the scientific understanding of natural laws."[16] Californians, often ahead of penological trends, supported these ideals with great enthusiasm.

Indeed, not only was a modern lifestyle and sensibility available to all people, it was *desirable* to all—even if the victims of neglect did not yet know it. The state was the mechanism to provide welfare and freedom to each individual. In fact, the state was obligated to accomplish this task, for its very stability depended upon the cohesion and participation of each and every citizen. In a 1959 *Nation* article, Terence Morris admonished his readers to take heed of precisely such wisdom advanced by Belgian social theorist Adolphe Quételet: "Society bears in its womb the embryo of every crime that is to be committed; it prepares for the crime while the criminal is merely the tool." Morris explained that no offender was ever "wholly free" from some "handicap" (social or physical) that carried "social significance." And as "(The criminal) is at unease with the world and has many needs. . . in the long run, the needs of the offender are the self-interest of the community as a whole."[17] If we could only but regulate the conditions of society that creates criminality, he seems to claim, we would be able to destroy any embryo of illegality or disobedience.

Consequently, the pathway to achieving a universal citizenship was not necessarily avoiding the fact that the offender was guilty—that is, declaring that she had no personal responsibility in crime—but rather recognizing that the social contract was still a "work in progress" whose promise had not yet reached everyone equally. Eliminating the poor by bringing them to a greater level of affluence, uncovering and eradicating the causes of criminal behavior, and integrating all individuals within the broad fabric of society would begin this process. And, it was in the whole community's self-interest to do so. In short, penal welfarists advocated the cultural improvement of the delinquent to be a democratic mandate. Educating workers, redistributing resources, and expanding economic opportunity were the means by which we might march steadily toward social cohesion and universal democracy.

Social Science Research and the Criminal Justice Practicioner

By the middle of the twentieth century, these developments were forging a new relation between the study of crime and the social sciences. More often the American problems of crime, of inequality, of education, of even simple conflicts at work were understood as *social* problems that might be solved by a "more highly socialized democracy."[18] A new focus on the social sciences and the regulation of social groups was something of a "new technology." Within it was the promise of increased control and dominion over problems like workers being ill adapted to industrialization and urbanization. No doubt the increased presence of women in the public sphere and their varied movements to articulate social needs helped this drive along. Women's participation in political arenas at the start of the twentieth century bolstered Social Progressives' aims. This strength derived from their involvement in civic associations and other organizations which created attention around and immediacy to a number of causes that overlapped with a therapeutic orientation to societal issues. Beginning with a general interest in philanthropy, women championed the rights of children, the need for temperance, and mothers' aid. Consequently, they built a platform for programs that utilized the state as an instrument to protect home and family. As women commanded more attention in the press and influenced campaign outcomes, political leaders began to recognize their importance as quasi-lobbyists and public rhetoricians in their own right. But beyond women's participation, the social science view also gained currency as a function of the academy. At the end of the nineteenth century the newly formed American Social Science Association began producing its own journal. One of its first volumes contained an article offering an inventory of social science courses being taught at universities ranging from Bryn Mawr to Harvard. In effect, the article argued for its own legitimization as a function of a growing number of colleges and universities teaching coursework that took a sociological perspective.[19]

In effect, social science research became a panacea. Much like Michel Foucault's account of the conversion of the insane asylum by medical personnel at the end of the eighteenth century, the crime control field experienced a revolution precipitated by emerging social scientists and a regulation of "the social."[20] Social questions and their answers became a primary feature of criminological thought and accordingly articulated specific approaches to penology. A positivistic discourse that prized observation, classification, diagnosis, and recommendations for cure took precedence. Specific kinds of schooling were required for this new perspective; and in California as across the nation, professionals began to enter the field specializing in corrections, counseling, and community treatment. For the first time, many of these professionals had college educations—some even with post-graduate degrees—in social work, public administration or some other related field. The "old-school" wardens typically had risen through the ranks: any formal education they possessed was secondary to their sense of themselves as professionals or the best way to do their jobs. In 1965, according to Charles Silberman, every warden in the state of California had climbed the seniority ladder. But by 1974, there wasn't a single head of an operating prison who had started as a guard. Not only had the majority of these wardens completed college, six of the eight held graduate degrees.[21] These changes tended to ensure reform in both penological thought and practice, but also brought a new level of expertise to the prison institution changing the very face of crime control quite radically.

During the middle part of the twentieth century, the goal of correctional professionals was to be a social practitioner that literally transformed "prisoners into enlightened citizens . . . ."[22] Unsurprisingly, as the theories of social science entered the practice of treating delinquent behavior, the work of crime control—this business of creating a transformation in prisoners—became mystified and somewhat obscured. It was not typically judicial authorities but penal experts who oversaw the processes of identifying, categorizing and treating criminal offenders. Eventually, the influence of social scientists—clinicians, probation workers, counselors, researchers, parole board members and the like—eclipsed "common" knowledge to the extent that their work became inaccessible to the layperson. The war against the delinquent mind became "un-winnable" without the insight of educated experts or specialists. When at one time "the leading principle had been *nullem poena sine crimen* ("no punishment without crime"), in the world of penal-welfarism the directive came instead to be: no treatment without diagnosis, and no penal sanction without expert advice."[23] Henceforth, decisions about sentencing, parole eligibility, suitability for particular rehabilitation treatments and so on were increasingly made by a limited set of individuals whose discretion was unparalleled from the perspective of twenty-first century criminal justice standards. Unlike today, the work carried out in the field was accomplished with little legislative or public oversight, and officials were trusted to fight crime and regulate crime control politics in relative isolation—as long as there were not significant scandals.

Also notable was the dearth of politicians who adopted crime control politics as a unique mode of running for or staying in office. While today crime is an issue that is almost never left out of political platforms or debates about how one could favorably change the state, through most of the twentieth century discourse by political hopefuls largely steered clear of the "crime card" to appeal to voters and constituents. This avoidance meant that crime and prison conditions, as well as the court system and the police, were largely removed from the public eye apart from the occasional prison escape or sensational court case. The common wisdom was that the professionals were doing their jobs and the public had no cause for worry. Perhaps the work of crime control was obscured also because crime rates stayed relatively constant until about 1963. By 1964 and the emergence of civil rights debates, this conventional wisdom was recast.

The Attack on Penal Welfarism

Public complaints and disenchantment with the penal-welfarist perspective began to appear in the late 1960s; but by the middle of the 1970s, the assumptions, conventions, penal ideals, and philosophical principles guiding the progressive project began to significantly crumble. New social attitudes questioned the purpose of government, while the use of correctional institutions to "alter the maladjusted" became deeply suspect. Indeterminate sentencing was now seen to be an exercise in coddling inmates that simultaneously encouraged inequity between prisoners who sometimes spent vastly different amounts of time behind bars for the same crime. The working ideologies that had one time fueled support for Progressives' penal approaches were now seen as antiquated and unpractical. Attacks of the model claimed that at best, its logic had no practical significance since inmates did not seem to be rehabilitated. At worst, critics argued, the model was immoral, coercive, and offensive to standards of fairness and impartiality so critical to maintaining legitimate authority. Critics called prison officials elitists and accused them of treating inmates like children or the mentally ill.

Many began to ask if it was even possible for a state institution to cure a convicted felon. And if it could, was this charge even appropriate?

The catalyst for such questions did not come simply from a particular conflict within the criminal justice system, new correctional leadership or modern discoveries about better approaches to confinement. Rather, the country experienced a number of very specific social, political and economic transformations that took place over a relatively short time. The decade of the 1960s marked realignments of long standing political constituencies which ultimately produced new social attitudes toward issues as diverse as race, support for welfare-state provisions, and trust in the wisdom and morality of state and national governments. Values and attitudes about the responsibility one had to his community began to shift alongside the growing costs of welfare state policies aimed at ameliorating the social and economic conditions of the poor and disenfranchised. Shifting economic realities altered public hopes that a "new capitalism" had been designed that might finally ensure perennial stability and ever expanding wealth. Consequently, the crime control field adopted a different set of meanings and possibilities. It was forced to grapple with philosophical questions about the effects and viability of punishment, the costs of electing prison as a primary response to crime, and the nature and cause of criminal behavior more generally. Approaches to crime and punishment today in part, grow out of, reactions to this rather volatile time. Current public discourse that addresses the relative advantage or disadvantages of the prison industry, the efficacy of private prisons, the poor condition of California's correctional system and even our very understanding of criminality cannot be divorced from such historical realignments.

Chief among the transitions California—and certainly the nation at large to varying degrees—endured during this time was a shift in the support for the programs and premises of the "general welfare-state," a term made popular in the late 1940s. Before the demise of the welfare state ethos, it had gained favor over the older political framework of "laissez faire"—a politics which interpreted state control of almost any civic or market function as a sort of necessary evil. Franklin Roosevelt championed the welfare state philosophy arguing the government was quite simply society's best tool to be used "as an efficient agency for the practical betterment of social and economic conditions throughout this land."[24] The same platform was broadly embraced by New Deal Democrats of the time who saw new regulatory laws and welfare state provisions as a means to ensure the historical edict of *liberty and justice for all*. The country invested in social programs for the unemployed, those with illnesses and/or disabilities, and veterans. It passed laws that aimed to safeguard workers by regulating minimum wage, maximum working hours, age restrictions for work-days, provisions to decrease poverty, liberalize social security benefits, and enable access to healthcare and housing. Furthermore, legislation initiated regulations to fiscal and monetary policy that would ensure optimum use of our market resources, resources being rearranged by new prescriptions initiated by John Maynard Keynes. In short, the spirit of these collective programs sought to restrict unbridled self-interest, tame Social-Darwinism, mitigate the brutality of unchecked capitalism, and move the state toward a new social order.[25]

While there was a fair amount of public debate, these policies garnered broad public support. Even though federal government expenditures directed toward social welfare, health and security stood at five million dollars in 1900, fifty years later that figure rose to two billion.[26] Similarly, while government held seven percent of the nation's capital assets in 1900, this percentage rose to twenty by 1950 and continued to grow.[27]

As these programs were introduced, state and national governments were poised to afford them. In 1940, the Gross National Product (GNP) had not yet reached $100 billion. But as the troops returned from WWII service and began to settle down, the economy picked up steam. Approximately twenty-five years later, GNP increased to $685 billion. The economy outperformed economists' most lofty predictions. Indeed, even after accounting for inflation, GNP had nearly tripled.[28] Confidence in domestic American markets began to swell. At the close of 1965 John M. Keynes was featured on the cover of *Time* magazine symbolizing public sentiment that the U.S. had finally triumphed over the unpredictable forces of market capitalism. President Johnson's budget director, Charles Schultze, boasted that although we were unable to "prevent every little wiggle in the economic cycle, we (could now) prevent a major landslide." The editors of *Time* added victoriously that "even the most optimistic forecasts for 1965 turned out to be low." If America could be said to have economic problems, they suggested "[these] are the problems of high employment, high growth, and high hopes."[29] Meanwhile, the economy kept growing—in 1966 the GNP picked up another $65 billion, in 1967 another $44 billion—until Richard Nixon found it wise to declare: "We are all Keynesians now."[30] In retrospect, there seemed little reason not to be.

The Limitations of the Welfare State

The rising costs of social reforms that paralleled the GNP, however, seemed to get exponentially expensive as time passed. In a five-year period between 1965 and 1970, the Department of Health and Human Services reported that the number of national households on Aid to Families with Dependent Children (AFDC) more than doubled to 2,208,000. By 1975, the program added yet another million more households to reach 3,498,000. The National Food Stamp program experienced a similar explosion. In 1965, it gave benefits to approximately 400,000 persons. By 1970, that number jumped to 4.3 million, and by 1975, to 17.1 million—a 427 percent increase in 10 years.[31] The state of California saw a similar trend. In 1965, there were 628,649 residents receiving AFDC.[32] By 1975, the number increased to 1,384,561. In fact, the number of California residents who received some kind of welfare in 1975 totaled 2,047,866, slightly more than ten percent of the entire state population. By the early 1980s, California ranked fourth in the nation for its total number of recipients of AFDC per 1,000 of its population.[33] In short, between 1969 and 1974, national public aid expenditures per capita rose by $80 billion.[34]

To make matters considerably worse, these growing state and national expenditures were coupled with a nation-wide economic slowdown. The old large-scale, fixed capital investments in mass-production systems that had been built without thought to fluctuating and flexible markets began to show signs of strain. The problem was these systems had been erected for an economic stability no longer present. As David Harvey explains, the lengthy post-war boom from 1945 to 1973 was built on labor practices that adhered to a version of capitalist production that by today's standards, was quite heavy and antiquated.[35] Those systems often relied upon new technologies that had developed during war years enabling the manufacture of automobiles, rubber, steel, and consumer electric goods.[36] These manufacturing arenas expanded creating strong and generally stable rates of growth enabling living standards to rise. Complimenting these economic arrangements, the U.S. government supplied fiscal and monetary policies that promoted relatively stable business cycles and the steady demand that large scale, fixed, mass production requires. Public investment in utilities and transportation increased and the nation spent money on programs like social security, healthcare, education and housing that worked in tandem to all but guarantee a stable social wage.[37]

But as the economic arrangements in the country shifted, widespread fiscal security began to evaporate, and the nation saw the restructuring of not only production but also labor markets. The mid-1970s brought with it employment practices that trended toward low-skill, lower-wage, and temporary work as opposed to full-time, benefit included, permanent contracts. Between the late 1970s and the early 1990s, plant closings eliminated four million high paying manufacturing jobs.[38] Corporations were moving manufacturing jobs off-shore to cash in on reduced labor costs. The power of trade unions stalled, and living wages and benefits were no longer on the rise. Three in five jobs between 1979 and 1984 paid $7,400 a year or less compared to only one in five jobs between 1963 and 1979.[39] The escalating cost of the Vietnam War produced rising military budgets, inflation kept creeping up and "credit crunches" seemed to be occurring more often.[40] California unemployment rates rose from 5.8 percent in 1960 to 9.9 percent in 1975.[41] The increasing social provisions adopted by the nation had created such structural rigidity, the only tool of flexible response government had left was the alteration of monetary policy, that is, the ability to print money whenever and at whatever rate officials deemed necessary. By 1980, national inflation would grew as much as 13.5 percent, interest rates topped at 21.5 percent and the cost of a gallon of regular gas increased from .35 (in 1970) to $1.19.[42]

As the Johnson administration ended its final year in office, it was blamed by critics for the increasing costs in both dollars and lives in Vietnam, failing to meet its own social policy goals, and the substantial damage it was seen to have inflicted upon the American economic system.[43] The mid-1970s marked severe unemployment, a harsh recession, and climbing deficits. Herein lay the entry point of a new age of cynicism that ostensibly closed the door not only on the postwar economic boom but also its political optimism.[44] The "new capitalism" was never really new, critics of Keynes would now gloat, and the economic scientists touting laissez-faire fundamentalism were now pointing to the 1970s as evidence for their indictment of almost all interventionism in economic markets. The "social welfare experiment" revealed, they argued, that shrinking the state and allowing the market to operate freely was the only way to sensibly achieve stability.

Political Realignments

The political ideas underpinning the Keynesian framework began to lose popular support as the economic crisis grew. Not so gradually, a new epistemology of social and political logic emerged, marked by a unique phase in the development of capitalist social relations. Herein, new articulations or linkages between the increasingly popular liberal discourses of free market capitalism and a set of fragmented race and class interests crystalized. Ideologically, the "conservative" themes of tradition, family and nation, patriarchy, self-reliance, and social order animated these reconfigured relations. The welfare state, which had not only been the mark of the modern approach to national citizenship over the last twenty years, but also the instrument to deliver that membership, was now "to blame" for inequity between citizens and a favoring of "special interests." The very ideals of social democracy, self-determination, empowering the disadvantaged through a commitment to civil rights—considered to be the pinnacle of the modern state by progressives—became the fodder for its attack. In fact, for many, these ideals eventually symbolized a penchant for identity politics, special preferences, and interventionist government policies—potent symbols that would eventually translate into criticism of penal policy and the prison institution.

Reactions to what Thomas and Mary Edsall have dubbed the "rights revolution," along with the use of divisive issues like race relations and taxes became part of an equation that eroded the Democrats' New Deal alliance with such a force, the political left in this country has never really been the same. Republican strategists, enflaming resentment toward the poor, people of color, youth culture, feminists and others, began to position voting blocks to react to highly-charged issues such as welfare policies, housing regulation, the decline in manufacturing work, the war on poverty, lawlessness and even school busing. As Republicans initiated a new brand of populist GOP politics, Democrats lost important swing voters: white, often Catholic, predominantly blue-collar workers from the North and lower income white southern populists from the South.[45]

Real material changes on the ground, of course, nurtured the restructured political coalitions. In truth, it was not until the middle part of the 1970s that civil rights gains came to full fruition, making it possible to genuinely measure the effects of that revolution. Its impact on working class whites was particularly potent since it was they who shouldered a good deal of the compromises and sacrifices mandated in the legislation. Resources that at one time were reserved solely for whites were now being lawfully redistributed—and significant changes in the demographics of the nation (whereby numbers of European white Americans continued to decline) meant that the population of people of color expanded, increasing anxiety for some whites. For the first time in history, whites competed with blacks for work, promotions, and on a large scale, prestige. Union apprentice programs were decreasing and more competitively awarded; parents had less control over where or with whom their children were being educated; and social remedy programs such as AFDC did not mitigate the problems they had been designed to solve. Where before there had been a desire to aid those in need, there now existed skepticism, anxiety, and territoriality. The discontent of families who felt they had to compromise their standard of living became a retaliatory motivation at the voting booth. State and federal programs to redistribute wealth and support social welfare such as Medicaid, subsidized housing, and welfare, were growing in cost. To add to all whites' frustration, the recipients of the new services were increasingly represented as undeserving and willing to manipulate the system for their own gain. The reference to the rhetorical trope of the American "welfare queen," in Ronald Reagan's 1976 campaign for president, touched nerves and inflamed anger by those who increasingly self-identified as Republican. By the time Reagan entered national office in 1981, the persuasive images he constructed of the nation's growing economic problems, the wastefulness of "big government," and the immorality of social programs meant to remedy poverty, racism, and segregation became the keys to unleashing a backlash that swept in Republican control for approximately the next decade.

National party politics began a new "amped up" chapter of competitive jockeying. The identity of Democrats and Republicans became polarized to a greater degree and symbolized two starkly different oppositional forces. For example, in the public mind the Democratic Party was imagined to prefer subordinate groups (people of color, women, the poor, illegal immigrants, gays) over whites, an immoral youth culture, anti-American values, social disorder and the irresponsibility of the poor and criminal. The GOP, on the other hand, was increasingly identified with religiosity, tradition, fiscal restraint, the nuclear family, individual responsibility, patriotism, and respect for authority.

Gubernatorial Politics in California and the Impact of Ronald Reagan

While Reagan played a key role in furthering the divergence between the two parties, the presidency was, of course, not the start of his political career or scarcely the beginning of two party competitive politics; indeed, he was an integral part of the social and political shifts some twenty years before he became Commander in Chief, ironically as governor of California. In 1966, he defeated Democratic incumbent Governor Edward "Pat" Brown in a landslide election. Reagan won by more than a million votes revealing, perhaps, that those in California were already beginning to grow weary of civic activism and progressive politics so symbolic of Brown's years in office. However, it may be more accurate to say that his win, odd as it may sound, signaled an increasing distrust of government itself, given the platform Reagan ran upon. Reagan's campaign developed a set of damaging images of Brown early on, capitalizing on what he saw as the immorality of student protests that began at UC Berkeley, unpopular civil rights legislation within the state, and his declaration of his status as a "citizen politician."

California is a unique arena to illustrate the struggles that were developing within national social policy and politics at this time. As Wallace Stegner has remarked, California is really "like the rest of the United States, only more so." The West has always had the reputation as a place where individuals can reinvent themselves—whether by way of a lucky strike in gold country or perhaps a break in Hollywood. California in the 1960s garnered this mythology with enthusiasm in headlines like: "California Here We Come—And This is Why," in *Life* magazine, "California: A State of Excitement," in the pages of *Time*, and "No. 1 State: Booming Beautiful California," in *Newsweek*.[46] The headlines were not entirely exaggerations either. No other state in the nation had a nearly free and open public school system, a set of rapidly-developing and well-supported public works projects including public parks, water and irrigation systems, highway construction, and a diverse and well-organized variety of social services. In 1962, the state claimed the distinction of most populous in the union luring close to 1,000 new residents per day. Indeed, the popular song "California Here I Come," would seem to be written with this time in mind. And yet, Californians faced the same economic fears and social anxieties alive on every Main Street across the country. In fact, some argue the state experienced the pain and struggle the nation as a whole endured in this tumultuous time, given its unique political demographics and character.

Because the state is so large—approximately 164,000 square miles—and has the greatest total population of any state in the nation, it is difficult to generalize about its people as a whole. But there is no denying the impact California has today and has had historically on social trends, national politics, and popular culture. Given its central place in the media industry, its large number of representatives in Congress, and the disproportionate share of electoral votes in national elections, even relatively low profile stories about Californians and state events gain national news coverage.

The announcement by Ronald Reagan that he would be taking to the campaign trail was one such story, perhaps augmented by his well-known role as a spokesman for General Motors and his fame as an actor. The gubernatorial election of 1966 is of interest here because it personifies forces wrestling for control at that historical moment as they appeared in the social events and political maneuverings of incumbent Brown and political newcomer Reagan. Reagan's successful entrance into California politics frames many struggles occurring over social and political questions across the country, but the race and its aftermath also puts into focus the effects a number of these struggles had later upon viewpoints of crime and corrections. Approaches to crime control and criminal justice philosophies found their emergence in the wrangling between parties in this race, which is to say, they suddenly appeared quite sensible in a moment in time when the country moved to retrench itself in patriarchy and tradition.

Reagan drew the distinction between he and Brown's positions on what the Republicans defined as moral issues. He painted Brown as an undisciplined leader who refused to get tough on college insurgents demonstrating against a new policy that barred organizing and fund raising for off-campus political activities. The protests at UC Berkeley began in the summer of 1964 when university officials passed a new policy banning the use of a small strip of sidewalk directly outside the Sather Gate main entrance for protests, the distribution of political leaflets and the overall activity encouraging what they deemed was civil disobedience. Students began passionately voicing their opposition to infringment of their constitutional rights to free speech. Breaking up a sit-in inside of Sproul Hall, police forcibly removed over 700 young men and women, resulting in what Kevin Starr has called the largest mass arrest in California's history. But student requests, protests and pleas made no discernible difference, as reversal of the policies were flat out rejected by the university administration. The fervor of the student coalition now grew even more intense and combined with anti-war protests at Berkeley, UCLA, and other college campuses statewide.

President Johnson, unable or unwilling to adhere to pledges he made on the campaign trail, escalated bombing into North Vietnam in early 1965.[47] Demonstrations erupted in Los Angeles and San Francisco at the federal buildings. Stanford students joined in the growing protest movement and even rank and file democratic organizations, such as the California Democratic Council (CDC), announced their opposition to the war—the first of such declarations by a national Democratic organization.[48]

Reagan expressed disgust over the protests and suggested the students either "observe the rules or get out." In his view, the students' disobedience flouted legitimate authority and their behavior trespassed on a code of ethics that was at the center of the academy. In contrast to Brown's handling of the civil unrest, he asked with indignation, "Will we meet (the students') neurotic vulgarities with vacillation and weakness, or will we tell those entrusted with administering the university we expect them to enforce a code based on decency, common sense, and dedication to the high and noble purpose of the university?"[49] Reagan publicly reasoned that if Brown could not keep a collection of hippie college students in check, he certainly was unfit to manage a state government—much less guide the moral compass of California.

Student unrest only aided Reagan's political viability and fueled his accusations that Brown was soft, indecisive, and unable to offer a firm hand in the face of what seemed like rapidly increasing social insurrections. In a blistering heat wave in August 1965, just days after Johnson signed the Voting Rights Act into law, the Watts section of Los Angeles broke into rioting after a routine traffic stop went awry. Police cars came under attack, three dozen lay dead—mostly Black men—over one thousand were injured, and most of the businesses in the area were burned to the ground. Although Brown was vacationing out of the country at the time, the blame still reached his administration when his lieutenant governor, Glenn Anderson, was faulted for failing to call in the National Guard before the mayhem reached grand proportions.[50] In addition, the strike on behalf of the National Farm Workers Association (NFWA) organized by Cesar Chavez in the San Joaquin Valley and three days of rioting in the Hunters Point district of San Francisco (over the police shooting of a sixteen year old) eviscerated any political capital Brown may have had left.

Reagan's campaign, however, had a second advantage over Brown's. He also seized upon the insecurities that new civil rights legislation, namely the Rumford Fair Housing Act of 1963, caused owners and landlords. The law outlawed racial discrimination in the sale and rental of housing for the first time in the western state. The advantage Reagan garnered, even then, was attributed to a "white backlash" against people of color, aided by anxieties over numerous new civil rights laws installed nation-wide.[51] But his campaign didn't gain ground as a function of blatantly racist rhetoric that blamed Blacks or decried new rights; instead, it had the effect of crystallizing white dissatisfaction with progressive change. The conservative lean within the GOP was growing stronger in California, and conservative ideas, even when Democrats advanced them, were gaining support. Between 1946 and 1966, Republican registration in Southern California grew by 125 percent.[52] As one voter put it, "I've had enough of this. . . these people (Negroes) burn and loot and get people killed in their riots, and we turn around and give them money. I am voting for Reagan. Brown has coddled these people too much[sic]."[53] Reagan cleverly steered the public's criticism in the direction of the break-down of *law and order*, as opposed to the faults of a certain set of people. This theme might have easily represented the flavor of his entire gubernatorial campaign, and was certainly one he lent to proponents of the "tough on crime" platform over the next decade. To those who claimed there was some kind of backlash, he reasoned, they needed to look at the facts once again. The reaction by folks was "nothing more than the concern people have for what seem[s] to be on the part of some extremists in the civil rights movement, the taking to the streets the issue of violence, of demonstrations, instead of an orderly process of appealing wrongs through legitimate channels. "To call this a white backlash I don't think is fair," Reagan protested. "I think this is a backlash, if there is such a thing, against this breakdown of law and order."[54] Perhaps the genius of Reagan's argument was that it directed anger at the object of legal fortitude, an enemy that could produce both rich allusions and plenty of fury without having to explicitly identify a human face.

Advocates of the new housing law defined its regulations as a stand against racism and an act of installing justice for all citizens. Brown felt confident that the time was truly ripe for a strong stand for civil rights— a stand that would affect private property and not just publicly-funded projects. He argued that race discrimination in California's housing industry thwarted "American principles of equality" and asked Californians to oppose the "serious injustice" of simply standing idly by while discrimination continued to undermine social order and equal opportunity.[55] The California legislature easily passed the Fair Housing Act in the spring of 1963, but Californians wouldn't have it. The state's real estate lobby mounted a successful initiative campaign (on behalf of Proposition 14) repealing the new law. Early polling showed that the public supported the initiative, a reality Brown just could not accept. He still believed that the cause for equality would win out; it was, after all, on the right side of history. The real estate lobby argued aggressively that citizens had the right to sell and rent their property as they pleased. In fact, the campaign for the initiative openly defended the right to discriminate. Reagan, lending his support for the proposition declared, "If an individual wants to discriminate against Negroes or others in selling or renting his home, he has a right to do so."[56] To the surprise of Brown and his advisors, Reagan's sentiments matched sixty-five percent of the electorate casting votes—an astonishing 2 to 1 margin. And while the California Supreme Court would later strike down the proposition as a violation of constitutional guarantees, the public's position had been made quite clear.[57]

Reagan won the election handily as Democrats buckled under the weight of feuds over the Vietnam War, student protests, and the right strategy to beat the broadly popular newcomer. Lu Haas, a press assistant to Brown at the time, summed up the state's mood when he suggested that ". . .by the time Pat Brown was being kicked out of office, the state had washed its hands, politically, of liberalism. It was dead."[58]

On January 5, 1967, Reagan took office using his inaugural address to emphasize his status as a *citizen politician*, a true member of the commonwealth, whose entry into office was a mandate against an autocratic power wielded by government—perhaps ironically against the power of government period. He seemed to chide the former administration as he spoke: "And let there be no mistake about this: We have come to a crossroad—a time of decision—and the path we follow turns away from any idea that government and those who serve it are omnipotent. It is a path impossible to follow unless we have faith in the collective wisdom and genius of the people. Along this path government will lead but not rule, listen but not lecture."[59]

Brown, contemplating his missteps after the election had been decided remarked:

> You don't realize that people who don't go to the university—they regard [it] as a sort of elitist organization, and even though I was tough, I was looked upon as soft. They tied it up with my opposition to capital punishment, and then you couple that with the Watts riots and I had been good to blacks. I had gone above and beyond the call of duty with fair housing and all those things. I had shown great sympathy to minorities. So you couple the abolition of capital punishment, the Free Speech Movement, and the Watts riots, and you add all three together, and I think they were absolutely disastrous.[60]

Although Brown may have been correct about the causes of his political demise, he failed to recognize the historical conditions that made Reagan's political rhetoric possible. Isolated insurrection, the Vietnam War, or a national economic crisis alone would not have ushered in a longing for more conservative ideals. Taken together—and in such a short period of time—these socio-political events and several others too numerous to list here (the assassinations of Martin Luther King, John F. Kennedy, Robert Kennedy, the new drug culture, the second wave of feminism, McCarthyism, Stonewall, to name a few) set the American stage for transformation much greater than any one man.

New Criminal Justice Realities in a Law and Order Era

Riding the wave of these changes, Reagan succeeded in reversing popular thinking about crime toward the old themes of punition and retribution. He refused to name social insurrections or racial protests as anything but criminal behavior, which transformed common rationales for civil disobedience into simple selfishness and defiance. The "war on crime" was no instance to show mercy, in his view, and social environment had nothing to do with criminal predilection. Brown had failed to understand this point, and Reagan captured the opportunities to underscore his error. Brown's rejection of capital punishment was a paramount example of Reagan using his position to paint him as weak. Indeed, when Reagan took office in 1967, there had not been a single execution in the state of California for four years, causing some to declare the state was in the midst of an unofficial moratorium. In his two terms as governor, Brown had granted clemency to twelve convicted killers, a greater number than any California governor in state history.[61] Speaking to the National Sheriff's Association, Reagan communicated a definitive position on crime and a proscription for the state's approach to punishment. His call for law and order turned former attitudes toward illegality on their head: "Let's have an end to the idea that society is responsible for each and every wrongdoer. We must return to a belief in every individual being responsible for his conduct and (treat) his misdeeds with punishment immediate and certain. With all our science and sophistication, our culture and our pride in intellectual accomplishment, the jungle is still waiting to take over."[62]

By the time Reagan left the governorship in 1974, law and order discourse had become code for reigning in defiant youth, soft on crime liberals, unruly people of color, and "activist courts." The phrase captured a sense of collective impatience with those unwilling to obey authority and expressed a failure felt by many to quell rapidly increasing crime rates. Frustration within the crime control field over a dearth of rehabilitative success, the growing cynicism and distrust in public officials, as well as debates over the true causes of crime had sharp consequences in both penal philosophy and practice. Increasing civil disobedience, rioting, Watergate and the like, all reflected the fact that lawlessness seemingly had no adequate solution.

There was little agreement about what ought to be done until a rather unequivocal point of view seemed to capture the academic stage of criminal justice scholarship in 1974. In December of that year, one of the field's most prominent scholars, David Rothman, declared soberly: "On all sides there is a startlingly unanimous view: incarceration has failed. Institutions cannot rehabilitate. We had better devote unprecedented energy and attention to alternatives."[63] This observation served as a theme for the scholarly texts of the field even up until the last fifteen years or so. The general bewilderment and frustration accompanying this acknowledgment appeared in the results of a number of research reports demonstrating that rehabilitative programs simply did not reduce recidivism. Although there was a long tradition of attempting reform, it would seem crime control officials were not making much, if any, progress.

Perhaps most detrimental to rehabilitation was Robert Martinson's well-known essay: "What Works?—Questions and Answers About Prison Reform" in which he analyzed 231 experimental studies of inmate treatment programs and produced the single declaration that "nothing worked,"—rehabilitation was a canard. Up to this date, Martinson's study was the most exhaustive of its type, and, ultimately, the most corrosive to the reputation of treatment programs. Examining all of the studies available both in the states and abroad between the years of 1945 and 1967, Martinson argued that, "With few exceptions, the rehabilitative efforts that have been reported so far have no appreciable effect on recidivism." And in some cases, he found, treatment actually *increased* the rate of recidivism. He asserted that most programs, aligned with penal-modernist principles, "[were] based on the theory of crime as a 'disease'—that is to say, as something foreign and abnormal in the individual that can presumably be cured." But in fact, he retorted, this theory is flawed "in that it overlooks—indeed, denies—both the *normality of crime in society and the personal normality of a very large proportion of offenders...*" [Italics mine].[64]

Martinson, in this quote, repudiates over a century of penal-welfarist thought. His contention crystallizes a shift in penal philosophy from a version of social determinism to the internalization of criminality as naturally occurring (a return to the penal sensibilities of an earlier era).

Criminal behavior becomes a rational, personal—even biological—phenomenon. According to his formulation, social disorder is a function of innately reproachable people who are reasonable and sensible.

Interestingly, however, while Martinson's 1974 essay is perhaps his most cited piece of work, some have argued that it wasn't his empirical research that brought down confidence in rehabilitation, but rather the shifts in social and political perspectives that made it possible for the work to even be considered relevant. In fact, a good deal of research revealed that the evaluative studies Martinson reviewed were methodologically unsound.[65] Even Martinson himself suggested as much in the original article himself. He also retracted a number of his conclusions in a 1979 article entitled "New Findings, New Views." But these details seemed obscured by the ideological tidal wave that repositioned offenders as beings closer to animals than people. Indeed, more and more discourse addressing criminals painted them as a predators that naturally pursued criminal opportunities. Crime was no longer a social problem but rather "a problem of the human heart" that is "permanent" and "absolute."[66] It was understood to grow inside the mind and body of the individual and poverty, joblessness, and socioeconomic disparities had no place in its ultimate root causes.

This version of criminality was later framed in the concept of *rational choice theory* put forth by Cornish and Clarke in 1986, and also in many popularized theories linking criminal behavior to biology. Instead of something a person was driven to do by outside forces, crime was something calculated by free will calculated with a logical, clear, awareness. Blomberg and Lucken complemented this perspective with new research in biotechnology that allowed us to record suspect patterns in genetics, brain functioning, and the nervous system. Once again it became possible to cite the popular Freudian idiom: "biology is destiny," albeit in a slightly new way.[67]

The policy trend of "getting back to justice" thrived in such an environment. Criminals were seen as rational actors in need of a harsh treatment. Policies referred to as "truth in sentencing," "law and order punishment," "zero tolerance," or "tough on crime," brought forth a new approach to treating offenders—at one time absolutely outside conventional rehabilitative logic—that the condemned individual ought to be punished for his or her crime against society according to the *severity of the act.* If illegality was consciously chosen, punishment that ameliorated the offender was pointless. The act of trying to rehabilitate an inmate's behavior is, of course, dependent upon a whole, free, autonomous, independent—indeed a "perfectable" individual. In the past, designing an individual plan for rehabilitation within penal-welfarism implied a conception of people as capable of control, as fundamentally able to change. But the penal practice of punishing offenders according to the severity of their actions revealed the frustration with and abandonment of that modernist idea. If human behaviors are contingent upon history, socio-economics, culture and a whole host of other social contexts, is it even possible to design an overarching program of treatment that would make someone a "better" person? What is the use of speaking about improving a person who is sane and makes an informed choice to commit crime? And, ultimately, who decides what constitutes progress or improvement? The *back to justice* sensibility never needed to grapple with these questions; its primary policy rationales began with retribution and deterrence and ended with incapacitation.

Since the late 1970s—and particularly during the 1980s and '90s—an inclination for punitive solutions to issues of delinquency has become more and more acceptable. Punishing convicts in ways that are painful, vengeful, and even physically harmful has gained favor. Theorists, writing about the "philosophy of retribution" argue that penal sanctions have often become "a kind of therapeutic theatre" wherein the offender is forced to express feelings of pain and moral shame.[68] Instead of society mobilizing a cure, some type of rehabilitation, or a way to alter the inmate's behavior or values, corrections officials use pain or shame as a substitute for eradicating delinquency. Often, harsh penalties have garnered support even when they do not seem to enable some specific crime control benefit. As one California public defender put it, "Lock 'em up and throw away the key," has been "as politically popular as God, Motherhood . . . [and] apple pie."[69]

Stepping back, a line can be traced from the law and order positions of Reagan in the 1960s to the popularity of "back to justice" penal policies decades later. Clearly, he cannot be solely credited with that macro shift in the crime control field, but that he marks the change with his discursive approach to questions of criminality during that time can hardly be debated. As civil disobedience grew and crime increased over the twentieth century, ideas about how to regard and treat defiant acts also changed. Those new realities affected and were affected by a larger set of events. The transformative social, economic and political shifts of the second half of the twentieth century frame a historical context to view the culture of criminal justice as requiring certain conditions to allow for changes in the philosophy and practice of crime control. The privatization of prisons or an increasing acceptance of an industry based upon growing prison populations thrives in a unique constellation of attitudes about offenders, purposes of punishment, and definitions of discipline. It is this constellation that gives meaning to serving justice or upholding the law in a specific historical moment. When one reviews the era of penal welfarism, it seems unlikely that the prison industrial complex could have gained ground given the attitudes surrounding punishment and the commitment to rehabilitation. The economic and political environment seems much less fertile for its assured growth. If this assertion is true, then key questions emerge: what specific conditions combined with "back to justice" policies or law and order attitudes to enable privatization to emerge? What events unique to California complimented this drive? What specific events made it possible for privatization to appear logical, prudent, and indeed innovative? The work in Chapter 3 addresses these questions, specifically as they reveal harsh economic realities in the state and budget crises within the expansion of its corrections department.

---

[1] For more on the history of penological modernism/penal welfarism see: David Rothman, *The Discovery of the Asylum: Social Order and Disorder in the New Republic*, (Boston: Little Brown & Co., 1990); Franklin Zimring & Gordon Hawkins*, Incapacitation: Penal Confinement and the Restraint of Crime*, (New York: Oxford University Press, 1995); David Garland, *The Culture of Control: Crime and Social Order in Contemporary Society* (Chicago: The University of Chicago Press, 2001). In writing this section, Garland's articulation of penal history spanning roughly from 1890 through 1970 has been extremely useful. I borrow his term "penal welfarism" in establishing the importance of crime control changes during this time period.

[2] David J. Rothman, *Conscience and Convenience: The Asylum and its Alternatives in Progressive America* (Boston: Little, Brown and Company, 1980) 43.

[3] Cesare Lombroso, *Crime: Its Causes and Remedies* (London : W. Heinemann,1911) vi-vii.

[4] Anonymous, "The Indeterminate Sentence," *Atlantic Monthly* 108 (1911) : 330.

[5] Frank Tannenbaum, *Crime and the Community* (New York: Columbia University Press, 1938) 19-20.

[6] Karl Menninger, *The Crime of Punishment* (New York: Viking Press, 1968). Excerpted in Rudolph J. Gerber and Patrick D. McAnany, eds. *Contemporary Punishment; Views, Explanations, and Justifications* (Notre Dame: University of Notre Dame Press, 1972) 179.

[7] Gerber & McAnany 179.

[8] Robert Hunter, *Poverty* (New York: The Macmillan Company, 1904; reprinted edition 1965) 25; 47. See also Sophonisba Breckinridge & Edith Abbott, *The Delinquent Child and the Home* (New York : Charities Publication Committee, 1912).

[9] Richard A. Cloward, Lloyd E. Ohlin, *Delinquency and Opportunity: A Theory of Delinquent Gangs* (New York: Free Press, 1960) 151. This citation relies upon the work of James Wilson wherein he surveys a number of leading scholars in the field of criminology. He asks what book or essay written before

1960 is the most significant on the subject of causes for crime. He reports that there is "remarkable agreement" by these scholars. Cloward and Ohlin's book is one of two texts most cited. See also on this theoretical thesis: W. Kvaraceus, W. Miller, *Delinquent Behavior: Culture and the Individual* (Washington D.C.: National Education Association, 1959) 68-69.

[10] Excerpt from a lecture given at the University of Naples, April 24 1901, reprinted in Stanley E. Grupp, ed., *Theories of Punishment* (Bloomington: University of Indiana Press, 1971) 231-33.

[11] Charlton Lewis, "The Indeterminate Sentence," *National Prison Association Proceedings* (1900) 175.

[12] As testimony to the popularity of probation, the Attorney General's report states that between 1915 and 1920 approximately thirty states either created or expanded probation policies. See U.S. Attorney General, *Survey of Release Procedures*, vol. 2, Probation (Washington, D.C., 1939) chap. 1.

[13] Frederick Wines, *Punishment and Reformation: A Study of the Penitentiary System* (New York : T. Y. Crowell, 1919) 221.

[14] Quoted in Malcolm Davies *Punishing Criminals: Developing Community-Based Intermediate Sanctions* (Westport: Greenwood Press, 1993) 29.

[15] Sheldon Messinger, "The Foundations of Parole in California," *Law and Society Review* 19 (1985) : 69.

[16] James C. Scott, *Seeing Like the State: How Certain Schemes to Improve the Human Condition Have Failed* (New Haven: Yale University Press, 1998) 4.

[17] Terence Morris, "Social Values and the Criminal Act," *The Nation* (4 July 1959) 9.

[18] Herbert Croly, *The Promise of American Life* (New York: Capricorn, 1909) 5; 22-25.

[19] George Stenmetz, *Regulating the Social: The Welfare State and Local Politics in Imperial Germany* (Princeton: Princeton University Press, 1993) 2. Emily Talbot, "Social Science Instruction in Colleges," *American Social Science Journal* 22 (1887) : 12-14.

[20] See Michel Foucault, *Madness and Civilization: A History of Insanity in the Age of Reason* (New York: Vintage Books, 1965).

[21] Charles E. Silberman, *Criminal Violence, Criminal Justice* (New York: Random House, 1978) 404.

[22] Andrew J. Polsky, *The Rise of the Therapeutic State* (Princeton: Princeton University Press, 1991) 81.

[23] Garland 36.

[24] Quoted in: Gregory L. Schneider, *Conservative Century: From Reaction to Revolution* (Maryland: Rowan & Littlefield, 2009) 6.

[25] Spiro, Shimon E. & Ephraim Yuchtman-Yaa *Evaluating the Welfare State: Social and Political Perspectives* (New York: Academic Press, 1983). Paul T. Homan, "The Pattern of the New Deal," *Political Science Quarterly* 51 (June 1936) : 181.

[26] Sidney Fine, *Laissaz Faire and the General-Welfare State: A Study of Conflict in American Thought 1865-1901.* (Ann Arbor: The University of Michigan Press, 1956) 379.

[27] Fine 378.

[28] U.S. Bureau of the Census, "Historical Statistics of the United States, Colonial Times to 1970," (Washington, D.C.: Government Printing Office, 1975), Table F1-5.

[29] Quoted in: *Time* 86 (31 December 1965) : 64, 67B.

[30] Quoted in: Charles Murray, *Losing Ground: American Social Policy, 1950-1980* (New York: Basic Books, 1984) 26.

[31] Department of Health and Human Services, *Social Security Bulletin, Annual Statistical Supplement, 1986* (Washington D.C.: The Brookings Institution, 1986) Table 204, p. 282; Henry Own & Charles L. Schultze, eds. *Setting National Priorities: The Next Ten Years* (Washington D.C.: The Brookings Institution, 1976) 340.

[32] California Legislature Senate Committee on Governmental Efficiency. "Welfare in California: Report to the State Senate." Sacramento, 1970.

[33] Department of Public Assistance, "Public Assistance: Facts and Figures," Sacramento, California 1975. "Total Population Estimates in California," CA.RAND.org. Rand California: California Statistics. Rand Corporation, n.d. Web. 13 May 2010.

[34] Murray 49, Appendix Tables 1 & 2.

[35] David Harvey, *The Condition of Postmodernity: An Enquiry into the Origins of Cultural Change* (Cambridge, Blackwell, 1990).

[36] Harvey 132.

[37] See: *California County Fact Book*. California: County Supervisors Association of California, 1968 13. Print. "Total Population Estimates in California." CARAND.org RAND California: California Statistics. RAND Corporation, n.d. Web 13 May 2010.

[38] Barry Bluestone, & Bennett Harrison, *The Great U-Turn: Corporate Restructuring and the Polarizing of America* (New York: Basic Books, 1988).

[39] Bluestone & Harrison 88.

[40] Ellis W. Hawley, "Challenges to the Mixed Economy: The State and Private Enterprise," eds. Robert H. Bremner, Gary W. Reichard & Richard J. Hopkins *American Choices: Social Dilemmas and Public Policy Since 1960* (Columbus: Ohio State University Press, 1986) 165. See also: Allen J. Matusow, *The Unraveling of America: A History of Liberalism in the 1960s* (New York: Harper and Row, 1984).

[41] "California Statistical Abstract," California: Department of Finance of the State of California, 1970. 43. Print. California Statistical Abstract. California: Department of Finance of the State of California, 1981. 22. Print.

[42] Thomas B. Edsall, Mary D. Edsall, *Chain Reaction: The Impact of Race, Rights, and Taxes on American Politics* (New York: W.W. Norton & Company, 1991) 17.

[43] Hawley 165.

[44] Harvey 142.

[45] Edsall & Edsall 4.

[46] Peter Schrag, *Paradise Lost: California's Experience, America's Future* (New York: New Press, 1998) 47.

[47] Jeffrey R. Lustig, "The War at Home: California's Struggle to Stop the Vietnam War," eds. Eymann, Marcia A. and Charles Wollenberg *What's Going On: California and the Vietnam Era* (Berkeley: University of California Press, 2004) 61.

[48] Lustig 61.

[49] Bill Boyarsky, *The Rise of Ronald Reagan* (New York: Random House, 1968) 139-40.

[50] Lou Cannon, *Governor Reagan: His Rise to Power* (New York: Public Affairs, 2003) 7.

[51] See opening comments in "The 1966 Election in California," *The Western Political Quarterly* XX: No. 2, Part 2 (June 1967) 547-550.

[52] Bell & Price 66.

[53] John R. Owens, Edmond Costantini, and Louis F. Weschler, *California Politics and Parties*. (London: The Macmillan Company, 1970) 149.

[54] Boyarsky 202.

[55] "Statement of Governor Edmund G. Brown on Human Rights," to a joint session of the Legislature, February 14, 1963. Thomas W. Casstevens, *Politics, Housing, and Race Relations: California's Rumford Act and Proposition 14* (Berkeley: Institute of Governmental Studies, University of California, Berkeley, 1964) 19-20.

[56] Lisa McGirr, *Suburban Warriors: The Origins of the New American Right* (Princeton: Princeton University Press, 2001) 205.

[57] Charles G. Bell, & Charles M. Price, *California Government Today: Politics of Reform* (Homewood, Illinois: The Dorsey Press, 1980) 65.

[58] Lucien C. Haas, *California State Archives State Government Oral History Program*, ed. Carlos Vasquez, (Department of Special Collections Oral History Program) University of California, Los Angeles, 1989) 75, 134.

[59] Ronald Reagan, "Inaugural Message of Ronald Reagan, Governor," (Sacramento, California: California Office of State Printing, 1967) 2.

[60] Jack Burby, "Governor Pat Brown, A Personal Memoir," *California Journal* (April 1996) : 47-8.

[61] Cannon 216.

[62] Ronal Reagan, Address: Meeting of the National Sheriffs Association, Las Vegas, Nevada, 19 June, 1967.

[63] David Rothman, "Prisons: The Failure Model," *The Nation* December 1974: 656-7.

[64] Robert Martinson, "What Works?—Questions and Answers About Prison Reform," *The Public Interest* 35 (1974) : 22-54. For other reports critical of rehabilitation see: Marvin Frankel, *Criminal Sentences: Law Without Order* (New York: Hill and Wang, 1973); Jessica Mitford, *Kind and Usual Punishment: The Prison Business* (New York: Random House, 1973); Norval Morris, *The Future of Imprisonment* (Chicago: University of Chicago Press, 1974); Leslie T. Wilkins, *Evaluation of Penal Measures* (New York: Random House, 1969).

[65] Walter Bailey, "Correctional Outcome: An Examination of 100 Reports," *Journal of Criminal Law, Criminology and Police Science* 57 (1966): 153-160; Charles Logan, "Evaluation Research in Crime and Delinquency: A Reappraisal," *Journal of Criminal Law, Criminology and Police Science* 63 (1972): 378-387; Wiilliam Wright & Michael Dixon, "Community Prevention and Treatment of Juvenile Delinquency: A Review of Evaluation Studies," *Journal of Research in Crime and Delinquency* 14 (1977): 35-67. For an overview of the Martinson controversy see: Michael Welch, *Corrections: A Critical Approach* (New York: McGraw-Hill, 2004).

[66] These are Ronald Reagan's characterizations as quoted in: Wendy Kaminer "Federal Offense: the Politics of Crime Control," *Atlantic* (June 1994) 102.

[67] Thomas G. Blomberg, & Karol Lucken, *American Penology: A History of Control* (New York: Aldine De Gruyter, 2000) 173.

[68] Jean Hamptom, "The Moral Education Theory of Punishment," *Philosophy and Public Affairs* 13: 211-240.

[69] Quoted in Malcolm Davies, *Survey Report: The Expansion of the Criminal Justice System and Penal System in California—Is Greater Coordination Required?* Bureau of Criminal Statistics Monograph Series. (Sacramento: Office of the Attorney General, California Department of Justice, 1988).

3

Economic Issues

It's unreasonable to expect to understand the California prison market without also understanding the particular economic context within which it arises. A market for prison products, services, or privately owned inmate beds must certainly have access to raw materials for production, whether those be unfinished goods or the bodies of convicted felons. Further, there must be complementary regulatory policies directing this commerce as well as a relatively stable customer base to turn a consistent profit. Clearly, not every product nor service can be sold within every location at any given time. Therefore, the prospect of a set of prison industries relies upon a set of contingent variables—a unique configuration of economic opportunities, as it were—that allows for a foothold in the business of confining people. As I show in this chapter, the alignment of several economic variables made it possible such for a prison marketplace to easily flourish as privatization became positioned to aid a complex set of forces not only economic, but also political. I argue that the prison market forms a unique matrix within the socio-economic relations contained in California. And, if the prison institution is a function that is too complex to be reduced to a simple restrictive social practice as I have suggested, its cost, its administration, its reach, its rationale—all of these must be elucidated in light of those productive advantages.

When private contracting emerges in California (its contemporary form begins in the 1980s), a peculiar political economic dynamic is also present. This dynamic is an arrangement wherein capitalism organically "consumes" the poor—mostly black and brown poor—who, for a whole host of reasons, are unable to be normatively absorbed into the labor market to earn a living wage. These poor can be said to be *produced* by the capitalist system where they are "relatively superfluous" from the standpoint of the labor market. But these individuals have not been ejected and disposed; indeed, they have been absorbed into a *new* social welfare system as it were, to be cared for in prisons that transformed in the 1980s and 90s into viable business ventures utilizing "criminal behaviors" to turn a profit. Looking at the features of California's economy during these years, several opportunities are present that while perceived as negative contributions to the state's overall fiscal health, represent inroads toward the blossoming of a nexus of hearty prison industries. The breakdown of the state's general budget, the collapse of welfare and social programs, the fiscal health of the California Department of Corrections, the shrinking number of available jobs employing young men with little education, the high recidivism rates unique to the state's criminal justice system, and even the influx of large numbers of undocumented immigrants have contributed to the privatization market. The work of this chapter is to explain how such variables endowed companies, Corrections Corporation of America or the GEO Group, for example, with the ability to expand their market shares and provide products that might "improve" California's economic stability. Is there a possibility California administrative officials offered both an invitation to aid this market while at the same time obstructing its success? To begin an examination, we need to consider a short geneology of the state's economic history in the context of the U.S. economy.

California Economy: The Early Twentieth Century

Features of the California economy read like a wish list for states not quite fortunate enough to be endowed with its abundance of natural resources or the applied ingenuity of its population. Few territories across the nation can lay claim to the beauty of California's pristine coastlines, which enabled the development of shipping and export businesses, its fertile soil, which allowed hundreds of varieties of fruits, vegetables and nuts to thrive, or its rich mining prospects, which generated riches from gold, natural gas, oil, and a vast array of minerals used in various national industries. The western climate has been called perfect, its available room to grow was (and still is) both spacious and serene, and its promise for generations included the prospect of striking a vein of gold, or, in later generations, a starry-eyed encounter with Hollywood glamour. The wealth the state has accrued can be traced back to not only the height of the gold rush of the 1850s, but also to the riches produced by agriculture, aerospace, and the entertainment industry.

While its true most states were experiencing the expansion of wealth at the start of the twentieth century, California was in an economic class

all by itself. There was no other place in the United States where more
worldwide trade took place. As a result, more riches were amassed for
its businesses from manufactured exports than in any other state in the
country. Its soil produced the nation's largest crop load which helped to
feed millions of hungry Americans. Even then, those crops were valued
at over $1 billion. California's rich fishing waters enabled the enormous
sardine industry of Monterey's Cannery Row. And the state was the
leading petroleum producer in the United States until at least 1936. Up
to the middle of the twentieth century, one fifth of the gold mined
throughout the world came from California.[1] It was not just a cliché to
head out West and improve one's lot. The bounty to be found in the state
seemed at times, simply too good to be true.

   Perhaps it was the aerospace industry that put California on the map
of lucrative industrial manufacturing enterprises. By 1956, the
production of autos and airplanes—its manufacturing predecessor—
employed more people in the Pacific-Southwest than any other industry.
Its origin went largely unnoticed when Glen Martin began building
aircraft in 1906 in an abandoned church in Santa Ana. Once World War
I began, Liberty Iron Works entered the field and produced planes worth
well over $1 million.[2] Shortly thereafter, Donald Douglas decided to
open an aircraft company in the sunny suburb of Long Beach,
California, believing it was perfect for the building and testing of new
planes. By 1932 he went on to sign one of the first contracts to produce
commercial aircraft for the carrier TWA; and by 1935, every single
plane manufactured in the United States was produced in California,
with the exception of those made by Boeing. As World War II increased
the demand for military aircraft, the demand on the industry grew. The
number of planes produced in the state at peak production topped
30,000, or an impressive eighty-two new machines per day, per year.[3]
The aerospace manufacturing base tripled during the war; by 1945,
federal government contracts to produce electronics and aircraft
technology grew to an unprecedented $8.5 billion—an astronomical
amount for that time. The products produced over the five-year span the
U.S. fought the war were valued at more than $9,000,000,000. Even
twenty years later, as production of aerospace technologies began to
slow down, more than one in every three Californians made some
product within the aerospace or national defense field.[4] In fact, the dense
population growth of Los Angeles County exploded from the migration
of workers and their families who moved to LA suburbs to take jobs in
aerospace factories. The only other manufacturing work in the city that
competed for that kind of space was the concentration of auto and tire
plants.[5]

By 1965, the success of so many of these industries made California wealthy. The ebullient economic report from then Governor of California Edmund Brown declared that the citizenry was marching through "the longest peacetime period of sustained economic advance in modern history."[6] New research on almost every economic front revealed California to be the undisputed leader in population, at the threshold of achieving the highest level of personal income in the nation, in the thick of the highest employment level in its recorded history and posting record rates of per capita income to boot. Given these impressive statistics, it seems hard to fathom that fewer than 50 years later the state would be struggling with a $10 billion budget shortfall and battling one of the highest unemployment rates (above 12 percent) in the country. It makes sense to wonder what fueled such halcyon times. How did the state achieve such prosperity only to have it stolen in less than a generation?

Economic Downturn: The Late Twentieth Century to the Present

In answer, we must look at the faltering of the American economy, certainly one of the most significant events of the twentieth century. The post-war period of the 1940s, 50s and most of the 60s marks the last historical era for which U.S. domination of world markets was a reality. While more than half of the entire world's industrial output between 1945 and 1955 was produced by American workers, by 1980 that figure had fallen to 21percent.[7] Today, the U.S. imports many more products than we export such that in 2008, the merchandise trade deficit reached an unprecedented figure of $840 billion.[8] In fact, the U.S. merchandise trade deficit with China, which reached a new record in 2011, continues to hamper economic growth. Never before has the nation recorded this level of deficit; in fact, no single nation's deficit has ever reached a larger proportion relative to the global economy.[9]

The first indications that American hegemony was beginning to fade came in the form of a stall in the structural competitiveness of U.S. manufacturing which had reigned supreme for at least 20 years following WWII. For the first time, Americans could no longer boast of unprecedented gains in productive output or exports. By 1967, the country began a downturn in industrial growth that ultimately placed it last among developed countries. While this downturn took a full 20 years to fully develop, the nation is still feeling its effects in the twenty-first century.

As I suggest above, one of the first indications of economic downturn was the reduction in American exporting. Tellingly, as our share of world production fell between 1953 and 1984, Japan's share rose from 3 percent to 15 percent during the same time period.[10] In a single decade, the value of foreign manufactured imports relative to domestic production exploded: the U.S. was no longer the supplier, but rather the consumer of more products than had ever entered the country in history. Recovering from the ravages of war, Germany, Japan, as well as South Korea, Taiwan, Singapore, Hong Kong and Brazil began exporting such a wealth of goods that by 1986, for every $100 spent on products produced in the U.S., we spent $45 on those produced elsewhere.[11]

Foreign exports were not necessarily better, but rather, they were able to benefit from a number of unique advantages. First, foreign companies employed production lines that paid extremely low wages in economies that had vastly lower standards of living. That work was taking place in much newer factories using modern equipment that had been rebuilt after wartime. As we became less and less able to compete with foreign markets that had lower cost margins, our industrial advantage collapsed. To make matters worse, the U.S. failed to coordinate corporate strategic goals with government regulation and develop research and development programs that might make our products unique and contemporary. Terminating investments in civilian industry, meant an aging civilian industry. Indeed, as our factories were crumbling and our workforce was becoming increasingly expendable, the U.S. government focused primarily upon spending money—which increased exponentially over the course of the next two generations—on military superiority. While the Europeans and Japanese were pumping their profits into their own domestic infrastructure and industrial dominance, we were sowing the seeds of decreased productivity and trade deficits.

As newly-industrialized countries penetrated Americans' lion-share of the world market for textiles, shoes, and clothing, and then expanded to ship building, petroleum and automobiles, U.S. domestic companies began to rethink their relationship to the American worker. In fact, the eroded productivity for U.S. companies left them in a bind: organized labor had negotiated wages and benefits to such a degree, those costs were eating into the bottom-line. It became clear that higher unit costs couldn't be passed onto the consumer given the pressure by competitors to keep prices low. In California, for example, average weekly earnings had grown from $104 in 1960 to $280 in 1979.[12] Working class power through unionization translated into the power to strike for an even greater slice of the economic pie. And strike California workers did, making the 1970s a highly volatile time for job walk-outs: the

Machinists struck for three months in 1975, the Lockheed space division orchestrated an 83 day walk-out in 1977, the automobile workers waged a three month dispute in 1978 and 20,000 Teamsters staged a walk-out in 1979.[13] California workers used strikes and aggressive bargaining, like their blue-collar counterparts across the nation, to secure higher average salary increases. And at times these increases topped national averages. Compared to national workers in non-construction jobs who secured a 3-cent per hour increase in 1978, their California counterparts drew an average increase of 21-cents—which further deepened the profit losses for California companies.[14] To add to the labor losses, the high value of the dollar decreased the cost of imports, making foreign products cost less and domestic products seem over priced. These pressures on American businesses intensified the crisis of international competition, but also weakened their standing in the world economy. By 1975, companies began to downsize, causing unemployment to rise to 8.3 percent across the country—an anathema given that less than a decade before the figure had been at less than 4 percent.[15] Other market assaults like the rise of fuel prices due to the oil embargo, the steady increases in wages (still rising even into 1979), tax increases and inflation—all of these drove profits for domestic non-financial corporations to less than six percent. This figure was a decline of more than a third from the high levels of the 1960s.[16]

Business and government leaders were initially taken by surprise. Approaches by corporations to alleviate the growing crisis ranged from "zapping labor," that is, pulling back the reins on wages and benefits to bolster the bottom line, to attempting to persuade government leaders to alter taxes and regulations through lobbying. Some companies simply got out of the production game altogether. Domestic markets for products like appliances and dry goods were becoming increasingly saturated by 1970, and it was clear that American companies had begun to exhaust new investment opportunities in products that had fueled the postwar boom. Almost every home in the country could boast of a modern refrigerator, a washing machine, a vacuum cleaner and other once uncommon "time-saving" devices. We seemed to have everything we needed—so what was there left to buy? This same story was unfolding in other advanced capitalist countries across the globe. As one market became saturated, others followed suit until the capacity to milk a majority of product lines dried up.[17] To maintain a decent profit margin while prices of competitive foreign goods continued to tumble, businesses were forced to expand output. Of course, this strategy had the effect of driving prices down even further as demand for the product weakened.

"Paper Entrepreneuralialism" and the Tactics of Global Capital

Businesses attempted a creative, if not suspect, response to these problems: "paper entrepreneurialism." The strategy became a way for cash-strapped companies to reinvigorate a dwindling bottom-line. Little more than short-term gambling, corporate executives engaged in investment and stock speculation with pools of finance capital that often generated more profits than did production. On the one hand, corporations used borrowed funds to gain a controlling interest in a firm and then nullify contracts, annul long-standing agreements with suppliers, and liquidate whatever else could bring in large profits. The result of these mergers and acquisitions was a hearty flow of cash that was generated by simultaneously downsizing factories and cutting employees deemed "redundant."[18] Conversely, corporations in need of capital were able to acquire it inexpensively by issuing their own company's shares at prices that were vastly over-inflated. Investors, eager to "speculate themselves a profit," rushed in to buy. The corporate community witnessed the explosion of investment and consumption, and both the U.S. and the international economies were boosted —albeit deceptively.[19]

Another response to the economic crises of this era was to market a new relationship to goods themselves. And herein the idea of "forward flight" and consumption for its own sake took hold.[20] Buying was an activity that marketers redefined. Consumers would now purchase goods simply because they could—and often because consumers *should* for the sake of the nation. When this new relationship to buying emerged in marketing and advertising campaigns, buying was an activity that was hailed as a strange new altruism to American businesses and even our own well-being. Advertising slogans declared, "Buy days mean pay days—and pay days mean better days!"; "Buy now—the job you save may be your own!" Or even: "Buy your way into prosperity!"[21] Today, as a function of the faltering U.S. economy, we see a resurgence of these tactics as companies claim their superiority by declaring their products are "made in America."

Within the new frames, if buying was not a gesture toward supporting American made products back then, it certainly became touted as a simple pleasure—a way of life—that we ought to enjoy for its own sake. Advertising became a rally cry of desire to *get* an object or live the life it made fantastically possible, as opposed to keeping or using that product to meet some practical need. Once these tactics became commonplace, objects were not recognized for their actual features, but rather for the signs offered to symbolize the meaning of their purchase. These strategies were really quite exceptional from the standpoint of an advertiser since selling a lifestyle was infinitely easier than bothering to explain the real details of what was actually being sold. For example, purchasing a pair of jeans might at one time have been about the quality of the fabric or the design features which allowed them to be useful and so on. But forward flight installed a different perspective. The product became a way to experience the signs of a lifestyle—to consume that lifestyle, to identify with that lifestyle, and to signify that lifestyle to others. In the 1970s and 80s, for example, Jordache jeans or Calvin Kleins signified a fashion forward attitude or an ontology that preceded the materiality of the jeans. Those jeans then became aligned with ideas that fueled their purchase over and above the utility of clothing one's body. Today, we witness the ultimate result of this practice: oftentimes the product itself is not even of much consequence, only the symbolic value of the thing seems to offer significant import.

There was one drawback to this marketing approach, however. Heightened consumption required cash, or at least credit. Without personal lines of credit to finance what one could not afford at point of purchase, increased consumption could not be sustained. Corporate genius rushed to respond, and rolling lines of credit were born. What freedom. Or was it? The price to be paid was in fact the extension of our own credit to the American economy. As Americans entered into debt, our payments funneled into corporate growth that allowed for the emergence of a new financial sector. Instead of working to collect enough money to buy a product, we now worked to get out from under the debt we accrued to own what we could not afford to buy. But the beauty of the arrangement, at least from the perspective of business, was that even though Americans were quickly going into debt, becoming slaves to their own consumption, all the while they believed they were gaining a certain brazen liberty.[22] As the 1970s ended, consumer installment debt began to steadily climb. By 1984, that debt in relation to income was approximately 14.5 percent nationally. By 1986, according to nationwide financial reports, the average debt carried by each American family was approximately $11,000 and growing "exceptionally fast."[23]

Economic Crises in California

While so many tremors were rumbling through the U.S. economic markets, California workers were in many ways shielded from a number of the hardest hitting attacks on civilian employment. The state was still adding employees in its manufacturing and service sectors even though growth had slowed considerably. Since the state had an already developed mining and fuel extraction industry, the oil crisis boosted its employment to extract oil even into 1980. Spending increases by the federal government on aerospace production grew an additional 14.2 percent in 1979 from the prior year keeping manufacturing employment deceptively secure. California workers posted growth in various industries producing fabricated metal products, non-electrical machinery, and electronic related instruments.

However, the economic crises that plagued the rest of the country would not spare California. By the first few years of the1980s, income inequity grew faster in the state than anywhere else in the nation, and median income for full-time workers stopped increasing for the first time since WWII. Diversified manufacturing positions in manufacturing ventures such as apparel, paper, chemicals, plastics and metals began to shrink until they comprised less than 8 percent of the manufacturing jobs nationwide. Weekly wages fell from $720 in 1969 to $594 in 1989 to $554 in 1997.[24] Between 1969 and 1997, weekly wages for California workers declined by about 40 percent. This decline meant that in 1997, the average male wage earner brought home about 23 percent less than did his 1969 counterpart.[25] As a sign of what was to come, purchasing power for low-waged workers began to shrink while that power for high wage earners—those at the 80th percentile of all income earners and above—gained at substantial rates. The middle income earners were disappearing, most to find permanent places within the lower percentiles of the wage scale.

Those stalwart industries such as aerospace production and auto-making that had at one time put California on the manufacturing map, began a steep decline. Chrysler shut down its assembly line in the City of Commerce in 1971, General Motors shut down two plants in 1982 and 1992. And Ford left Pico Rivera and Milpitas in 1980 and 1983 respectively. By 1995, aerospace companies cut 60 percent of their workforce from peak employment numbers of 1988.

Not only work in manufacturing, but also disappearing were jobs in industries based on natural resources. Canning and logging hit labor peaks in 1979 and were being replaced with service positions in industries like retail trade, health services and finance.[26] Agriculture jobs also peaked in 1982 along with work in the mining of metals, oil and gas. But as has been discussed in great detail elsewhere, the new service positions being added in this phase of economic history simply could not substitute for those lost jobs. Service jobs typically paid less, produced less, and were far less exportable than traditional products we once sold to our global neighbors. What California and other states were seeing was the development of a very different kind of economy that was permanently downsizing for those at the mid to low range of the earnings spectrum. The less educated and the less skilled were increasingly finding it difficult to secure living wages and the middle classes were shrinking as the very rich and the very poor increased exponentially.

Today, the average service position in California pays a little less than $10.00 per hour or an annual salary of $20,800 for full-time work—a full $2,000 below the official poverty line.[27] Such jobs are multiplying in fields like retail sales, food preparation, and leisure and hospitality. Job seekers are typically between 25 and 64 years of age, work full-time hours, and are disproportionately Latino. The work is a far cry from post-war jobs available when General Motors, for example, had the distinction of the largest private American employer in the country. The work at GM, though never glamorous, at least paid enough to raise a family and perhaps even take a week or two of vacation after enough seniority had been accrued. Unionization was obviously a key to access such benefits. On average, according to one UCLA study, union workers earn about four dollars more per hour than non-union employees.[28] But, higher wages, like many of the benefits safeguarded by union membership, all but evaporated in many professions. As business struggled to recover profits, unions themselves were blamed for the ails of the economic problems of the 70s and 80s. And thus organizing for the welfare of workers is something of an anathema in this generation. To many, unions symbolize bloated salaries, crooked politics and injury to "forthright" business. While California has one of the highest unionization rates in all industry groups in the country (ironically with the exception of manufacturing), that rate is only about 18 percent—a little over half of what it was in the post-war period.[29]

It's pretty clear that business interests in the state have no intention of going back to post-WWII arrangements with labor either. More than 700 bills have been introduced in nearly every state in the U.S. to push back gains made by unionization. According to the National Conference of State Legislatures, there has been huge increases in legislation designed to force unions to dismantle collective bargaining, limit a union's abilities to collect dues from employees or make it more difficult for employees to unionize. Given that California's legislature is controlled by Democrats (who havely traditionally supported such policies), collective bargaining seems relatively safe for now, but the budget deficits have made this arrangement less secure in recent years as proposals to rollback pensions for public employees have gained momentum. Studies by the Conference Board, a business research group, demonstrate those growing trends. In the late 1980s, corporations surveyed agreed with the following statement about 50 percent of the time: "Employees who are loyal to the company and further its business goals deserve an assurance of continued employment." Ten years later, the rate of agreement with the same statement dropped to just 6 percent.[30]

California historian Dan Walters names the conglomeration of these new economic realities I have been detailing the "post-industrial hybrid." He notes that as the state transformed over the 1970s and 80s a set of economic arrangements seemed to implode. As I note above, factories producing automobiles, tires, lumber, and steel shut down; industries that stayed solvent did so by cutting wages and benefits, restructuring their wage schedules or outsourcing many traditionally in-house positions with seasonal, temporary, or part-time workers.

It's unsurprising that poverty rates during this same period began to grow in the state peaking in the mid-1980s and then growing once again in the mid-1990s. Between 1969 and 1993, the percentage of the state's poor families grew from 9 percent to 18 percent. And although the state has seen the rate decline since (today the rate stands around 13 percent), it has never returned to its pre-1970 levels.[31] More alarmingly, while poverty is measured by using a nationally-determined figure of total income, the high cost of living in many of California's counties skew the official tallies of the poor. Adjusting for living costs, the rate jumps five percentage points for more than ten different state regions, making the actual poverty rate in Los Angeles county, for example, 26 percent.[32]

The Special Case of Demographics within California

As these shifts were taking place, California was also contending with a significant demographic transformation that had, and continues to have, considerable consequences for its economy. The state's popularity as a destination for newly arriving immigrants—both legal and undocumented—has been unparalleled. Between 1960 and 1995, the number of immigrants living in California increased six-fold making one in every four residents in the state foreign born—the highest number since 1890. By 1989, while the number of male immigrants within the U.S. workforce stood at approximately 8 percent, a full 29 percent of California's male workforce was comprised of immigrants. As the state reached the end of the 1990s, this figure rose to 36 percent.[33] Indeed, in the 1990s, half of all new workers in the state were recent immigrants and 80 percent of these were either Hispanic or Asian—with the former comprising the larger number.[34] Compared to demographic statistics in 1969, this was a five-fold increase.[35] Most immigration to California in the 1950s was from either Canada or Europe with the remaining newcomers entering from Mexico. But over the last thirty years these figures have reversed: while Europeans and Canadians make up a dwindling 10 percent of newly arriving immigrants, Mexico and Central America's share has climbed to above 50 percent. Although there are no precise or direct counts available of those who are in the state illegally, best estimates are that 2.6 million illegal immigrants call California home.[36] Today, California's labor force includes approximately 1.8 million undocumented immigrants—the highest concentration in the nation—and more of these male immigrants (93 percent) are found in the California labor market than native-born males (81 percent).[37]

As these immigrants arrived, however, white native-born residents have moved out. Over the last several years in fact, California has lost more of its native population each year than it can reproduce. Between 1994 and 2004, 70 percent of all domestic migrants leaving the state were white.[38] According to Lee Green, this development means that between 1990 and 2000, immigrants and their children made up not just a portion, or even most of California's growth; they accounted for virtually all of it. Of the 4.2 million people added to California over those ten years, the net gain generated by the native population was just shy of 90 thousand—fewer than the number that typically attend the Rose Bowl game.[39] Today, the net gain of immigrants to California makes it the most ethnically-diverse state in the country.

Not surprisingly, this fact has had significant effects upon the state economy. To begin, the influx has contributed to significant income inequality among California citizens because the immigrant population's wages are disproportionately lower than those of the native born. According to Deborah Reed, about 67 percent of all immigrants occupy the lower half of the wage distribution. Research shows that while three of every four immigrants in the state are of working age (25-64), they have been largely ill equipped to compete for high-paying positions since most lack a high school diploma and skills coveted by employers. An estimated 3.8 million people in L.A. County alone can barely read, write or speak English. In fact, a study by the United Way shows that 53 percent of working age L.A. residents have difficulty reading street signs, filling out a job application, and reading a bus schedule. The study concluded that Los Angeles has the highest rate of "so-called undereducated adults of any major US metropolitan area."[40]

Native-born workers who are less skilled, less educated, or of color have suffered economically as a consequence. Work has become sparse, as the competition for lower skilled jobs grows more fierce. While immigrant wages nationally are equal to or even higher than those of similarly skilled natives, studies show that immigrants working in California typically earn lower wages and are in greater competition for those dollars. Supporting this finding is a research report by the Rand Corporation, co-authored by McCarthy and Vernez, that documets that wages for native-born high school drop-outs were between 10 and 16 percent lower ($2,250-$3,800) in the 1970s as a function of immigration. By the 1980s, as many as 200,000 natives were unable to find work, causing many of them to simply stop trying. As increasing numbers of immigrant job seekers have entered the state, and as the state's relative supply of lower-skilled workers has grown, the competition for the pool of jobs they pursue has intensified, driving wages downward. Tellingly, the industries that have the greatest concentration of immigrant workers are those that used to be inhabited in great numbers by low-skill, less-educated individuals born in the state. Today, there are as many immigrants in manufacturing jobs as there are native-born. The jobs that have replaced the traditional blue-collar positions are now often being filled by immigrants as well: work in social services, accommodations, food services, construction, wholesale trade, and agriculture typically pay lower wages and offer few, if any, benefits. Since African-Americans are more likely as a group to occupy what some reports call "adversely affected educational categories" (which amounts to saying they earn fewer degrees as a group) and because racism undermines their perceived suitability for a number of private sector service jobs, their job opportunities have also been even fewer. According to Tony Duster, work in the service industries carries with it many more racist hiring practices. As opposed to industrial positions, wherein interpersonal interaction with the public is seldom a part of the day to day routine, service employment often requires more face-time with customers or trade clients. For employers who believe the public perception of race will make a difference to their bottom-line, any person of color put forward as the public face of the company is perceived as a potential liability.[41] As a result, there is a disproportionate negative effect of the job crisis in California on its African-American residents; and it seems naive to believe that their poverty rates in the state, second only to American Indians, are unaffected by such trends.

In sum, significant immigration patterns in California, as well as specific demographic features of the particular immigrants making up those patterns, has made crucial impacts upon the economy. When immigration explains up to 40 percent of the rise in male wage inequality in California, it is impossible to account for the working life of a Californian without also recognizing the impacts of the absolute decline in income at the mid-to-lowest levels of distribution.[42] But, of course, the central question we've been working towards answering is: how do these facts affect prisons, prison privatization, and criminal justice trends that impact who becomes incarcerated?

Making Sense of a new Economy and Criminal Justice Realities

The details of California's economic history are significant for at least two reasons. First, the growth of the Department of Corrections & Rehabilitation and its number of facilities is linked to the economic restructuring that has taken place over the last 30 years. As the prison population has grown exponentially in the state, so too have the pressures to find a feasible—which is to say, affordable—method to house these growing numbers of prisoners. Private contracting of prisons entered the list of available options only when the prison system experienced two simultaneous strains: decreasing funds and increasing inmates. Therefore, the distressed political economy of the state serves as a significant basis upon which private prisons stood a chance in the California legislature.

While I want to be careful not to argue that the reorganization of the economy is the direct cause of a rise in inmates in the state's prisons, it is well documented that incarceration *is* a phenomenon that strikes mostly poor offenders.[43] As the state has "downsized" its social welfare sector and communities have had increasing difficulty providing safe, secure, and stable spaces to raise families, it has simultaneously expanded its criminal justice sector and augmented in particular its penal institutions.[44] The faltering economy, therefore, is one explanatory factor in the rise in California state prisoners. In fact, incarceration may be understood as a tool to organize the growing class of poor in California.

Some argue the system of capitalism needs the poor and may create these classes by way of policy or crisis. A counter response is that the poor directly threaten the capitalist system by defying or calling into question the social relations that support ordered work and the ideology that undergirds those relations.[45] In this way, the poor, in contrast, harm capitalism. An interesting argument by Christian Parenti suggests not only that both of these claims are simultaneously true, but also that, "Prison and criminal justice are about managing these irreconcilable contradictions."[46] Which is to say that the poor are a needed factor in capitalist growth, but also an absolute liability to its smooth reproduction. This perspective has significant implications for our understanding of how political economic conditions are not just an occasion to decry a crisis, such as high rates of poverty or homelessness, but an opportunity to manage, indeed control, a whole capitalist society.

For example, it's clear that those at the median to bottom levels of income distribution have grown in number over the last three decades and although the cost of living continues to rise, wages have stagnated or fallen. The hope to better one's conditions through professional advancement has not held great promise across all sectors of employment. It has become more difficult to feed, clothe, house, and provide healthcare for an average family. Under these circumstances, there exists greater risk for poverty, troubled homes, and illegality— especially of youth. Dropouts, according to a 2009 statewide briefing, cost California $1.1 billion. The reason is apparent: high-school dropouts are more likely to commit crimes than those who remain in school. This claim, that "[d]ropout prevention is crime prevention" is not particularly new, but the equation points to the risk teens face when families and communities are unable to provide a safe, quality education.[47] A descent into drug culture, gang culture, or simply isolation has proven to increase one's chances of becoming a ward of the California criminal justice system. Once this occurs, a cycle has been initiated that statistics reveal is genuinely difficult to escape. Records show most inmates return to prison almost as soon as they are released, more than half after about two years. Recidivism rates, now at about 70 percent, are so high and skew the national averages to such a degree, the Federal Bureau of Statistics calculates the U.S. recidivism rates both with and without California.[48]

Michel Foucault has called the dynamic of high recidivism part of "a curious mechanism of circular elimination" present in the prison institution. In this cycle "society eliminates by sending to prison people whom prison breaks up, crushes, physically eliminates; and then, once they have been broken up, the prison eliminates them (once again) by 'freeing' them and sending them back to society; and there, their life in prison, the way in which they were treated, the state in which they come out, ensures that society will eliminate them once again, sending them to prison . . .[49] Part of what is elucidated here is that the conditions offenders face once they are released ultimately contributes to their greater chances of returning to jail. And once they return, it's clear that the prison institution has indeed become the force that perennially organizes their social, economic and cultural life. They become reformed by the idea of incarceration and its sensibilities. In short, it becomes their cultural touchstone. One national study examining the conditions of prisoners after release revealed that once they leave a correctional facility, they have a 13 times greater risk of death than the general population. These individuals died of drug overdoses at 12 times the rate of the general population, were the victims of homicide at 10 times, and took their own lives at three times the rate.[50] In California, more than 75 percent of parolees have drug and alcohol problems upon release and another 10 percent are homeless.[51] According to a five-city survey completed across the state, 60 percent remain without a job as well. Two-thirds of employers stated they would not knowingly hire an ex-offender regardless of the crime they committed. In fact, 40 percent checked records to ensure that recent hires were not ex-cons.

Even when those who have been released do find work, their ability to earn is often hampered. Researchers from Princeton University found that when paroled, prior inmates earned only half as much as people of the same background who had not been in prison and have "virtually no prospects for advancement." Lack of a formal education is one of the primary reasons for this predicament, which is unsurprising, since half of those released from California state prisons are functionally illiterate. To be clear, there exists a complicated relationship between poverty, the penal institution, and the larger restructuring of California's political economy.[52] But the negative apects of the prison institution described at the start of the nineteenth century which predicted that it would create a "marginal" population of delinquents is now simply viewed as an inevitability. Not only is it accepted as fact, but also it's simply common sense to view the delinquency effect of imprisonment and the poverty effect of a fractured economy as a problem to which prison is a suitable response.[53]

The California State Budget and Correctional Institutions

The economy in California, however, is not just an indicator of shifts that have taken place for individual citizens in relation to the prison institution, it also demonstrates changes that have occurred institutionally. Economic transitions set the stage for many of the issues that have been plaguing the state's budget and consequently, the financial health of the California Department of Corrections and Rehabilitation (CDCR). The CDCR is the largest agency drawing its funding from the State's general fund. As a result, the CDCR is dependent upon the health of that fund for the livelihood of 66,000 employees—their salaries and benefits—as well as the payments for medical, dental and mental health costs for inmates and supplies to maintain each of the department's facilities. I will return to the specifics of the CDCR later because it is from this agency that so many of the state's financial pressures derive. And if private contracting of California prisons was adopted to solve any problem, it was to decrease these pressures. But for a moment, let us focus on the California budget more generally.

Until November of 2010, when voters in the state finally amended the rule, California was one of only two states requiring a two-thirds majority of the legislature to pass a budget. This two-thirds majority measure, passed in 1978, was originally put into place to reign in spending and tax increases via Proposition 13. But as a result of its adoption, legislative gridlock has problematized the budget process, endowing a small minority with the power to block passage of a working budget—in many cases to achieve spending increases for pet programs and projects. Even as late as last year, for instance, Republicans in the California Senate blocked over twenty bills simply because they said Democrats "broke promises that sealed the summer's budget pact." Since no one party has responsibility for unpopular budget decisions, each one blames the other and refuses to compromise.

Other changes brought on by Proposition 13 were just as significant to the state's fiscal health: assessed property values were rolled back to 1976 levels, property tax was capped at 1 percent, and limits were put on the amount one could be assessed for the growing value of property. As a result, the state grew much more reliant upon the vitality of income taxes and the overall health of the state's economy to produce revenues. Since Proposition 13 dramatically altered the amount the California legislature could collect in property taxes, the state has gathered less of these revenues than the average for all other states since about 1977.[54] In good economic times, consequentially, there is a higher intake of revenue and a sigh of relief; however, in low revenue years, alternative sources from non-wage generating strategies such as stock options and capital gains have been crucial. It took years for the impacts of these changes to the state's public finances to truly be felt, but between the 1980s and 1990s, budget pressures began to mount in ways never before seen. The recession in the early 1990s sealed the insolvency that had been brewing for years and the first major deficit of more than $10 billion in the general fund appeared in fiscal year 1992-93.[55]

The growing problems in the state budget meant programs and departments dependent upon its funds were obviously also feeling the pinch. Simultaneously, as the state began to run out of money, the consequences of public policies aimed at "getting tough on crime" meant that the number of inmates in the CDCR was rising rapidly. The corrections annual operating budget grew faster than the entire

California state budget as a whole in the 1990s: the CDCR increased 14 percent per year between 1984 and 1994 compared to a 7 percent year increase for the state budget overall.[56] These increases resulted in corrections becoming a cash cow. Today, California spends more than any other state in the nation on imprisonment —over $9 billion according to the CDCR's own web-page. If costs were reduced to simply align with the average other states spend per year, the savings would be $4 billion every year.[57]

Increased cost to simply feed and care for inmates was the first challenge to the department. Most corrections departments spend about $32,000 per inmate per year for care and housing; California spends around $49,000 and has had consistently higher rates for years. If the state could have simply stopped the increasing numbers of inmates or reduced the overall recidivism rates, they might have been able to gain some ground on the spending in the late 1980s. But the prison population has shown no sign of significantly decreasing over the last 30 years. In 1980, the CDCR was responsible for 23,511 offenders; in 1988 the population increased to 64,000 prisoners; in 1998 the population had more than doubled to 154,000. By 2004, the total grew to 162,500,[58] and today, the department cares for approximately 171,000.[59] To put this into perspective, researchers Franklin Zimring and Gordon Hawkins reveal in a 1994 study that from about 1981 onward, both the raw numbers of inmates and the imprisonment rate per 100,000 increased in California without interruption. At year-end in 1985, the prison population had more than doubled since 1980; by 1990, the population doubled once again. In short, even though the state built 21 new prisons between 1981 and 2001, at the end of that twenty-year period, to merely remain at almost twice their design capacity, the CDCR still needed to build one new prison a year, every year, until the incarceration rate radically shifted.

In 2010, such a shift had still not occurred; indeed, adult prison facilities were running at approximately 180 percent of their designed capacity. Perhaps as a sign of things to come, between 1985 and 1995 the CDCR reported that the Los Angeles County jails began to house approximately 350 "floor-sleepers" who used foam rubber mats on the concrete because there were no vacant cells with available cots.

But state prisons were no better off. For a little more than a decade, prisoners at fourteen facilities (which account for almost half of all state prisons) have been housed in what were once day-rooms—communal areas for mingling, watching TV and playing cards. This move came after triple-bunking the inmates in each available cell no longer accommodated the increasing numbers. As I noted above, most of the overcrowding can be attributed to high recidivism rates—more than half of all inmates return to custody within two years.

The "Three-Strikes Your'e Out" law passed in California in 1994 ensured that those who returned also stayed for longer periods of time. Over 40,000 offenders in the prison population are repeat offenders. About a quarter of the inmates being held in California are "three-strikers"—most involved in a non-violent offense when sentenced with their third strike. I will examine the three strikes law in greater detail in the following chapter, but for now it is sufficient to note that over 55 percent of second and third strikers are convicted of a non-violent offense, and most of these are for drug and property crimes.[60] This means that the mandated sentencing for these offenders does not come cheap. The Justice Policy Institute estimated that the number of three-strikers added to the system between March 1994 and September of 2004, just the first 10 years of the new law, would cost California an additional $8.1 billion to incarcerate.

California voters, however, refused to change their position on the law even after they witnessed its increasing costs. In November 2004, with the financial stakes clearly debated, voters were asked to amend the Three-Strikes law. In a ballot measure entitled Proposition 66, it was proposed that a third-strike apply only when a conviction was for a serious or violent felony. But the public voted it down, even though the net savings to the state would have been several tens of millions of dollars immediately after its passing and several hundred million dollars annually as the law matured. Looking back, it's not completely surprising the proposition failed at the polls given that the campaign against it had a relatively easy task: stir up fear of crime and violence as well as panic over the release of "dangerous" inmates. And, given the cultural tone of post-9/11—which at that time had been only a short three years beforehand—public anxieties were still heightened. In hindsight, the defeat of the bill marks the public's preference for (a perception of) security over fiscal realism and the notion that the state's budget deficits could be seen as, "someone else's problem."[61] Over the past year, as I will explain in Chapter 4, California voters finally amended the law, but the effects of this change have yet to be studied.

In the summer of 2009, after several beleaguered inmates brought lawsuits accusing the state of cruel and unusual punishment, a panel of three federal judges ruled that the governor would need to reduce the inmate population by approximately 40,000 allowing the facilities to be at 137 percent of their original designed capacity. The order proclaimed that in failing to provide constitutionally adequate medical and mental healthcare, the state had created "criminogenic" conditions which encouraged prisoners and parolees to commit more crime. Although a plan was advanced to alleviate the overcrowding and some measures have already been adopted to decrease the inmate numbers (principally sending thousands of inmates to private prisons out of state, a point I will address in Chapter 6), Governor Arnold Schwarzenegger suggested that the federal panel had no business in the state's corrections issues and in late 2009 he filed an appeal to the U.S. Supreme Court to make that case. The court heard arguments in November of 2010 about the dire conditions inside the facilities. Some of the evidence included grisly details of prisoners found "catatonic in pools of their own urine" and "hanged to death" in cells with windows "obscured with smeared feces."[62] I will return to the decision by the court and its ramifications upon the California Department of Corrections later in this work, but for now, it's enough to recognize that clearly the state's overcrowding problems garnered the attention of the highest court in the country.

Exacerbating the shortage of funds to care for inmates has been a considerable increase in healthcare costs over the past 20 years. The inmate population, like that of the entire U.S., is aging. The price of prescription drugs and treatments continue to rise, and court mandated services have had to be absorbed into the budget. Prisoners tend to have health problems more frequently than the general population, and in addition to their unhealthy lifestyle habits, they typically have had inadequate healthcare over the course of their lives. One in five has a serious mental illness; one in three is infected with hepatitis C; and the number of those infected with HIV/AIDS is five times higher than the national average.[63] The state also spends money on "permanently medically incapacitated" inmates. These are individuals who are, for example, semi-paralyzed, on breathing tubes, or unable to walk. Californians pay over $50 million to treat these offenders a year—between $19 million and $21 million simply for prison guard salaries, overtime, and benefits. Most of the ailing inmates are shackled with steel bracelets around their ankles to the safety rails of their beds.[64]

Even though the state has spent large sums on healthcare, it apparently has not been enough. After reports found that one in five prison doctors had either been disciplined by the California Medical Board or sued for malpractice and several inmates were either denied proper care or simply not getting any care, a range of law suits were filed. In one case, an otherwise healthy young inmate had a tooth pulled and died six days later from an infection that rendered him unable to breathe.

In addition, according to a federal court report released in August 2004, at one California facility four of the eight doctors had either had criminal charges filed against them, lost privileges at community hospitals, or had been diagnosed with mental health problems. And lest it be proposed that these doctors were simply under-paid and thus lacking motivation to provide adequate care, records show that the average annual salary for each physician was approximately $177,000.[65]

The federal government has stepped in more than once to remediate the state's healthcare programs and declare the services it renders sub-par. In 2005, for example, a federal judge noted that not only had the state admitted its own prison conditions were unconstitutional, but also on average an inmate needlessly died every six to seven days due to issues in its medical delivery system. In short, the court claimed that the state had failed to comply with mandates ordered in the past and it was clear conditions were not going to improve unless the system was dramatically overhauled.[66] Consequently, the control of the healthcare programs within the entire state prison system went into receivership in 2006, supervised by the U.S. District Court Judge Thelton E. Henderson. As a result, the state's costs for inmate healthcare skyrocketed. To simply compare spending before and after the court took over the healthcare program reveals a difference of more than a billion dollars. In 2010 alone, the state spent more than $1.5 billion for inmate medical care.[67]

Along with the climbing medical costs, the price to simply provide guardianship has increased significantly. The salaries and benefits of the California Corrections and Peace Officers Association (CCPOA) grew substantially in the 1990s as the ranks of prisoners began to swell. Between 1984 and 1994, 25,900 new prison employees were added to the CDCR, a larger number than were hired for all other state departments combined (16,000).[68] In the mid-1990s, Governor Pete Wilson signed labor pacts that increased guards' take-home pay by eleven percent—increases that were typically larger than those given to other state employees. The next Governor of California, Gray Davis, also negotiated a contract with the union that hiked salaries a striking 37 percent over the course of five years and added a retirement benefit (able to be taken at age 50) that paid 90 percent of an employee's salary per year.[69] The raise increased the base take-home pay before overtime to an average of $65,000 a year, up from $21,000 in the early 1980s. As a point of comparison, the average yearly salary for a credentialed public school teacher in California at the time the raises were granted was about $47,000. One difference between salaries of prison guards and teachers, however, is that teachers must have a college degree and a year of post-graduate training. Prison guards require a high-school diploma and four-months training.

The Logic of Private Prisons in California

After reviewing so many of the economic realities that have transformed the state, why is it that private contracting appeared at the moment it did in California? The first private facility opened its doors in La Honda in 1986. Its appearance was not accompanied by large-scale public attention or great debate. The facility housed low-risk inmates in a community setting. What was it about the prison that uniquely met the demands of the new economic structures beginning to develop and the pressures they were putting on state agencies? My argument suggests that the dramatic and rapid changes in the California economy in combination with state budget shortfalls and financial liabilities within the CDCR signaled a breakdown in the state run penal system that had few options at the time. The resistance to private contracting by the CCPOA was seemingly the most potent complication to the widespread adoption privatization. But in 1986, there was much more support for alleviating the growing burdens of incarceration, and the CCPOA was still a political force in its infancy.

As demand for prison cells grew, a second private facility opened in Baker, a desolate desert city midway between Los Angeles and Las Vegas. From these beginnings, the state contracted with private firms to run seven additional facilities bringing the total to nine by the late 1990s. The prisons fulfilled a number of different needs. First, public authorities were feeling the crunch: they could not construct prisons quickly enough to accommodate the growing inmate numbers, but they also faced a shift in public sentiment toward penal institutions more generally. Mainstream political ideology, citizen movements favoring revenue restrictions and expenditure controls, as well as faltering cultural commitments to "treating" offenders stood in the way of easy approvals to building new prisons. Even prisons that *were* being built had changed philosophical underpinnings—the prison was no longer a place to change behaviors; instead, it was rather somewhere to warehouse people. As governmental power in this modern period was being discredited and often rejected, the superiority of the free market and its advantages of healthy competition were being championed. The private sector was lauded as the instrument to reinvigorate the heavy and bloated processes of bureaucracy. When public and private sectors were obliged to bid against one another, so the argument went, the public sector would be forced to pay attention to its performance more carefully.[70] In short, the ethos guiding the acceptance of private contracting suggested that being motivated by profit was inherently more efficient than public provision. Private companies, motivated by self-interest, would be bound to provide imprisonment with greater cost savings.

Furthermore, privatization avoided cumbersome and rigid procedures of government construction and finance. Private contractors had greater flexibility to choose sites, personnel, and building plans as well as the latest technology and architectural designs. While government generally funded new prisons by issuing bonds, private companies could use a slew of financing "cocktails" including lease purchase or even lease-back arrangements that spread the costs of construction and operation over a set period of time. Finally, and perhaps more attractive still, were the savings that could be produced by non-unionized workers and less strident labor policies. Since private companies hired, fired, promoted, set salaries, and awarded benefit packages according to their own prerogatives, labor costs could be tightly monitored to complement the bottom line.

In all, the topography of economic features within California comprised an opportunity for private prisons to initially appear with very little fanfare in 1986. Not until the CCPOA gained a critical mass of political capital did the question of whether or not private contracting should continue, or grow, become a topic of debate. The CCPOA would ultimately be the brakes on the growth of private contracts as it rightly recognized that the care of California inmates was the lynchpin to their livelihoods. To surrender that responsibility to private hands meant— and still means—the death of their unionized power. Once the corrections system had amassed a large enough number of prisoners and those prisoners began to represent a resource to several various interests—not only prison guards and private companies, but as we shall see, those elected to and seeking office—offenders emerged as a commodity to argue over. The state, inundated with an ever-larger population of inmates, unmanageable budget deficits, and marked changes in the political economic conditions structuring labor markets, allowed in-state privatization—for at least several decades—to buttress these conflicting realities.

---

1 John W. Reith, "The Mineral Fuels," ed. Clifford M. Zierer *California and the Southwest* (New York: John Wiley & Sons: 1956) 213.

2 Reith 293

3 Governor Gray Davis, *Economic Report of the Governor: 2000* (Sacramento, California: State Capitol, 2000) 29.

4 Governor Ronald Reagan, *Economic Report of the Governor: 1968* (Sacramento, California: State Capitol, 1968) vii.

5 Harold Meyerson, "Striking Home," *Los Angeles Times* 7 Dec. 2003: M-1; M-3.

⁶ Edmund G. Brown, *Economic Report of the Governor: 1965* (Sacramento, California: California Office of State printing, 1965) I-III.

⁷ Bertrand Bellon & Jorge Niosi, *The Decline of the American Economy* (New York, Black Rose Books: 1988) 12.

⁸ Central Intelligence Agency. "The World Fact Book: United States." Nov. 2010. Web. 7 Nov. 2010.

⁹ Lawrence H. Summer. "The U.S. Current Account Deficit and the Global Economy," The 2004 Jacobsson Lecture. Washington D.C., 3 Oct. 2004.

¹⁰ Bellon & Niosi 27.

¹¹ Bennett Harrison & Barry Bluestone, *The Great U-Turn: Corporate Restructuring and the Polarizing of America* (New York, Basic Books: 1988) 9.

¹² Edmund G. Brown, *Economic Report of the Governor: 1980 Statistical Appendix* (Sacramento, California Office of State printing: 1980) A-18.

¹³ Edmund G. Brown, *Economic Report of the Governor: 1980* (Sacramento, California Office of State printing: 1980) 11-13.

¹⁴ Brown *Economic Report 1980*, 11.

¹⁵ Anthony S. Campagna, *The Economy in the Reagan Years: The Economic Consequences of the Reagan Administrations* (London, Greenwood Press: 1994) 5.

¹⁶ Philip Armstrong, Andrew Glyn & John Harrison, *Capitalism Since 1945* (Oxford, Basil Blackwell, 1991).

¹⁷ Harrison & Blueston 10.

¹⁸ Robert Brenner, *The Boom and the Bubble: The U.S. in the World Economy* (New York: Verso, 2002) 86-7.

¹⁹ Brenner 189.

²⁰ I am using the term "forward flight" from the work of Jean Baudrillard. He suggests as consumers move on a forward flight toward new things to buy, they ought to recognize that purchasing is not so much about *having* an object [for long], it is about *obtaining* it—about consuming it *as a purchase. The System of Objects* Trans. James Benedict (New York, Verso: 1996) See especially chapter 4.

²¹ Vance Packard, *The Waste Makers* (Pocket Books: 1969) 17.

²² Baudrillard 160.

²³ George Deukmejian, *Economic Report of the Governor: 1985* (Sacramento, California Office of State printing: 1985) 29. See also Harrison & Bluestone 17.

²⁴ Deborah Reed, *California' Rising Income Inequality: Causes and Concerns* (San Francisco, CA: Public Policy Institute of California, 1999) 14. Figures are adjusted to 1997 dollars.

²⁵ Reed 14. Statistics are adjusted to 1997 dollars and represent civilian males ages 18-54 who worked at least 13 weeks during the year and were not self-employed.

²⁶ Stephen Levy, *California Economic Growth: Regional Market Update & Projections 1988* (Palo Alto CA, Center for the Continuing Study of the California Economy) 25.

²⁷ California Budget Project, *A Growing Divide: The State of Working California 2005* Sacramento, California: California Budget Project, Sept. 2005) 9.

²⁸ Patrick McDonnell, "Union Membership Increases in the State," *Los Angeles Times* 8 Sept. 2009: A-9.

[29] Nancy Cleeland, "Unions Gain Ground in Golden State," *Los Angeles Times* 31 Aug. 2003: C-1; C4.

[30] See Peter Gosselin, "If America is Richer, Why Are Its Families So Much Less Secure," *Los Angeles Times* 10 Oct. 2004: A-1; A-26-7.

[31] Public Policy Institute of California, "Poverty in California" March, 2009. Web. 23 Dec. 2010.

[32] Public Policy Institute of California 1.

[33] Reed 39, 51.

[34] *California Economic Growth: Short Term Uncertainties, Long Term Trends* (Palo Alto: Center for Continuing Study of the California Economy, 1991) Key-3

[35] Reed 39.

[36] Hans Johnson, "Illegal Immigrants," Public Policy Institute of California: Dec. 2010. Web. 23 Dec. 2010.

[37] Johnson 1.

[38] Rodriguez B-11. As one resident commented in a letter to the *Los Angeles Times* ". . .Any educated, experienced professional with the means to do so is getting out of Dodge." "Pretty soon," another writer remarked, "California will be full of nothing but millionaires and the people who mow their lawns." See: "Is California a Nightmare or Still a Sweet Dream?" in "Letters To The Times" *Los Angeles Times* 3 July 2004: B-20.

[39] Lee Green, "Infinite Ingress," *Los Angeles Times Magazine* 25 Jan. 2004: 14. Green also points out that while the combined birth rate for U.S. citizens and immigrants living in California who are not Latino has dropped to replacement level, the birth rate for Latino immigrants from Mexico and Central America averages more than three children per mother.

[40] Jean Merl, "Study Finds Rampant Illiteracy in L.A. County," *Los Angeles Times* 9 Sept. 2004: B-1; B-8.

[41] Tony Duster, "Crime, Youth Unemployment and the Black Urban Underclass," *Crime and Delinquency* 33: 2 (April 1987) 300-316.

[42] Reed 39, 51.

[43] This fact was plain in 1967 in a report to President Johnson entitled "The Challenge of Crime in a Free Society," just as it is today. The report stated, "The offender at the end of the road in prison is likely to be a member of the lowest social and economic groups in the country." *The Challenge of Crime in a Free Society: A Report by the President's Commission on Law Enforcement and Administration of Justice* (Washington D.C.: U.S. Government Printing Office, February 1967) 77. That is, for the same offense, a poor person is more likely to be arrested, and if arrested charged, and if charged, convicted, than a middle or upper class person. Numerous studies have substantiated the link between economic class and imprisonment. Increasing rates of incarceration have been positively correlated with decreasing social welfare programs and stable employment paying a living wage. The earliest of these studies appeared in the well-known criminologist E. H. Sutherland's text: *Principles of Criminology* (Philadelphia: Lippincott, 1939). Readers interested in this line of study might also see: Ronald Goldfarb, "Prisons: The National Poorhouse," *The New Republic* 1 Nov 1969: 15-17; Nils Christie, *Crime Control as Industry* (New York: Routledge, 1993); Jeffrey H. Reiman, *The Rich Get Richer and the Poor Get Prison: Ideology, Class, and Criminal Justice* (New York: John Wiley & Sons, 1998).

[44] My argument follows from Loic Wacquant's work. See: *Prisons of Poverty* (Minneapolis: University of Minnesota Press, 2001).

[45] Steven Spitzer, "Toward a Marxian Theory of Deviance," *Social Problems* 22 (1975): 643.

[46] Christian Parenti, *Lockdown America: Police and Prisons in the Age of Crisis* (New York, Verso: 1999) 238.

[47] Seema Mehta, "California Briefing: Dropouts Cost the State $1.1 billion, Study Finds," *Los Angeles Times* 24 Sept. 2009: A-14.

[48] Office of the Governor, "Prison Populations & Recidivism." Dec. 2010. Web. 20 Dec. 2010.

[49] Michel Foucault, "On Attica," *Foucault Live: Collected Interviews, 1961-1984*, ed. Sylvére Lotringer, trans. Lysa Hochroth & John Johnston (New York: Semiotext(e), 1996) 114.

[50] Alan Zarembo, "Prisoners Face High Death Rate After Release," *Los Angeles Times* 11 Jan. 2007: A-19.

[51] Jenifer Warren, "Panel Calls Prison Policies Costly Failure," *Los Angeles Times* 14 Nov. 2003: B-1.

[52] This idea has also been explored by Loic Wacquant. See: "Deadly Symbiosis: When Ghetto and Prison Meet and Mesh," ed. David Garland, *Mass Imprisonment: Social Causes and Consequences.* (London: Sage, 2001) 82-120.

[53] Michel Foucault, "The Punitive Society," trans. Robert Hurley, in Paul Rabinow, ed., *Michel Foucault: Ethics Subjectivity and Truth. (The Essential Works of Michel Foucault, 1954-1984 Vol. 1),* (New York: New Press: 1997) 26.

[54] Tracy Gordon, *Fiscal Realities: Budget Tradeoffs in California Government.* San Francisco, CA: Public Policy Institute of California, 2007) 31-32.

[55] California Citizens Budget Commissioner, *A 21st Century Budget Process for California* (Sacramento, CA: Center for Governmental Studies, 1998) 11-12.

[56] Data compiled by the California Legislative Analyst's office. See: Steve Lawrence, "Prison Building Boom Grows Amid Questions," *The Daily News* 30 September 2004.

[57] Dan Walters, "Prisons Still eat into California Budget," *Sacramento Bee* 11 Jan 2010.

[58] State of California, Little Hoover Commission, *Beyond Bars* 31; "Facts and Figures," California Department of Corrections and Rehabilitation Home Page. 17 Nov. 2004. Web. 20 Dec. 2010.

[59] However, since the CDCR and Governor Jerry Brown began shifting low-level felons to County jails under the new realignment plan in 2011 (a plan I discuss in Chapter 6), the total number of inmates actually being overseen by the CDCR has shrunk.

[60] See: California Department of Corrections & Rehabilitation, "Corrections: Moving Forward," Published by the CDCR Office of Public and Employee Communications, Sacramento, California, 2009) 19.

[61] Greg Krikorian, "Three-Strike Law Has Little Effect, Study Says," *Los Angeles Times* 5 March 2004: B-1, B-10.

[62] Adam Liptak, "Supreme Court Hears Arguments on California Prison Crowding," *The New York Times* 30 Nov. 2010.

[63] Jenifer Warren, "Relatives of Dead Inmate to Sue State," *Los Angeles Times* 30 Sept. 2004:B5.

[64] Jack Dolan, "Sick Inmates a Threat Only to State's Budget," *Los Angeles Times* 2 March 2011 : A1.

[65] Tim Reiterman, "Scathing Report on Prison Doctors," *Los Angeles Times* 11 Aug. 2004: B-1, B-7.

[66] "California Healthcare Services: Fast Facts," *California.Gov Homepage.* 4 Jan. 2011. Web. 3 Feb. 2011.

[67] Denis C. Therlault, "California Finds That Prisons Aren't so Easy to Cut," *San Jose Mercury News* 23 March 2010.

[68] Dan Pens, "The California Prison Guards' Union," eds. Daniel Burton-Rose, Dan Pens & Paul Wright *The Celling of America: An Inside Look at the U.S. Prison Industry* (Monroe, Maine: Common Courage Press, 1998): 134-139.

[69] Dan Morain, "Guards' Raises Could be Higher Than Expected," *Los Angeles Times* 4 March 2004: B-6.

[70] Richard Harding, *Private Prisons and Public Accountability* (Buckingham: Open University Press, 1997) 145.

4

The Political-Legislative Sphere

As socio-political and economic transformations within California and across the U.S. impacted penal philosophy and practice, a set of assumptions about the definition of appropriate punishment and crime fighting was turned on its head. This chapter argues that because certain political and legislative trends emerged in California starting in the mid-1970s, a shift occurred in the criminal justice field that allowed the notion of privatizing prisons to become not only logical, but laudable.

The first of these trends was a "new penology" or what has alternatively been called "actuarial justice,"[1] and more simply, "managerialism."[2] I will examine the ways this approach developed, how it utilizes specific penal practices and cultural realities, as well as the ways private contracting capitalized upon its wide appeal.

Next, I consider the ubiquity of populism within the penal field and how this trend has created a new stage from which to govern for both political candidates and elected officials. I discuss, in particular, the case of the "Three Strikes and You're Out" law in California and look closely at its development as a rhetorical event shaping both criminal law and the power of specific special interests. It becomes clear that although there are more mandatory sentences like "Three Strikes" in the state than ever before, many of these sanctions have been adopted without solving any of the purported problems they were meant to address. I suggest that perhaps the addition of several different interest groups now involved in the process of writing penal policy is to blame for the problem of the state adopting penal policies that do not actually address penal problems. It would seem that far from the long-standing tradition of penal experts and criminal justice officials directing the round-up, conviction, and care of offenders, the collection of interested parties in crime and criminal sanctions today continues to expand.

Finally, I explore the development of a movement for victim-rights and its implications upon the relationship between citizens and the state.

I claim that the installation of "victimhood" as a rhetorical trope has not only initiated a new touchstone for morality and solidarity in contemporary California culture, but also has ratcheted up the levels of appropriate punition and retribution. The "tough on crime" policy trend summarized in Chapter 2 owes much of its popularity to simple public exasperation. In fact, the trends discussed in this chapter must be understood in light of a "floating" preponderance of public frustration, anger and retribution toward crime, criminal actors and the seeming failure of crime control workers. As this acrimony fueled calls for harsher sentences, more spending on law enforcement, and a heightened derision toward criminal offenders, it created significant inroads toward the market of private contracting.

These three trends have shaped the agenda of criminology in the state and influenced administrative decisions, policy initiatives, and the "commonsense" knowledge of crime control actors. They have also organized public opinion and created patterns for solving long-standing socio-penal problems such as overcrowded prisons and the perversity of those often referred to as the "underclass." Ultimately, I suggest that the shifts in the crime control field that correspond to criminal justice policy and the activities of legislating in California have allowed for private contracting to appear both sensible and advantageous.

California's New Penology

Perhaps the novel idea put forth by David Rothman in 1974 foreshadows the trend toward managerialism best.[3] In his essay entitled "Prison: The Failure Model," he bemoans the death of rehabilitation and then suggests that as we accept the new reality that we will never solve the problem of crime, we might be well served to simply consider creating nationwide crime insurance policies to protect against its inevitability. He writes:

> For failure in such areas of hazard as fire or automobile accidents, we have . . . devised sensible ways to respond. Fire continues to take lives and property, but there is little new that we are going to do in this area. There is no public demand for bigger fire departments . . . despite the fact that 12,000 people die annually in fires, which is precisely the number that die in homicides. Rather, we accept the continued presence of fire in our society, and respond essentially with an insurance scheme. Citizens and businesses carry fire insurance—not as a cure for the problem, but as a means of protecting themselves as best they can against losses. It is time, I believe, to transfer this mode of operation to the area of crime.[4]

Reading Rothman's prescription some thirty years later, one may not be struck as much by his suggestion that we advocate for state/federal financing of crime insurance for all would-be victims (although the notion could be construed as odd), but rather at his utter resignation that crime is now simply an unsolvable problem. In context, his acknowledgment flies in the face of decades of confidence that with the proper approach, given the right societal circumstances, criminal activity could be all but banished. Rothman's claims reveal that as far as criminological theory was concerned at the time of his writing, we lost the war on crime. And if we could not eliminate it, managing the effects of its inevitability became the next best thing. The new invocation might read: the time for fighting crime (and attempting to repair criminals' lives) is past; instead, we must now simply prepare for its inescapable impact. Whereas the old penology of penal-welfarism concerned itself with the individual offender—his responsibility, his fault, his moral sensibility and diagnosis—the new penology would invest in techniques that identified and managed those classes calculated to be most dangerous.[5] In this light, prison becomes a simple holding tank as opposed to a place where an inmate works through a treatment or program to help him return to his community.

Five years after Rothman's essay was published, California formally recognized this new purpose for its prisons in the text of the state's penal code. The term "rehabilitation" was officially removed from the document marking the point at which one of the reigning hallmarks of penal-welfarist thought simply faded away. The state's shift in 1976 from indeterminate to determinate sentencing complimented this changed understanding of California's prisons. Instead of judges making individualized decisions about prison terms (minimum and maximum lengths) on the basis of an offender's history and crime and then handing the responsibility for inmate release over to a parole board, they were now bound to hand down specific sentences according to particular crimes.[6] From 1980 on, state after state began a campaign to mandate minimum prison sentences ensuring that those who broke the law were not only largely punished through prison time, but also sentenced for longer periods of time.

The move to systematize penal sanctions recognized the same purpose that framed the new penology. The management of crime required not a focus on the unique, upon the specific, but rather on patterns of similarity, on schemes of classification that could calculate criminal distribution. Here then, we see this new approach of managerialism functioning systematically: it abides by an ethos of rationality and efficiency, and has as its objective the control of at-risk *populations—not individuals.* Classes of offenders are designated, their risks categorized into particular types and levels of danger, and then those profiles demand a given set of surveillance, punition, or control approaches. Incapacitation becomes about the reduction of crime in the aggregate as opposed to reorienting a broken individual into civic life. Crime is measured in a body of units, as a set of potential acts to be controlled for the community's protection. Therefore, moral character becomes less pressing than the liability offenders represent to others.

While the language of managerialism (that is, the way it is described) uses actuarial terms, its aims are typically tied to economic concerns. To regulate populations effectively, we install the best crime control measures that ensure the greatest reduction of crime per dollar spent.[7] Given such logic, wardens are more than heads of prison facilities; they evolve into something of a "business-scientist" conducting operations research and systems analysis to innovate methods of crime control that will yield more security for less investment.

Actuarial Justice: An Exemplar

One exemplary model of actuarial justice might be the New York City police department during the 1990s. During this period, William Bratton headed the agency and gained widespread notoriety for his novel policing approaches and managerial style. Bratton suggested the formulation early on that a present-day "department doesn't just try to solve individual crimes." Instead, he explained, "We counter crime patterns and dismantle criminal enterprises."[8] Under his watch, reforming New York's boroughs entailed turning neighborhood police stations into "profit centers" where "profit" was understood to be the statistical reduction of crime. He combined a whole host of evaluative criteria used by police to measure whether crime rates were increasing and then translated their aggregate into a "bottom line." This bottom line was so important, it became the prime indicator of the department's success. Such a streamlined management approach could compete against any corporate firm, he boasted, prompting him to "pit [his] command staff against any Fortune 500 company," as a means to prove its superiority. As Bratton won the hearts of New Yorkers and gained the mantle of "CEO of the NYPD," his crime control methods drew the attention of Californians. Intrigued with his innovative principles, the LAPD took very little time to invite him to move west and work his magic in Los Angeles, where he was appointed the new chief of police over nine years ago.[9] And while he left the job in 2009, his crime control approaches are a lasting legacy for California law enforcement. Techniques like "realtime" information that targets gang violence and terrorism, crime mapping and immediate assessment programs still motivate standard operating procedure for the bulk of state's police departments.

Similar to its law enforcement agencies, California's penal institutions show signs of the new penology. Both the LAPD and the California Department of Corrections and Rehabilitation (CDCR), for example, use a program called COMPSTAT (short for COMPuter STATistics or COMParative STATistics). The program first gained favor within the NYPD and was one of the hallmark policing features Bratton brought with him to Los Angeles. It operates, according to department web-pages, to ascertain "crime trends" and fit particular criminal problems to viable solutions. To read about how the state's police departments use the system is curiously akin to hearing business executives explain a corporate systems analysis plan within a cybernetic program. As COMPSTAT is initiated, it is fed "statistical data" to be analyzed. Then, "personnel" are "deployed," and each manager becomes "accountable for results" to increase the "effectiveness" of the department's output.[10] Similarly, the CDCR claims to use COMPSTAT to accomplish statistical analyses of its management and performance, but it's also lauded simply as a "management philosophy." The program allows the department to identify, intervene, and implement what is called "proactive counter measures to minimize a drop in operational performance as early as possible."

Using Technologies to Fight Crime

In addition, systematizing the practice of incarceration and surveillance within corrections departments has meant using a wide range of technologies. The Strategic Offender Management System (SOMS) consolidates all the existing databases on current and past offenders, for instance, and Global Positioning Satellite technology (GPS) monitors parolees—in particular every sex offender on parole in the state of California as well as selected high risk parolees linked to gang activity. Similarly, the department has put in place biometric identification systems and telemedicine programs to help facilitate efficient tracking of prisoners and cost-effective medical treatment. The availability and proliferation of federal and state crime data-bases has made it possible to track more kinds of crime, specific variables of those crimes, and the disposition of millions of cases at the stroke of a key.

The Bureau of Justice Statistics reports that all 50 states use some variation of the Master Name Index, Criminal History File, fingerprint records and data bases that supply numbers of arrests, disposition, and admission to correctional facilities. Most states also chart the use of these data-bases by maintaining transaction logs that offer an audit trail of all inquiries, responses, updates, or modifications to the records currently held. It's estimated that federal data bases contain some 55 million criminal files—up 20 million in just the last ten years—on about three-million persons which account for almost one-third of the country's adult male population.[11] California, though challenged by the huge numbers of offenders to be processed, is still continuing to transfer "DNA fingerprints" of convicts into the central CODIS (Combined Index DNA Indexing System) file at a rate of up to three-thousand a year. Many of these federal data-bases are available to any person willing to pay a fee, enabling almost anyone the opportunity to acquire information about any person ever finger-printed. In short, it's not necessarily that these systems are totally fool-proof in fighting and/or managing crime, but rather that the breadth of technologies used to manage deliquent or suspect populations are so ubiquitous.

The business of crime control has not just gained new technologies, it has assumed a stance that replicates the logic of those technologies. Penal institutions are systems to be managed to meet strategic planning or to compute crime problems, but they do not speak all that much about the prisoners themselves. The goals are focused rather upon public accountability, public safety, and a "bottom line." These trends reveal clear shifts in criminology within California institutions: modes to achieve public safety reposition the role of the offender, widen the scope of the proper governance of crime control, and revolutionize the manner by which we measure success.

But it is interesting to note that as success becomes normatively measured in actuarial form, that is, as a function of data that demonstrates streamlined operations to control groups considered a societal threat, the statistic has become something of a tool to see a whole criminological reality, as it were. Anklets, bracelets, home detention, boot camps, chain-gangs, high security campuses—all of these technologies allow for the statistical tracking of populations while constructing a type of knowledge about levels of efficiency within a system. Similarly, systems of organizing the work of crime control, described above, are the defining features of efficient punition. Not particular programs of rehabilitation, of treatment, of ex-convict reorientation, but rather the application of strategic classification and differentiation of criminal classes. Penal knowledge is thus reframed as a mode of reasoning wherein the idea of rehabilitation, if it is considered at all, must prize what the department refers to as the "scientific rehabilitation model" or "evidence-based treatment" (utilizing an evidence based system for addressing parole violations "allow[s] agents to scientifically weigh an offender's risk level," according to the CDCR). Within this logic even old markers of penal success or failure carry with them new interpretations.

For example, recidivism rates, once used to measure the effectiveness of penal policies, now serve to indicate risk for given populations. The data signals whom ought to be targeted by crime control workers for surveillance, but also how likely a group of offenders might be to commit additional crimes given their histories. Similarly, drug testing, traditionally used to reveal deviance in an offender or the need for intervention and/or counseling, has become merely a cue that reveals the propensity for an offender to commit dangerous crime.[12] Lastly, prison, probation, and parole are not means to treat or reintegrate prisoners who have broken laws, but rather means to detain would-be delinquents and reduce "risk" to our communities. Mandatory minimums, Three Strikes laws, restrictions upon parole, "zero tolerance" policies, "truth in sentencing" mandates are all focused upon simply enforcing restrictions on a statistically compiled population, and in many cases do not even have any measurable effect upon crime reduction.

The "Three Strikes" law in California, for example, was touted by the California's Attorney General, Dan Lungren, as the means by which violent crime dropped 26.9 percent during the first few years of its implementation (the law was implemented in 1994). In an report " Three Strikes and You're Out—Its Impact on the California Criminal Justice System After Four Years," the mandate was celebrated as the mechanism allowing California to mark its, "lowest murder rate since 1970 and its lowest overall crime rate in thirty years."[13] But these claims were, in fact, patently false. Studies showed that crime had begun a steep decline in 1991, a full three years prior to the law being passed. Indeed, the reduction in crime levels occured not just in the state of California, but also across the U.S. in large metropolitan cities like New York and Chicago.[14] Moreover, while "Three Strikes" was meant as a mandate to increase the deterrence effect upon and incapacitation of repeat offenders by decreasing their numbers on the streets, research showed that the proportion of felony arrests attributable to that target group were negligible. Before the law came into effect, 13.9 percent of adult felony arrests were of offenders targeted by the law. After the law was passed this number fell to 12.8 percent of all felony arrests—a decrease of 1.1 percent.[15] Simply put, contrary to the claims of Lungren and then Govenor Pete Wilson, there was no statistically significant decrease in criminal arrests of the population of delinquents the law promised to target. Three Strikes had little or nothing to do with the drop in crime in California during the mid-1990s.

The New Penology and the Underclass

Given that the supervision and tracking of populations is so commonplace, perhaps it is unremarkable to suggest that the regulation of what has been referred to as the "underclass" is also accomplished by the turn towards the new penology.[16] But it is significant in this discussion if only to suggest that privatization of prison facilities requires a demand for prison space, and such a need is readily met when it becomes *rational* to detain and manage a "troubled" class of potential assailants or even large groups of undocumented immigrants. The term "underclass" has, of course, been used for decades, owing its formulation to a distortion of the work Oscar Lewis conducted on poverty back in 1959.[17] Suggesting that once a "culture of poverty" is formed it may take on a life of its own, Lewis explained that the elimination of poverty *per se* would not necessarily mitigate all the manifold issues associated with being poor. But political leaders, such as Daniel P. Moynihan and more notably Ronald Reagan, took up Lewis' material in ways that framed poverty as nothing less than a moral defect and twisted his idea of a cycle of poverty into an ironclad, no escape, cultural dynamic.[18] The term's rhetorical value was to define problems of economic neglect and racism on an interior cultural defect that had a "life of its own." Consequently, government leaders using the term, as did Moynihan, were released from both fault and the responsibility to change public policy that might exacerbate conditions of poverty. In short, the discourse of actuarial justice or managerialism has become an opportunity to effectively articulate the purpose and scope of this mode of governing—or perhaps neglect of governing—for within it, the underclass becomes just one more segment of the population in need of regulation and separation for the sake of the safety of the rest of us.

In sum, the trend of the new penology calls for a criminal justice practice that promotes the belief that crime can not be cured. It opts for managing the violence and delinquency we must resign ourselves to endure. It avoids concern for unique character or morality problems within the psyche of offenders and eschews clinical treatment for a statistically-proven, results oriented, system of risk reduction. Primarily because expertise in sociological issues or human treatment programs is unneeded in this milieu, a demand for simple holding cells is completely rational. Frontline employees of private facilities have no specialized knowledge of criminal behaviors and they possess no skills requisite to rehabilitate or reintegrate troubled offenders back into a community. As a whole, private facilities offer no education, no vocational training, and no substance addiction programs. Nor do they need these programs. Their value is simple economics: mass detention for the most prisoners at the least cost. Therein, private contracting of prison beds meets the demands of the new penology in that the mission of privatization is nothing greater than incapacitation—providing cost effective, systematically-managed facilities to state and federal clients.

The Rise of Penal Populism

If managerial approaches within the crime control field direct us to manage populations, the notion of penal populism suggests that those populations are not just interesting to criminal justice officials, but to a variety of special interests for various purposes. The term *penal populism* emerged from the work of Sir Anthony Bottoms who apparently coined the concept "populist punitiveness" to explain influences on criminal justice and punition in modern society.[19] In his words, the idea captures "politicians tapping into and using for their own purposes, what they believe to be the public's generally punitive stance."[20] But in the wake of the wide use of the concept in the 1990s, the rather difficult term "populist punitiveness" gradually transformed into the current expression "penal populism" and has come to loosely represent a larger set of practices than first conceived by Bottoms. My use of the concept in this chapter follows John Pratt's work in *Penal Populism,* arguing that the term accounts for the ways in which a "stronger resonance" exists today between the government and individuals, political groups, and criminal justice organizations that reside outside the formal bounds of governing institutions. All of these parties claim to initiate and manage penal policy—and this managing is accomplished conceivably on behalf of public interest. In addition, Pratt suggests that the establishment officials (including governmental, judicial, criminological, and penal) who once controlled criminal justice practice in sacred isolation, must now share those responsibilities with these new groups of interested parties. Since the height of penal-welfarism, the power to manage penal institutions, write criminal justice policy, or police the streets has drastically shifted towards a type of "democratization." That is, we now see an unparalleled level of participation at every step of the work of crime control by the state legislature, unions, associations, executive branches of California government, lobbyists, the public, and of course, the media. Decisions about criminal justice policy are often made on the basis of self-interest, political gain, and the erratic tide of public opinion. While the work of researching, writing and debating penal policy, in particular, may have criminologists or penal experts' participation, over the last few decades, they have increasingly become ignored, repudiated or pressured to alter their positions on key policy issues.

Part of the transformation began during the assault on rehabilitation and treatment programs that ultimately gained a reputation in some circles of being a thinly veiled attempt at social cleansing. The penal practitioner, typically holding some type of social science degree, had too much discretionary power, critics such as the American Friends Service Committee argued, and was influenced by paternalistic motives. Once convicted, penal officials reduced every inmate's behavior to diagnostic information as a means to design an indeterminate sentence. This term might commit the inmate to rehabilitation for six months, perhaps a lifetime—there was no way to predict. It was this kind of open-ended sentencing that was being declared patently unfair by critics of the status quo. Not only did indeterminate sentencing pave the way for inconsistency between offenders who committed the same crime, according to the argument, it also encouraged the abuse of power. Sentencing was often both racist and sexist and focused too much on the offenders' specific circumstances as opposed to issuing uniform penalties. To continue allowing the "experts" the sole purview of penal decisions was to indulge their arrogance. What the system needed was oversight, centralized standards, and reviews of court and appellate processes. Calling for checks and balances within the penal system, the American Friends Service argued:

> The authority given those who manage the system, a power more absolute than that found in any other sphere of law has concealed the practices carried on in the name of the treatment model. At every level—from prosecutor to parole board member—the concept of individualization has been used to justify secret procedures, reviewless decision-making, and an unwillingness to formulate anything other than the most general rules and policy. Whatever else may be credited to a century of individualized-treatment reform effort, there has been a steady expansion of the scope of the criminal justice system and a consolidation of the state's absolute discretionary power over the lives of those caught in the net.[21]

Couched in these terms, the indeterminate sentence and the professionals overseeing its use became a symbol for tyranny for those who desired change to the traditional sentencing schema. The critiques revealed deep ruptures in the crime control field, but also suggested that the mechanisms once hailed as the means to protect and serve the ailing prisoner less than a decade before were now precisely those representing systematic oppression. But what the critics launching these attacks could not have foreseen was that as the work of drafting law, reviewing its effects, or deciding on inmate treatment became open to more hands, it simultaneously became de-professionalized and vulnerable to pressures from a great many special interest groups. Criminal justice decisions became matters to be negotiated by lobbyists, union officials, the legislature, public opinion polls, and political hopefuls. The discontinuities of the decisions that have been made over the years mark the struggles between all of these players in the populist process. Private contractors, in fact, were able to enter into the dialogue on corrections once this change took place because as a single-issue lobby, they finally had meaningful structural access to those in the seats of power and decision-making. In short, as crime control discourse has become more politicized and subject to more voices, it has also meant that those with more power or leverage get more chances to frame the conversation.

Technology and Populist Discourses

As crime control experts were asked to cede ground to allow others to enter the domain of criminal justice decision-making, both the content and form of discourse addressing these kinds of decisions began to shift. These changes shaped alternative constructions of penal knowledge and included more voices than had ever entered the conversation in this county's history. By means of television, radio, film media, and later, electronic communication devices of the late twentieth century, crime became an object of entertainment, commodity and political power.

Television news programs have, of course, been capitalizing on the public's fascination with crime and violence for at least the last thirty years. They have expanded their coverage of murders—particularly gang killings in California—rape, sexual assault, and more recently, pedophilia and child pornography. Between 1989 and 1993, coinciding with the expansion of California's prison system, crime stories on the national networks (ABC, CBS, NBC) grew four times in number.[22] In fact, crime was the leading story on U.S. network news in 1993— exceeding those on the economy, healthcare and even war in Bosnia.[23] In addition, the resonance between local news programs and local newspapers grew as the former often used the latter to fill out its line-up. For example, when the *San Francisco Chronicle* ran a front-page headline warning that a teenage homicide arrest rates were up a record 87 percent in northern California, local nightly news programs quickly seized on the story. Only later was it revealed that the crime figures had been skewed in the newspaper's story. By comparing the number of juveniles referred to the probation department that year for homicide (a total of sisxteen) to the number of juveniles who had been referred for *attempted* homicide (three), the statistics appeared to jump dramatically. In retrospect, juveniles arrested for homicide had not increased at all in 1993, even though the truth of the matter seemed less interesting than the sensationalism of yet another crime scare.[24]

Complementing news reports of increasing crime has been inexpensive and easy to produce reality-based law and order programming such as America's Most Wanted, Rescue 911, American Detective, Cops, Unsolved Mysteries, Inside Edition, and Hard Copy. These shows have not only proliferated to foment a concern over crime—at a time when crime rates in both the U.S. and California have actually dropped—but they are also an index of the types of reflexive public discourse becoming so popular over the final decades of the last century. How are issues of criminal justice altered when there are so many ways to participate in conversations that take up law and order?

First, they have encouraged citizens to insert their own voice into many of these shows that are often precipitated upon audience participation and decision-making. Also they have raised the value and import of the average citizen's reasoning, observations and perspectives. In the case of *law and order* crime show formats, public sensibilities become a touchstone for common knowledge about criminal justice issues and their proper solutions. Notably, a number of these shows invite the public to call into the program to aid in the search for and conviction of perpetrators they identify in their episodes. In so doing, the average person becomes an adjunct to the official agencies fighting crime as s/he engages in surveillance of some would be convict.

Second, citizens have gained power over armed forces and crime control officials through everyday personal technologies. Over twenty years ago, a single individual using his Sony Handycam altered not only the course of policing in the LAPD, he sparked a fire that literally burned neighborhoods of Los Angeles to the ground. George Holliday recorded nine minutes of the Los Angeles police beating Rodney King in 1992, spurring dramatic reforms in the department which had a reputation for abuse and racism. Used in the criminal trial of the four officers, the video proved to be the panoptic device that reorganized

LAPD policing policies and triggered mass rioting when not-guilty verdicts set the officers free. Consequently, the department has some very different operating procedures and teaches its recruits early on that once they become officers, they must think about their jobs in a radically different way. "Police now work in a YouTube world in which cell phones double as cameras. . .helicopters transmit close-up footage of unfolding police pursuits, and surveillance cameras capture arrests or shootings . . ." The central shift the King beating brought about is the recognition that ". . .Someone is always watching."[25] As citizens utilize simple and increasingly ubiquitous recording and distribution devices to capture crime or violence, they become armed with the capacity to hold police and others accountable, organize responses, and demand change.

Once the world-wide web became widely used in the U.S. in the 1990s, this phenomenon expanded. A seemingly endless set of channels opened up for crime control to be discussed, debated and used in various advocacy campaigns by almost anyone. While these channels may not have had the primary purpose of selling a product or producing crime story based entertainment, they expanded the opportunities for the public to "talk-back," interact with one another, and disperse and consume information pertaining to criminal justice. Use of the internet by law and order groups, victims' rights organizations, think tanks, state and federal agencies, and ordinary citizens became a platform to argue on behalf of a given criminal justice issue, weigh-in on legal or penal decisions or simply advocate for new policies. Open chat rooms provided the means to communicate with likeminded individuals, access data and research, become educated on heretofore-unknown criminal trends or correctional policies, and organize movements for change. Add to this the capacities afforded by the most recent popular technological trends: social networking, twitter, and as I mention above, YouTube, and we see how complex and overarching the forces fueling penal populism have become.

But these modes used to communicate about criminal justice issues have also had impacts upon the *content* that can be transmitted through their channels and thus suggest a third implication of penal populism. Most of our electronic media have left the printed word of the literary epoch to either reinvent itself or simply die out. The truth content of communication messages, their value as information per se, is eclipsed by the easily remembered adage, by slogans, by sound bites and sensational images. The sensibility of the linear, analytical structure of the written word is especially unpopular where image and fragmented, pithy, sayings abound. Average consumers of public discourse have no time nor little interest in wading through dense content, or lengthy texts that might help them to comprehend the implications or background of a given penal policy. In present-day campaigns for criminal justice laws, it's the slogans or images that constitute meaning and action. Within these, a comprehensive and compelling rallying call is born that quite often functions to appease public discontent or express collective anger. Slogans like "Three Strikes," "Zero Tolerance," and so on, or laws/programs named after victims of crimes such as "Meagan's Law," or the "Amber Alert," are not useful for their explanations of the facts of a given policy, nor for their ability to help us think about crime problems and their solutions. They are therapeutic, aesthetically-pleasing and rhetorically-compelling. While we have more power to interact and advocate within these technologies, we are not always able to think critically about how as we use them they may alternately be *using us*.

In short, communication technologies, mass media outlets, and the ease with which the majority of citizens have access to these discursive forms have meant that the truths about crime and crime control are shaped and regulated in drastically different ways than in the era of penal-welfarism. The tools link personal ideation, conversation and interpersonal interaction with what Wayne Munson rightly calls "the mass mediated spectacle of modernity."[26] They have literally changed the way information and knowledge about crime, criminality and penal propriety is created and exchanged, and they have redistributed the power that derives from that process.

Populism and the Use of Crime to Govern

If it is true that penal populism has become widespread, how does such populism effect the activity of governing by public officials? According to Jonathon Simon, states such as California are not necessarily facing a crisis of crime and punishment, but rather a crisis of governance; and crime, perhaps more than any other issue today, is a privileged method with which to govern.[27] That is, where at one time political actors focused upon such issues as housing, education, and social justice to gain appeal and persuade citizens, they now turn to concerns over crime, violence, terror, and their control. The use of crime to govern—to direct the course and/or conduct of populations—has been particularly effective in places like California, where the electorate is so diverse, few issues have the power to unify and galvanize voters' support. But the "Three Strikes" bill, which became popularized partly from the October 1993 killing of twelve-year-old Polly Klaas, offers a ready example of the populist nature of crime control politics and the ways it has been drafted as a means to organize power.

The report of Polly's late night abduction from a slumber party in the small town of Petaluma, California, was more than most parents could bear. FBI agents, local police officers, 200 to 300 search-and-rescue personnel and huge numbers of ordinary citizens combed the county looking for her. While kidnapping cases are always tragic, the publicity given Polly's story was rare. She was an innocent, a neighborhood girl who became America's stolen child. News of the crime spread quickly and became the center of popular public anxieties. The story was carried across all local channels and then nationally on *E! Entertainment*, *MTV News*, and *America's Most Wanted*—which covered the case at least five different times. The *Los Angeles Times*, as well, featured the event on the front page no less than half a dozen times and in a unique turn, actress Winona Ryder offered a $200,000 reward for Polly's return.[28] But after six weeks and no signs of young Polly, most began to give up hope. Then, on November 30, 1993, authorities arrested Richard Allen Davis after an unlikely phone tip caused police to revisit the details of a suspicious late night run-in with the offender six weeks earlier. He finally confessed to killing Polly after prints linked him to a piece of furniture at the scene.

Once the news broke, the public seemed to collectively mourn. Polly's memorial service was attended by an estimated 1,400 and broadcast live by both CNN as well as local television stations. There were appearances by Linda Ronstadt and Joan Baez, who sang a special rendition of "Amazing Grace." Remarks by President Clinton were read; state dignitaries and government officials delivered speeches of regret but also promised renewed efforts to come down hard on violent crime.[29] Anyone watching the events of Polly's service could see that if it wasn't clear before the funeral, it was absolutely plain after: Polly's story was the fuel that lit the national fire to increase harsh penalties on repeat criminal offenders in California.

Davis had been in and out of prison for much of his life and constituted what would have been considered a "Three Strikes" offender. Public officials and citizens asked what was the use of our current prison sentences if Richard Allen Davis could be out on the streets and commit this cold-blooded murder. Polly's death became the symbol of and the rationale for the state and federal gauntlet to be lowered upon the heads of anyone who was a repeat offender. And while the bill was originally written for another young girl who was murdered in Fresno, California, the killing of little Polly ultimately served as the fodder to acquire the needed signatures for balloting. Support for the

"Three Strikes" bill was so strong, advocates could not print petitions fast enough for citizens to sign. In short order, several other states passed versions of the same measure, while President Clinton recommended his own "Three Strikes" law at the federal level.

With so much public acclaim for "Three Strikes," political actors took notice. To be accurate, the bill's original author, Mike Reynolds, garnered support early on from the National Rifle Association (NRA) and the California Correctional Peace Officers Association (CCPOA)—California's prison guard employee union. In hopes of rerouting popular fervor over gun violence, the NRA decided to offer a meager sum of money in the event that the bill might triumph at the ballot. According to Tim Gest,

> The NRA had been successfully warding off gun-control measures in Congress, state legislatures, and city councils for many years, but the battles were getting tougher. The NRA could make a plausible case that gun control was an ineffective anticrime tool. But that argument was losing appeal as more Americans, particularly police officers, were falling victim to firearms violence . . . NRA leaders, recognizing the advantage of taking an aggressive anticrime stance, started a national drive called CrimeStrike to campaign for tougher prison sentences and to protest unwarranted parole releases . . .[the] three strikes idea was one of the first beneficiaries of CrimeStrike.[30]

As start-up seed-money, the "Three Strikes" campaign received $5500 from the NRA's CrimeStrike program, but would ultimately receive about $130,000 in total. The CCPOA, standing to benefit from policies that mandated inmate to guard ratios—and thus laws that might increase inmate populations—would eventually give well over $100,000. But by October of 1993, Reynolds obtained twenty-thousand of the 385,000 signatures needed to qualify the measure for the 1994 November ballot, and he wasn't entirely sure how he would make up the difference.

At the same time, the California governor's race was heating up. With low approval ratings and a faltering economy, Republican incumbent Pete Wilson would not be offered easy passage back into gubernatorial office. He needed a compelling campaign appeal, an emotional narrative to secure the widest block of voters. Polly's killing offered such a narrative and Wilson soon threw his support solidly behind the Strikes measure. But Democrats who controlled the state legislature buckled at the governor's bid to use a "tough on crime" posture as his defining campaign issue, particularly as Three Strikes gained public support. Democrats knew that, put on the November ballot, the bill might tip the scales of conservative voters who would come out to the polls to make their voices heard. And if large numbers of conservatives showed up, it might seriously handicap Democrats' chances to unseat the Republican governor.

A strategic move was needed. Democrats made the decision that they would support whatever version of the bill the governor favored so as to neutralize any tough on crime stance that might distinguish Wilson from a Democratic candidate. Not only did the Democrats bow to Wilson's choice of the final draft for the bill, the Speaker of the House at the time, Willie Brown, made a deal with the original author of the measure, Mike Reynolds, that was particularly sweet. He offered legislation that would automatically place Three Strikes on the ballot so that Reynolds did not have to actually go to the effort and incur the cost of collecting the balance of signatures for its qualification. But of course there was a price to be paid. The bill would have to be placed on the June ballot, at the time of the party primaries in the state, as opposed to November which decided the gubernatorial election.[31] As Franklin Zimring notes, "In effect, the executive and legislative branches of the California government . . . swallowed the outside-the-beltway version of the Three Strikes whole because the Governor and the legislature were unwilling to concede the high ground on getting tough to the other side in the political campaign to come."[32] The bickering over the bill's ownership confirmed that the power and prestige it was set to award was a valuable commodity indeed. It therefore failed to be rigorously debated and scrutinized by lawyers, academics, social scientists and corrections officials. Both the elected district attorneys of Los Angeles and San Francisco opposed the bill as well as the defense bar and the judiciary. It had no support from criminal justice experts and ironically, was almost identical to other laws already on the books—so in essence it was legally unnecessary. Even those within the legislature admitted that the bill was badly flawed. But in the end, most surrendered to political pressure and voted in its favor.[33] In March of 1994, the California legislature passed and Governor Wilson signed AB 971, the "Three Strikes and You're Out" law. It's of note that the bill California passed is far harsher than other states' versions and researchers estimate that ten times as many persons have been sentenced to prison under its auspices than in all other jurisdictions with "Three Strikes" laws combined.[34]

After the bill became law, Marc Klaas, Polly's father, remarked that although he didn't care for the bill's final content, he did not have much choice in the matter of its adoption. As he put it, by the time the measure was submitted for a vote, it was "gaining the momentum of a freight train running down hill—it was a done deal." The fact that officials were endorsing the bill had little to do with its specifics, he explained, "politicians jumped on three strikes whether they believed in it or not."[35] The political capital represented by the tragedy and the public policy written to assuage it ensured that the "stage" used to support and pass the law would be shared and politicized. As a clear instance, both California Senator Dianne Feinstein and Governor Pete Wilson eulogized Polly Klaas at her memorial. Neither had ever met the little girl. Her death, and the crime it symbolized, became a moment to govern through. "It was mind boggling," Marc Klaas would later remark, "my little girl was dead and here were these politicians launching campaigns at her memorial service."[36]

The Contradictions of Populist Criminal Justice Policy

Approximately five years after the bill became law, researchers evaluated the effectiveness of "Three Strikes." The results were striking. Most of those who qualified for a "third strike" were arrested for petty drug or property crimes, not violent felonies. In fact, the offense of a person convicted of a "third strike" was less likely to be a crime of violence than for a defendant with no strikes at all.[37] In the words of the study: "If all the people arrested for felonies who met the criteria for California's third strike eligibility were to disappear from the earth without a trace, the felony crime rate in the cities we studied [Los Angeles, San Francisco, San Diego] would go down by between three and four-percent." However, the report continues, "The actual crime savings attributable to special treatment of second and third strike cases will inevitably be less than the maximum possible impact, meaning that the potential savings for third strike enhancement is much less than three-percent."[38] These findings suggest that the law is doing little to decrease the crimes it was designed to combat. In hindsight, perhaps the campaign for the bill never had that decrease as its purpose to begin with once it entered the hands of political interests. In the end, what was accomplished was the creation of a law that united a multitude of individuals and organizations behind a single symbolic policy. That advocacy reassured the public that something was being done about the threat of violent offenders, even if it has ultimately changed the degree of public safety in California.

The populist nature of California crime control and the way political actors govern through crime alters the public interpretation of crime. The crime story, the issue of public safety, and the ominous and eminent threat of violence become translated into an effective appeal to voters. That appeal solidifies support for specific special interests and mobilizes political power to create more and more criminal justice legislation. One is compelled to ask whether some of our crime policies have all that much to do with genuine crime control, or whether they simply fill a need for the public to feel that something is being done to combat criminal activity. Alternatively, one might ask if some crime control measures serve various political interests that need a galvanizing issue to gain public support and/or popularity. Either way, private contracting benefits. Private prison companies benefit from our addiction to mandatory sentencing or "tough on crime" policies. As public expenses increase because prison commitments grow, as trial rates rise and case processing times increase, demand for more prison space grows. As prison space becomes scarce, the state, unable or unwilling to meet those demands, turns toward private contractors.

Victims' Rights: A New Morality?

A final trend to examine in socio-political policy affecting California is the emergence of the victim as an object of discourse within the criminal justice system. The drive to recognize victims of crimes began in the 1970s when the Warren Court was pressed to respond to calls for more humane treatment of offenders. Several court cases fueled a potent prisoner's rights campaign which fought to establish respect for inmates' constitutional rights as well as create reforms for both suspects of crimes and defendants in court cases. Many believed these rights "for criminals" were expanding far too broadly and therefore a movement to expand "victims' rights" began to take shape. According to advocates for victims, if an individual was an object of a criminal act, that individual ought to have a role in criminal justice proceedings. At the time, victims had no standing in criminal prosecution, their voices were not heard at any step in the process, and they were essentially "invisible casualties" of unfortunate circumstances. Additionally, victims were not always told whether or not a person was arrested or convicted in their case, they had no idea if any of their property was recovered, and they were not allotted compensation for loss or missed work. As a result of pressure put on the high court through a number of landmark decisions, victims' rights and restitution became a significant focus of policies within the criminal justice equation by the early 1980s.

In 1982, the President's Report of the Task Force on Victims of Crime released a set of recommendations that lead to a flurry of attention on the role of the victim in state and federal crimes. Perhaps a bit on the dramatic side, the report declared: "Something insidious has happened in America: Crime has made victims of us all. The specter of violent crime and the knowledge that, without warning, any person can be attacked or crippled, robbed, or killed, lurks at the fringes of consciousness."[39] The text admitted without apology or question that the system could do nothing to halt this set of circumstances and as a result, we had no choice but to reword the Sixth Amendment of the Constitution to acknowledge the position of the victim. The proposed change would declare: ". . .the victim, in every criminal prosecution shall have the right to be present and to be heard at all critical stages of judicial proceedings."[40] In addition, the report recommended that laws be passed at the state and federal levels to ensure that victims' personal information be protected, that they have legally privileged counseling not subject to defense discovery or subpoena, that parole be abolished, that victim impact statements be required at the time of sentencing, that restitution to victims be mandated, and that any money acquired by the offender–whether by windfall or labor—be forfeited to h/er victim.

California was one of the many states to swiftly enact a number of these policy changes—in fact before the report's recommendations were published. That same year California voters adopted Proposition 8 (not to be confused with the same-sex marriage initiative passed in 2008 in the state) named "The Victim's Bill of Rights." The proposition granted victims the right to be present and express their view at felony sentencing hearings as well as parole hearings. Apparently not satisfied with the first set of statues, nine years later, Californians passed another Proposition, number 115, entitled "The Crime Victims Justice and Reform Act." This act added additional safeguards to victims including a declaration—unneeded in the opinion of many law-makers—that criminals would be afforded no rights exceeding those granted by the federal Constitution. The law also decreased the number of times a victim was subject to testify in a given case, accelerated trial times and effectively increased sentences for offenders.

But what was the real intent of these measures? And how did they affect the criminal justice process in California? According to the National Institute of Justice which produced a report studying the effects of Proposition 8, California judges, at least, saw no real purpose for the law beyond public denunciation of crime and criminals and "law and order" posturing by legislators. A full two-third of those judges questioned believed the allocution statute (the right of victims to speak at sentencing hearings) was completely unnecessary. In the words of one judge: ". . .By the time a victim comes to court, a well-prepared probation report having been reviewed by a well-prepared judge leaves little room for modification of an intended decision. A victim's emotional appeal to the court cannot carry more weight in place of the facts and criteria."[41] Instead of seeing the law as a means to help victims, most judges remarked that they were suspect of its political intent: "'Victims Rights' is a political issue and gets a lot of good press for 'Law and Order' candidates," stated one. Another remarked, "I thought it was a law and order legislative act to give legislators an image rather than change sentences. . . " A third asked: "What was the intent? to influence the court? to allow victims opportunity to express their views of courts and procedures and sentences? . . . I don't know the intent of the law."[42]

But if there was confusion about why the law was passed to begin with, there can be no denying its effect upon criminal justice proceedings in the state. From a legal perspective, crime stopped being an issue between the state and the offender. Instead, it entered a matrix that included the offender, the state and the object of the crime—the victim. For the first time since we began to recognize the rise of the social contract within the nation state and establish the objective nature of criminal law, Californians began to allow—perhaps even honor—a personal, decidedly emotive, subjectivity in questions of criminal justice. Allowing a victim of crime to become part of the legal process of sentencing through victim impact statements, for example, injected the criminal court process with an unabashed emotional appeal. Once the victim entered into court proceedings, deliberations became a legitimate space for hate, love, grief, sorrow, and despair to be expressed. The change is "without exaggeration," according to legal scholar Hans Boutellier, "the most important post-war development in the practice of criminal law."[43]

Additionally, Boutellier argues that the valuation of "victim-hood" in contemporary court practices constitutes what he terms a new communal emblem that binds citizens together.

> In a pluralistic society, solidarity, the central notion of the social constitutional state, can no longer be based upon a common identity we have recourse to in addressing each other . . . Nor is it necessary to seek a higher order—God, Nature, the Community, Man, Rationality, the Nation or History—that enables us to be social. The awareness of each other's vulnerability is enough to establish a public morality. The only thing that counts in a secular, liberal society is that people are vulnerable to humiliation and cruelty, pain and suffering; the extent to which we show ourselves to be sensitive to other people's experiences of this kind determines the morality of our culture.[44]

Here then, Boutellier suggests that what unifies us becomes a new touchstone for moral behavior: that recognition that to survive in this world we must protect against threats of violence, crime, and terror that are *now* ever-present. Even when social bonds fragment and our common identity as members of a state or nation take on less value than our individual interests, backgrounds, racial or ethnic histories, class status and so on, the threat of crime and terrorism—of being the victim of some catastrophe—has become the binding lubricant of social solidarity. Morality is thus defined by respecting our common vulnerability. Morality is enacted by protecting that vulnerability. The relatively-recent national campaign advanced by the Office of Homeland Security: "If you see something, say something" serves as one example of institutionalizing such a "morality." We join together to defend our well-being, our community is constructed from our stand to watch out for one another.

Identifying with Our Victims

Perhaps the recognition of interest in and solidarity with victims of crimes fueled *New York* magazine in the mid-1990s to do a feature expose on the phenomenon. Cases in which victims of crime as well as "good Samaritan" bystanders turned the tables on their attackers were shown as evidence of a still-developing consciousness wherein citizens joined together to "take the law in their own hands." Several stories of victims "pull[ing] out guns they did not have permits for and blast[ing] the thugs" expressed a pointed communal outrage.[45] One of these cases included a man nick-named "the subway Samaritan" who stabbed two men robbing a passenger on the train. After killing one, to popular acclaim, he disappeared. Another story of an electronics engineer, Bernhardt Goetz, who shot four teens on a N.Y. subway in 1984, became particularly infamous. In Goetz's videotaped confession, he voiced definitive pleasure in attacking the boys who had reportedly assaulted him. Far from feeling any sympathy for his assailants, he explained that his problem at the time was simply that he ". . .ran out of bullets," according to his testimony.[46] The shots he fired ultimately paralyzed one of the boys, but still he rose to the status of folk hero in the wake of the publicity over the case. The public outrage was clear— members of the community identified with Goetz—and any harm done to the boys was perfectly justified. The jury in the trial agreed; Goetz was acquitted of attempted murder and assault and convicted only of carrying an illegal firearm.

A closer look at American popular culture reveals that identifying with those who are victimized and/or identifying oneself as a victim has a certain cache. Much like the mass mediated images of crime and police investigations mentioned above, television portrayals of those who admit to and seek help for their addictions (or those who have been a victim of cruel or violent circumstances) are often sought after, revered, and respected. Recently solved kidnapping cases like Jaycee Lee Dugard abducted in California in 1991, or Elizabeth Smart, who disappeared in Salt Lake City in 2002, represent obvious examples of public attention. But there are also everyday victims that the public is invited to watch, become familiar with, and talk about around the "water-cooler" the following day. Reality shows like "Intervention" or "Celebrity Rehab," talk shows modeled after Dr. Phil or Oprah Winfrey, and even make-over programs like "The Biggest Loser" or "Dr. 90210," are all predicated upon a therapeutic culture wherein "victims" are dissected, analyzed and potentially helped. As participants in this culture, we are encouraged to know the current talked-about victims, have an informal working knowledge of the terms that describe their plight (such as post-traumatic stress disorder, bi-polar syndrome, radioactive iodine and so on), and methods used to treat these individuals. The knowledge is not used solely to understand another person, although this is important, it is also used to recognize our own potential as a victim—lest she one day be you or me.[47] In other words, as the public focuses on the victim, lessons are learned about being vigilant against potential threats and how one treats certain kinds of "victimization."

Privatization and Victimhood

The link between the sensibility of victimhood, what we might call its moral directive, and the phenomenon of private contracting may not be direct, but it is nonetheless insidious. As the victim position is heightened through legislation that guarantees certain rights to citizens or a popular ethos that encourages individual identification with those who are suffering, victimhood draws strength from the unity afforded by fighting off some enemy in the form of a person, force or condition. As individuals come together to fight off "adversaries," they may experience more solidarity, but in the process a social order is constructed that divides up victims and perpetrators in absolute terms. Herein lies the context for demonizing offenders. In contrast to penal-welfarism, an era that aimed at the ideal that the "sick" prisoner was sent to prison to be cared for by a social collective (even if a prison facility it did not always live up to this ideal), inmates today are mostly imagined as a motley bunch who do not deserve the "luxury" of three meals a day and a roof over their heads. When those sent to prison are understood as opponents, as antagonists, their care, their rehabilitation, their humanity is obscured. An offender's humanity often becomes an after-thought.

A turn toward private contracting is not *caused* by a greater focus on victims, but it is surely helped by the trend. When moral behaviors can be defined by acting on behalf of just *one* set of individuals in society, when it becomes appropriate to deny humanity to those who are sent to prison, then prison privatization—if it exploits inmate labor, if it allows for the poor treatment of prisoners, or if it is run by those who could care less about the well-being of folks it releases back into society—is not problematic. In fact, those behaviors are also unremarkable when they issue from state managed facilities—and so if state facilities can no longer hold all of the convicted felons, we have little choice but to adopt other alternatives such as privatization. In either case, the result is similar, we have a group of people deserving of care, of protection, of compassion, and a group that is not: a blueprint for division, separation and neglect.

---

[1] Malcolm Feeley & Jonathon Simon, "Actuarial Justice: the Emerging New Criminal Law," *The Futures of Criminology*, ed. David Nelken (Sage: 1994) 173-201.

[2] See Malcolm Feeley & Jonathon Simon, "The New Penology: Reformulating Penal Objectives and Implications for Penal Growth," *Proceedings of: Growth and Its Influence on Correctional Policy-Perspectives on the Report of the Blue Ribbon Commission,* Berkeley, CA, July 1991.

[3] I will use the terms managerialism, actuarial justice, and the new penology interchangeably in this chapter.

[4] David Rothman, "Prisons: The Failure Model," *The Nation* December 1974: 658.

[5] Feeley and Simon, *The New Penology* 66. I am using the pronoun "he" here with the recognition that not all offenders are male. However, the bulk of those sentenced to prison in California was, and still is, a phenomenon affecting mostly men.

[6] Michael Tonry, *Sentencing Matters* (New York: Oxford University Press, 1996) 4.

[7] Daniel Krislov, "Ideology and American Crime Policy, 1966-1996: An Exploratory Essay," *The Crime Conundrum: Essays on Criminal Justice*, eds. Lawrence M. Friedman & George Fisher (Boulder: Westview, 1997) 115.

[8] William J. Bratton, "How to Win the War Against Crime," *New York Times* 5 April 1996: A-17.

[9] "NYPD, Inc.," *Economist* 7925 (20 July 1995) 50, and "The C.E.O. Cop," *New Yorker* 70 (6 Feb. 1995): 45-54.

[10] The Los Angeles Police Department "COMPSTAT" 2008. Official Website of the Los Angeles Police Department. Web. 4 Feb. 2011.

[11] Loic Wacquant, *Prisons of Poverty* (Minneapolis: University of Minnesota Press, 2009) 66.

[12] Feeley & Simon, *Actuarial Justice* 179.

[13] See also additional statements about the effectiveness of the law in: Pete Wilson, "Three Strikes' Law Truly Makes California Safer," *Los Angeles Daily News* 9 Mar. 1997: V-3. Dan Lungren, "Our Tough Law Works," *USA Today* 24 Feb. 1997: A-10.

[14] Franklin E. Zimring, Sam Kamin & Gordon Hawkins, *Crime & Punishment in California: The Impact of Three Strikes and You're Out*, (Berkeley: Institute of Governmental Studies Press, University of California, Berkeley, 1999) 69-70.

[15] Zimring et. al 78-84.

[16] Feeley and Simon, *New Penology* 72-3.

[17] Oscar Lewis, "The Culture of Poverty," *Scientific American* 215 (1966) 1-16.

[18] See Patrick Moynihan, "The Negro Family: The Case for National Action," *The Moynihan Report & the Politics of Controversy*, eds. Lee Rainwater & William Yancy (Cambridge: MIT Press, 1967). In 1965 Moynihan authored a position paper during his tenure as assistant to President Johnson on domestic affairs. The paper, known as the Moynihan Report, discussed the crisis of the Black family and its social pathology grounded in cultural characteristics.

[19] John Pratt, *Penal Populism* (New York, Routledge: 2007) 2.

[20] Anthony Bottoms, "The Philosophy and Politics of Punishment and Sentencing," *The Politics of Sentencing Reform*, eds. Chris Clarkson & Rod Morgan (Oxford: Clarendon, 1995) 40.

[21] American Friends Service Committee, *Struggle For Justice: A Report on Crime and Punishment in America* (New York: Hill & Wang, 1971) 39-40.

[22] Robert Lichter and Linda Lichter, 1993—*The Year in Review: TV's Leading News Topics, Reporters and Political Jokes* (Washington, D.C.: Media Monitor, 1994); Robert Lichter and Linda Lichter, 1999—*The Year in Review: TV's Leading News Topics, Reporters and Political Jokes* (Washington, D.C. :Media Monitor, 2000).

[23] Steven R. Donziger, ed., *The Real War on Crime: The Report of the National Criminal Justice Commission* (New York: Harper Perennial, 1996) 69.

[24] Donziger 72.

[25] Joel Rubin, Andrew Blankstein, Scott Gold, "LAPD's Change in Focus: The King Video Ushered Police into a YouTube World," *Los Angeles Times* 3 March 2011:A-1; A-10.

[26] Wayne Munson, *All Talk: The Talkshow in Media Culture* (Philadelphia: Temple University Press, 1993) 6. While Munson is addressing the phenomenon of talk-shows in this quote specifically, he captures the ways that new media, and new ways to use old media, increase the opportunities for populism to take hold in contemporary society. In so doing, it becomes easier to recognize the points of intersection between governing officials, special interest groups and ordinary public citizens.

[27] Jonathon Simon, "Governing Through Crime," *The Crime Conundrum: Essays on Criminal Justice*, eds. Lawrence M. Friedman & George Fisher (Boulder: Westview, 1997) 171-189.

[28] Joe Domanick, *Cruel Justice: Three Strikes and the Politics of Crime in America's Golden State* (Berkeley: University of California Press, 2004) 118.

[29] Domanick 126.

[30] Ted Gest, *Crime & Politics : Big Government's Erratic Campaign for Law and Order* (New York : Oxford University Press, 2001) 191.

[31] Franklin Zimring, "Three Strikes, You're Out: Crime in California," *The Economist* 15 Jan. 1994: 30.

[32] Franklin Zimring, "Populism, Democratic Government and the Decline of Expert Authority: Some Reflections on 'Three Strikes' in California," *Pacific Law Journal* 28 (1996): 243. 1996.

[33] Samuel Pillsbury, "Why Are We Ignored? The Peculiar Place of Experts in the Current Debate About Crime and Justice," *Criminal Law Bulletin* 31:4 (1995): 311.

[34] Zimring *Crime and Punishment* 5.

[35] Gest 195.

[36] Dominick 127.

[37] Zimring et. al. 2; 39.

[38] Zimring et. al. 22

[39] United States, President's Task Force, *Victims of Crime* (Washington D.C., 1982) vi.

[40] Andrew Karmen, "The Situation of Crime Victims in the Early Decades of the Twenty-First Century," *Visions For Change: Crime and Justice in the Twenty-First Century,* eds. Roslyn Muraskin and Albert R. Roberts (New Jersey: Prentice Hall, 2002) 39. See also: Lawrence Friedman, "The Crime Movement at its First Decade," *Public Administration Review* 45: 790-794.

[41] Edwin Villmoare & Virginia V. Neto, Victim Appearances at Sentencing Hearings Under the California Victims' Bill of Rights, U.S. Department of Justice: National Institute of Justice (Washington, D. C.: U.S. Government Printing Office, 1987) 37.

[42] Villmoare & Neto 37.

[43] Hans Boutellier, *Crime and Morality: The Significance of Criminal Justice in Post-modern Culture* (Boston: Kluwer Academic Publishers, 2000) 47.

[44] Boutellier 15.

[45] Eric Pooley, "Frontier Justice: Fed Up New Yorkers Are Taking the Law Into Their Own Hands," *New York* 23, July 1990: 34.

[46] Quoted in: Wendy Kaminer, *It's All the Rage: Crime and Culture* (New York: Addison-Wesley Publishing, 1995) 26.

[47] Kaminer 13-17.

5

Taking Account of Ideologies

It's useful to recognize that we never react to crime itself, but rather to our *thoughts* about crime. Those thoughts are formed and framed by the discourses used to represent them and the perceptions to which those discourses give rise. Criminal justice policies take their shape, then, as solutions to crime problems, but we shouldn't forget that these problems have already been defined with a given rhetorical character. Perspectives about appropriate punishment, similarly, are not so much dependent upon the contours of criminal action or even institutional directives, but by "less obvious social and historical circumstances," as David Garland has written, which rely upon "political discourses . . . specific forms of knowledge, legal, moral, and cultural categories, and specific patterns of psychic organization or sensibility."[1] Given these observations, the issues relating to privately-contracting prisons are also already guided by particular forms of consciousness, collective perceptions and socio-cultural meanings that emerge in a given historical time and place. Acknowledging the penological, the managerial, or even the economic nature of privatization without also accounting for the sociological or discursive conditions of its emergence gives us only part of the picture.

Thus, this chapter focuses on the social processes of meaning making that have functioned to produce patterned themes in support of private contracting of prisons in California. I claim that at least three specific themes have become, to borrow a term from cultural critic, Stuart Hall,[2] "ideological conductors" serving to energize the drive toward privatization in the state. Taken together, the themes have allowed for a mythology to emerge around the notion that utilizing private prisons is a simple matter of adopting a neutral, efficient, and cost effective corrections option. It has allowed supporters of privatization to argue that "private prisons are just like any other private institution: they're a little nicer, a little more efficient, a little less bogged down by bureaucracy, and they're here to add a touch of quality to the dregs of the American prison system."[3] But of course this simple perspective obscures the history of the political and economic factors allowing for privatization that have been detailed in previous chapters. It covers over the ways in which the prison system in California has ignited a whole set of industries which depend upon the continued mass incarceration of its citizens and it conceals the racial and class biases inherent in the arrest, conviction and imprisonment of those citizens. To realize these exclusions, we must investigate how the stories supporting privatization disallow such details.

In service of unpacking the evidence for the discourse underwriting private contracting, I use textual evidence found in criminal justice documents such as legal opinions, California law and legislative records, artifacts of public information and entertainment, criminal justice scholarship, and the discourse found on criminal justice blogs. These texts reveal the strategies through which the logic of privatization travels and becomes both legitimized and natural. In so doing, I trace a set of analytical themes that have impacted the ideological bounds of reasoning in those discussions and arguments. This approach assumes that examining the ways that policy, scholarship, and public opinion intersect offers an entry point into a conversation about the salient issues of incarceration. It also suggests that as a "snapshot" of those significant concerns at a specific historical moment, we can recognize why certain policy solutions adopted to address those problems appeared to be reasonable.

The first theme I discuss might be understood as a persistent *culture of fear* that is pervasive in California culture. The discourse representing this thematic suggests that there exists in the state an ever-present risk to life and limb and public danger is not just a function of crime, but also simply everyday life in California. While public opinion polls since at least 1966 show that as a nation we have grown more and more afraid of becoming victimized, real levels of crime have been dropping— consistently—to reach their lowest levels since the U.S. began keeping records. This drop means that on average, the public is safer today in virtually any U.S. city than they were in the early 1970s. Despite this fact, Californians have drastically increased "tough on crime" policies, the types of crimes punishable by prison, and the time needing to be served for a great number of offenses. The anxieties arising from the culture of fear have fed a tremendous expansion of the state prison population between 1979 and 1999 by a factor of seven.[4] But the significant question I am concerned with is how this phenomenon has provided fodder for privatization. I make sense of its emergence by describing the characteristics of the large-scale fears within the state, some of their possible causes and how they have affected—and continue to affect—the discourses and sensibilities of criminal justice policy-making that aid and encourage private contracting.

The second ideological theme addressed in this chapter is one that is not necessarily new, but reinvigorated by the public knowledge of the various crises in both California's governmental braches and the California Department of Corrections & Rehabilitation (CDCR). The discourse carries within it traces of Governor Reagan's historical attack in the 1960s on the state's seemingly monolithic and dysfunctional "big government" that I detail in chapter 3 and couples with a rather mystified construction of the neutrality of the free market as a panacea for institutional ineptitude. Curiously, while the last decade has laid bare more fraud and corporate corruption than has perhaps been seen in this century, the belief in the rationality and naturally superior order of privately-owned and managed business—over and above government management of almost any public service—has triumphed. Indeed, the discourse surrounding the preeminence of the free-market system has proven to be tireless even in the wake of the worst recession in this country since the Great Depression. My claim is that where privately-contracted prisons are favored over publicly-managed prisons, one will also recognize rhetorical appeals that borrow from this ideology and reveal that part of the attractiveness of privatization arises simply because it is a for-profit agency and not owned or controlled by the public or its officials

A final theme explored in this chapter demonstrates the exaggerated images of criminality itself. Upon inspection, race and class are central elements of the very classification: criminal. Indeed, after controlling for a number of significant factors, research shows that the size of California's Black population is a stronger indicator of the percentage of Black incarceration than even its rate of violent crime.[5] Compared with white youths, people of color in California are 2.8 times more likely to be arrested for violent crimes, 6.2 times more likely to be tried in adult court, and a full 7.0 times more likely to be sentenced once they arrive there.[6] Empirical data suggests that the California criminal justice system often relies less upon identifying and treating those who break the law, than upon unconscious tropes of criminality which depend upon race and/or class. I examine the images of criminals Californians imagine they are incarcerating and show that in fact these images do not fit the profile of the average offender. Finally, I explain how the tropes serve to naturalize a need to increase prisons, which ultimately has enabled private contractors to serve as a source for more beds.

In short, this chapter aims to demonstrate that ideological discourses resonate with the actual mental, emotional, material, and cultural conditions of individuals who form opinions encouraging the privatization of California state prisons. Adopting private contracting is more than a material shift within the institution of corrections; in addition, it is a mark of symbolic struggles being played out within the discourses that represent crime and corrections, a struggle that affects not only all aspects of criminal justice in the state, but the cultural realities of Californians themselves.

The Culture of Fear Defined

California's private contracting gained acceptance as a function of an increase in Californian's fear of crime. Heightened insecurity over crime, a relatively new phenomenon on the list of social issues, became prominent during the mid-1980s. In fact, although fears about crime entered into national public discourse during the 1960s—specifically, scholars suggest, during the Barry Goldwater presidential campaign of 1964, those fears did not overcome other American concerns for approximately another twenty years. Climbing steadily, poll numbers show that by 1994, Americans ranked crime on public surveys ahead of every other social issue including the economy, the deficit, international relations, government spending and pollution.[7] In that same year, a poll published by Gallup revealed that more than 80 percent of respondents believed that crime was the most serious threat to individual rights and freedoms in the United States.[8] And if there was any doubt about whether or not the issue was worth the money we spent to solve the problem, even though the costs of criminal justice that year totaled three-quarters of a trillion dollars, 75 percent of citizens queried believed we were not spending enough.[9] This belief was despite the fact that between 1980 and 1999 the federal budget for criminal justice more than doubled.[10] It is also significant that between these same years the prison population in the United States increased approximately six fold. Today, there is no other issue besides the economy and perhaps Islamic terrorism consistently receiving more public attention than domestic criminal violence.

Barry Glassner has suggested that public fear is not only at an all time high level, but also seems to be increasing.[11] Fear of crime combined with a whole host of other types of fears have transformed Americans into a people whereby the phrase, "Be careful" is key to our "cultural imagination." These words are a sign that "safety has become the fundamental value of our times," according to Frank Furedi, a writer who has also chronicled Glassner's main claims. He continues by noting "passions that were once devoted to a struggle to change the world (or keep it the same) are now invested in trying to ensure that we are safe."[12] Both Glassner and Furedi dub this national mindset a "culture of fear"; others, such as Mike Davis, who has written about the culture of California, have named it the "ecology of fear." No matter the label, what might be understood as an ever-present, oftentimes intangible anxiety, has seemingly penetrated our psychic geography. Here, crime exists in citizens' minds as a series of menacing archetypes and abstract enemies; it preys upon one's consciousness as images of danger that could strike at any moment. The surprise attacks on the World Trade Center, and other acts of terrorism both here in the U.S. and abroad over the last decade, have only heightened such concerns.

The Culture of Fear in California

In California, a mixture of unique "dangers" contributes to this mindset. In Los Angeles County, for example, citizens contend with one of the largest, if not *the* largest, concentration of gangs in the United States.[13] It's rare for a week to pass without a report of at least one assault or murder at the hands of gang members, and typically these stories feature innocents like a child caught in crossfire or a local teacher being gunned down on the way home from a trip to the grocery store.[14] Perhaps the greatest threat arising from gang activity is becoming a victim of crime simply by being in the wrong place at the wrong time. But as the nightly news broadcasts seem to imply, there may be *no right place or time* to avoid harm when it comes to the ubiquity of gang violence. Attempting to do something about "the terror" caused by criminal street gangs, California legislators passed a substantial number of laws throughout the 1980s and 90s to combat this burgeoning mayhem.[15] But in spite of these laws public apprehension over drug trafficking, graffiti, witness intimidation and random violence have not significantly decreased. In fact, to the surprise of many, one of the state's more upscale areas, Orange County, reported an increase in the early 1990s of the number of gangs and tagger-crews (from 192 to 341). The number of identified gang members also grew from approximately 12,000 to 21,328. The increases seemed to reinforce the threats of living in an urban area, while indicating that no secure place existed no matter how far one might travel from "danger zones."

Californians also experience anxieties associated with the large influx of illegal immigration. Besides being a hotbed of gang agitation, the state is one of the most significant gateways for Mexican and South

American illegal immigration in the country. Additionally, the border California shares with Mexico has seen increased armed conflict between warring Mexican drug cartels whose long-standing drug trade arrangements seem to have unraveled. As a result, competition for the control of certain trafficking routes used to gain entry into the U.S. has caused increased violence. The killing has taken almost 40,000 lives—including over 300 Americans—since 2004. The ongoing battle to curb the flow of drugs, illegal passage of immigrants, and often both simultaneously, has kept border officials scrambling. According to at least one confidential California Department of Justice study, authorities are losing that battle in that at least 60 percent of the members of the 18th Street Gang in southern California (a gang with approximately 20,000 members) were found to be in the state illegally.[16]

Crime committed in California by illegal immigrants, however, is complicated by immigration sanctuary policies which actually prohibit officers from inquiring about an individual's citizenship status. A policy dating to the 1970s, Special Order 40, bars any officer from "initiating police action where the objective is to discover the alien status of a person." Protocol, therefore, dictates that California police may not question any person about his or her immigration status and may not notify federal immigration authorities about those illegal immigrants who break the law (apart from a felony infraction or a *series* of multiple misdemeanors). Here, then, police work becomes complicated by the complex relations between federal immigration authorities, local police departments and the sticky politics involved in issues of illegal immigration within the state. The firestorm across the country launched over Arizona's bill (SB 1070) passed in 2010—which requires police to check the immigration status of people they lawfully stop and suspect are in the country illegally—points to the kind of sensational debacle police forces in California would like to sidestep. In fact, police are so sensitive to the political blowback, they will hardly even speak on the record about Special Order 40. As one LAPD captain put it, "We can't even talk about it. . . . [p]eople are afraid of a backlash from Hispanics."[17] The result is that illegal immigrants who commit crimes, even those who have been deported but return and break the law once again, are not necessarily arrested. Indeed some might say they have something of a safe haven. Consequently, the criminal activities within which illegals engage are not always as easily dealt with by authorities. When these offenders are caught, there is more *red tape* and close inspection of protocol for potential deviations from Special Order 40 than with other routine arrests. Citizens are not only fearful of serious crime committed by illegal immigrants, but also their petty crime—for example, driving a motor vehicle without insurance and hitting a motorist—which could cost them pain, suffering and money. California residents have lived with the ironies and frustrations of these arrangements for a long while and recognize that competing policies and/or goals of federal, state and local government agencies do not always ultimately translate into the safety of ordinary citizens.

One final unique apprehension of California residents is dealings with the police. Police brutality and misconduct in the golden state was perhaps most sensationally revealed over 25 years ago in the videotaped beating of Rodney King by Los Angeles police officers. The dark shadow of the court trial left public perceptions of police departments in the state at best, less credible and at worst, downright criminal. Scandals that erupted in the Los Angeles Rampart Division came shortly thereafter—not nearly long enough after the King incident to repair the public relations damages the trial wrought. Several officers in a particular squad assigned to fighting gang activity were found to be committing drug crimes themselves and then framing known gang members for their illegal activities. After one officer finally took a plea deal, it was discovered that approximately 70 officers in that division were engaging in misconduct. The 2009 shooting of Oscar Grant on New Year's Day by a Bay Area Rapid Transit officer (BART) added another dose of bitterness to the mix. Grant, allegedly resisting arrest, was stretched out in a prone position and unarmed. According to reports, Officer Johannes Mehserle stood, drew his gun and shot Grant once in the back. A new hailstorm began and the public relations efforts started once more. Perennial events such as these have sullied the reputation of the police force and caused citizens to question whether officers are truly present to protect and serve—or simply command and harass. Today, significant numbers of complaints of excessive force, discourtesy, bias, and unauthorized imprisonment persist. In the second quarter of 2010, citizens filed 1,132 reports with the Los Angeles Police Department (LAPD) claiming alleged misconduct by department officers. Within that three-month period alone, Los Angeles County received 595 allegations of unauthorized force and false imprisonment as well as over 100 claims of biased policing, including racial bias.[18] The Los Angeles County Sheriff's Department has similarly faced scrutiny over the excessive use of force by deputies—to such a degree that the Federal Bureau of Investigation is now investigating cliques of deputies' brutality against inmates and the cover-ups of these crimes.

Perhaps the most egregious detail about a potential complaint filed against law-enforcement in California is that officers may sue those who do so for defamation of character. A California statute (California Civil

Code 47.5) provides officers with a structured protocol to bring suit against any citizen who files reports of alleged police misconduct.[19] It is no small thing, therefore, to report police misconduct or brutality when not only can a claimant be named in a defamation lawsuit, but also he or she has no right to be represented by a lawyer in such a case and virtually no right to appeal a decision found to be unfavorable.[20]

It's understandable then that many Californians are preoccupied with safety and vigilance in the face of potential risks; to the common person, it's simply practical equipment for living. Whether or not a person has been an actual victim of crime does not seem to be a significant factor in that preoccupation; for violence can seemingly touch anyone who inhabits the culture of fear. Taking children to the park could be a trip to the emergency room given the incidents of razors being placed in park jungle gyms. Driving down a public interstate could put you in the line of fire by a disgruntled driver (two real-life crime trends in the state of California).[21] Gone is the time when danger or crime was merely a problem of urban areas, the underclass, or unusual circumstances. Instead worry about crime has graduated into a persistent and nagging thought. Furedi argues that although we have considered ourselves long since enlightened, "[n]ot since the Dark Ages has there been so much concern about organized"—and I would add disorganized—"forces of evil."[22]

It's no surprise, therefore, that safety and security have become significant growth industries. For if the world is riskier, we must arm ourselves with products and services to ensure our families are protected. Records indicate, for example, that California sales of firearms have surged.[23] Security companies continue to proliferate boasting of their readiness to respond to intrusions at a "moments notice." Gated security for suburban developments—which as of 1994 accounted for an estimated one-third of all new communities built in southern California[24]—is spreading for those who can afford it, encouraging a new level of social exclusion in our cities. Security video devices monitor everything from work-outs at the gym, suspicious shoppers browsing in the mall, to potentially abusive baby-sitters in the form of furry stuffed animals with hidden cameras. Youngsters are not fully armed today without a cellular phone—"just in case of an emergency"—and it has become commonplace to see pepper-spray dangling from a key-chain. The reigning wisdom seems to be that if the incidence of crime cannot be controlled, the well-advised should invest in the most up-to-date devices for their own defense.

The Irony of Fearfulness in California

Of course, the irony of Californian's preoccupation with fear is that it is largely unfounded. In fact, according to the California Criminal Justice Statistics Center, "Californians are more likely to be victimized by an accident in their own homes than they are by crime."[25] Even though a majority of citizens will claim that crime rates have continued to rise with no restraint, actual incidences of crime have dropped not only in California, but also across the U.S. One reason for the misperception might be what Hindelang and his colleagues refer to as the "crime-is-rising-at-a-distance" phenomenon. Individuals, according to this research, often estimate crime within their own neighborhoods with some accuracy, but consistently misjudge property crime risks, changes in crime rates and the frequency of crime outside of areas within which most of their daily lives are spent.[26] It would seem that while we see our own city as reasonably safe, places we have little experience with appear more ominous. And although we may have little direct experience ourselves with becoming a victim of crime, it still seems to be an ever-present and increasingly significant threat.

Nonetheless, the reality is that the crime rate in California peaked over thirty years ago in 1980 and has been decreasing steadily ever since. Data from 1989-1999 show that crime declined at a faster pace in California than it did across the United States as a whole (by 48 percent while the national rate fell by 31 percent).[27] This drop was in spite of the fact that the state had a dramatic increase in population during the same period. In fact, the number of people added to the population of California during those years grew faster than in the six most populous states in the U.S., indeed faster than the entire country (up 14.8 percent compared to 8.8 percent and 10 percent respectively).[28] In just one ten-year period (between 1988 and 1998), serious crime rates fell a striking 35.3 percent. Over the past year, homicide rates in Los Angeles dropped to levels not seen since 1967 when the city had almost 30 percent fewer inhabitants.[29] Even the smaller municipality of Compton in Los Angeles County—known more for its "gang-banging" and drive-by shootings celebrated in gangster rap lyrics than for the safety of its streets—recorded the lowest levels of homicide since 1965.[30] Add to this a decrease in property crime—even vehicle theft, again at levels not seen since the 1960s—decreases in burglary, which has fallen 71 percent since 1980, and declines in the rates of assault and robbery which also continue to decrease, albeit at a slower pace.[31] In sum, violent crime in large cities in southern California (those with over one-hundred thousand inhabitants) came down 70 percent over the last decade—and this was an 18 percent decrease *over the national average.* If awards were handed out, two California cities, Torrance and Glendale, both in Los Angeles County, would take the prize for the largest drops in violent crime in the nation.[32]

But while these statistics ought to allay citizens' fears and calm worries about being victimized, they simply never seem to be absorbed by the general population. One has to wonder what stands in the way of the average Californian discovering and acting upon this information. For if crime really has been falling—in fact, even if crime was simply remaining at a constant rate—residents' anxieties about being victimized must not be a reaction to the amount of crimes committed or their character, but rather to the interpretation of their urgency. So how do they become so "urgent"?

Mass Media and the Culture of Fear

One way to make sense of this phenomenon is to recognize that as our culture has become permeated by electronic mediums of communication, public discourse has been transmuted by the boundaries and structural requirements of those mediums. That is, the very framework of television, or the World Wide Web, for example, bends the content it communicates to itself. When 90 percent of Americans, according to one study, consider the most important source of information about crime to be the mass media, this fact cannot be inconsequential.[33] The fact that the public is getting most of its information about crime from mass-mediated forums means that knowledge about crime and criminal justice work is subject to the metaphors that regulate those mediums—perhaps the most popular of which is television. The sixty-second sound bite, the sensational image, the truncated analysis are the forms through which we learn about criminal behaviors and illegalities in our culture (as well as what ought to be done about them), forms governed by competition for ad revenue and air-time. As violent crime provides spectacular images in abundance, its portrayal within the televisual is a logical, if unfortunate, marriage.

Research shows that the portrayals of violent crime in films and television have escalated over the past thirty or so years, correlating with the rise in public anxieties over victimization.[34] Throughout the 1990s, the three major networks (ABC, CBS, NBC) devoted more programming minutes within their nightly newscasts to crime than any other single topic.[35] Between 1989 and 1993, the number of crime stories on these networks quadrupled to reach 1,632 or nearly five stories per evening.[36] Even in the wake of declining crime rates, the networks continued to press crime and violence as the most important news story—tied only with those reports on the war in Kosovo. In 1998, fully one-third of all crime stories focused on murder, nearly four times the number devoted to the impeachment trial of President Clinton.[37]

To put those stories in context, less than two-tenths of one percent *of all arrests* are for the charge of murder. However, statistics show that on average, for every single event of violent assault, nine property crimes are committed. Nonetheless, approximately 28 percent of all crimes featured in nightly newscasts are stories featuring homicide, not stolen property. Furthermore, offenses committed by corporations or by government officials, which some argue have the most widespread effect on Americans, are typically not even categorized as "crime stories." As Jeffrey Reiman points out, the public is harmed far more as a result of crimes like price fixing, consumer deception, or embezzlement than all the property crimes in the FBI crime index combined. He continues by saying, "Yet these far more costly acts are either not criminal, or, if technically criminal, not prosecuted, or, if prosecuted, not punished, or if punished, only mildly."[38] The point here is that ideas about how to think of crime are not natural; mass media shape our very definitions of what constitutes a criminal act. Those definitions typically exclude the behaviors that genuinely affect the largest number of citizens in lieu of focusing on street crimes committed by one perpetrator upon one victim.

This tendency is also accompanied by news media's proclivity to focus upon certain kinds of crime victims. In cases where victims are shown, they are predominantly female, white, and affluent.[39] However, victims of most violent crimes are poor men of color who live in urban areas. In California, those with the highest risk of becoming a victim of crime are Black teenage men between the ages of 16 and 19. These individuals are four times more likely to be injured by aggravated assault than an average aged white person and a full 50 percent more likely to be a victim of violence than white teens.[40] But broadcast news audiences learn quite early whose victimization counts. When crime stories feature white women as the most typical victims of crime—the very same group who report the lowest levels of victimization—we see "minority" victimization as simply normal. The incidents of crime, the types of crime and the depictions of victimization lead television audiences to particular interpretations of the crime problems in California: who the offenders are, what crimes are most common and who ought to be afraid. Although a complicated relationship exists between public anxieties and public discourses focusing upon crime, it is possible to draw a couple of conclusions. Beckett and Sasson's studies, which parallel George Gerbner's basic findings, indicate that those who watch the most television tend to be more fearful and mistrusting. While they warn us that there is always the danger of conflating causes and effects, that is, are fearful people drawn to violence on television? Do they selectively expose themselves to frightful content? Or is there some type of selective retention of what those viewers already believe to be dangerous? The researchers ultimately argue through empirical assessments that the greater amount of time one watches television depictions of crime and/or news broadcasts of actual crime stories, the greater the chances that he or she will view the world as a place where crime consistently occurs. Those viewers will also tend to believe there is a need to become "tough on crime," and that the identities of criminal offenders are the same groups of violent, black and brown men we see portrayed repeatedly on nightly newscasts. [41]

Government and the Culture of Fear

Perhaps media programming ought to be understood in the context of another factor in the arousal of anxieties over crime: the discourses of government officials and political leaders. Michael Flamm advances an interesting argument about the manner in which "law and order" language originally entered into the speech of political candidates and office-holders. He suggests that conservatives, who had relied for some time upon anti-communist discourse in the 1950s to articulate political attacks upon liberals, began to run into road-blocks with these same appeals. In the aftermath of John F. Kennedy's strong showing of political might toward communist forces, claims of his being "soft" were no longer useful. Strategies shifted to mark the beginning of a new articulation of conservative platforms. These began to take the shape of a vocabulary of "law and order" which borrowed from the mantra of "peace through strength" serving anti-communist discourse. This vocabulary became the amalgam that represented fighting back against domestic illegality, civil disobedience, and a paternalism or lenience offered to criminal offenders by a "liberal" criminal justice system. More extreme conservatives went as far as to argue that communist agitators had fomented riots breaking out across the country, thereby linking together the attack against communism and crime. [42] But ultimately what stuck from these struggles was a politics fashioned out of blaming progressive foes for weakness in the face of crime and a failure to maintain authority.

In the more recent past, Democrats have recognized the power of *law and order* appeals to voters and have prudently adapted these to their own interests. The more reactionary the response to crime, it would seem, the more sensation focused upon the public official. Bill Clinton recognized this power in both his 1988 and 1992 campaigns, and in fact signed an expensive crime bill into law in 1994 that funneled approximately $24 billion to local law enforcement agencies across the country. The funds added 100,000 new police officers to the streets and gave an additional $7.7 billion to states to build new prison facilities. California's share of the grant awards from the bill was over $100 million for the hiring of "Cops on the Beat" (additional officers for police and sheriff's departments) and an additional $3 million for corrections "boot camps," according to a brief released by the California Legislative Analyst's Office in 1996. The flurry of attention on the federal bill manifested within weeks in a poll that showed 37 percent of Americans citing crime as the most important problem facing the country. That percent rose to a startling 52 percent in August of that same year, immediately following the passage of another federal crime bill adopting the "Three Strikes You're Out" mandates that had been making huge waves in California. When the tab was totaled, between 1980 and 1999 the U.S. had doubled both the number of dollars we were spending nationally for criminal justice expenditures as well as the number of law enforcement officials fighting crime across the country.

Once government officials begin paying attention to crime or victimization, and that activity is covered by the mass media, how does it affect the average citizen's viewpoint of crime? Is there a link between citizen apprehension and a focus on crime by state or federal leaders? Perhaps unsurprisingly, the research suggests that as politicians pay more attention to crime issues, and this attention garners media coverage, the percentage of Americans who say that crime is the most important problem we face consistently increases. Similarly, as less attention is paid to the issues of crime by political leaders, public concerns decline. Thus, when the public has a broad interest in crime, Katherine Beckett argues ". . .it appears that the public is *following the leadership of politicians* and the media, not the other way around"[italics mine].[43]

While Beckett's logic makes sense, it would be unwise to imagine that state or federal political leaders have free reign to shape media coverage or public opinion on social or political issues. The vast numbers of mediums for public discourse are themselves contentious sites of struggle with complex internal relations and unique institutional demands. Every social actor competes for the acceptance of his or her rhetorical message, even though clearly not everyone has an equal chance to have a voice in that competition. That being said, it's clear that government officials have a special place in the ongoing contest. Researchers have found that not only are their comments not checked as closely for truth content,[44] but also a full 72 percent of all sources offering information for television network news programs consist of government officials, political institutions or groups.[45] In short, the culture of fear has found powerful allies in government leaders and the mass media. The two forces combined have directed public attention, shaped the frames through which it interprets danger and risk while supplying solutions that rely upon the expansion of the prison institution.

Effects of the Culture of Fear Upon Criminal Justice

The increased attention upon crime coupled with the increased use of law and order discourse has had ripple effects throughout the entire crime control field. In truth, the shifts that were brought about by so much public preoccupation over crime had been coming for some time, but by the 1990s, a consensus had formed crystallizing long-standing dissatisfaction with penal-welfarism and a sense that crime and violence had grown out of control. Once the Determinate Sentencing Law passed in California in 1976, over 1000 new measures became law that established offenses never before on the books and often made sentences for existing offenses more punitive. Public opinion became harsher, sentencing codes were altered to reflect mandatory minimums, determinate sentences became a mainstay and presumptive sentencing stipulations became increasingly common. Parole was abolished in over a dozen states and probation now had a more limited use for a designated set of crimes. Juveniles began to be tried as adults and the country witnessed a resurgence of the death penalty. As the field transformed, not only were more bodies being added to California prisons, but also the populations of prisons across the nation also began to increase. After remaining relatively constant throughout the 1970s, prison commitments to adult arrests between 1980 and 1989 increased from 196 per 1000 to 332 per 1000.[46] Data for 1986 show that the U.S. state and federal prison population actually began its climb in 1973. By the start of 1990 this population was 293 percent above the 1972 level, requiring eleven new medium-sized (500 beds) prisons *each month* to accommodate the additional 58,700-person increase from 1989 to 1990 convictions alone.[47] By 2003, more than 2.2 million people were incarcerated in the United States—a rate of 482 persons for every

100,000 people in the country, a 304 percent increase between 1980 and 2002.[48]

Even the expansion of prison facilities between 1978 and 1988, which brought the addition of over 200,000 beds nationwide, could not match the pace of prison commitments. State prisons were operating at an average of 115 percent of design capacity while federal facilities were being filled at over 150 percent their original bed capacity.[49] In all but nine states, prisons were found by the federal courts to be in violation of constitutional standards due to overcrowding, making it quite clear that, indeed, public authorities were having difficulties getting facilities built to house these growing numbers.[50] In California, the incarcerated population grew nearly six times its original number between 1977 and 1995. Zimring and Hawkins reveal in a 1994 study that from 1981 to 1994, both the raw numbers of inmates and the imprisonment rate per 100,000 increased without interruption in California. At year-end 1985, the prison population had more than doubled since 1980, and by year-end 1990, the population doubled once again. These figures suggest that California's rate of expansion during these years was so rapid, no other jurisdiction in the country could match its pace. Zimring and Hawkins write: "no state ha[s] ever added 75,000 prisoners or increased prison and jail populations by 115,000 in one decade."[51] Astonishingly, however, the records show that even though the state's prison population rose 58 percent between 1989 and 1999, its crime rate plummeted 49 percent. And this drop was occurring nationwide even before incarceration rates began to soar.

Over this last decade, the state prison population has declined slightly (down approximately 5,000 from its highest recorded numbers), but facilities are so overcrowded, the decreases have hardly made a dent in available bed capacity. As was mentioned in Chapter 3, these conditions prompted a lawsuit that made its way to the U.S. Supreme Court. In May 2011, the Court ruled against the state of California in an opinion declaring the system's institutions were so egregious, their conditions amounted to cruel and unusual punishment. As a result, California was directed to shed over 30,000 inmates from its prison rolls by 2013, to reduce the inmate population to a hearty 137.5 percent of the system's capacity. The state still grapples with this directive by continuing to shift non-violent offenders to county facilities, but the struggles over what to do with so many inmates are far from over. As I will explain in Chapter 6, predicaments like these have put upward pressure upon the expansion of private contracting in California.

One other consideration is worth noting here. Given the skyrocketing population, the costs of the harsher policies over the last thirty years have been striking. As the length of sentences began to increase, and zero tolerance programs became more popular, it would be accurate to say that Californians wanted incarceration. And they didn't seem to care how much it would cost. During the 1980s, the California state budget grew by approximately 9 percent per year. But corrections spending increased by about 19 percent per year. The annual cost to house, feed, and care for each inmate at the turn of the millennium grew to approximately $25,000, a figure constantly compared to that of educating a child in the state's K-12 system: a mere $7,200 by comparison.[52] In 2008-09, the average annual cost for each inmate grew to $48,536 as healthcare allocations alone for adults grew 100 percent from 2006. In all, between 1998 and 2009, the CDCR's budget grew an astronomical 6.8 billion, from $3.5 billion to $10.3 billion.[53] While we cannot say that a culture of fear and the popularity of law and order discourses solely caused these effects, it's clear that rising fears and anxiety over crime and victimization had a significant role in the growth of crime control agencies. Today, we see the fruits of that explosion: billions of dollars spent, unheard of recidivism rates and overcrowded conditions so perverse they have been deemed unconstitutional.

One point is certain. The culture of fear has constructed a frenzied and anxious discourse loosened from the factual moorings of declining crime rates within the state. And in retrospect, it has wreaked havoc on the California budget as was predicted by criminal justice experts, criminology scholars and credible research organizations across the state. Citizens, informed about crime predominantly through media depictions of perennial street violence, have reacted as any person who feels threatened might. They have become alert, watchful and careful. They have voted to lock up threats to their safety—even when the state cannot afford it. They have chosen harsher punishment for would-be offenders and invested in security for their homes and family members. And they have largely ignored the fact that many of these choices have not genuinely decreased their fears. The overcrowding of California's prisons and the cost of the crime control system in the state are really unsurprising when one examines these in the context of the public discourse fomenting anxiety over becoming a victim. It's a wonder the state isn't more in debt over the costs of punishing offenders.

Furthermore, the growth of industries that center around incarceration is a logical development from the standpoint of capitalist political economy. The pressure upon prison institutions to grow in California aligns perfectly with the appearance of private prisons. As this "solution" came forward, it was heralded as a prudent and rational means to address economic and logistic issues otherwise unmanageable by the CDCR. The culture of fear, however, tells only part of the story of adopting private contracting; the whole notion of private prisons being "private" adds fuel to both their image and acceptance.

The Mystification of the "Free" Market

The culture of fear was buttressed by an additional rationale that must also be addressed here because it overlaps and borrows from its logic. The fear of crime in California also brought with it a public cynicism that diminished the faith citizens had in the criminal justice system more generally. Confidence in criminal justice workers and their ability to adequately punish those convicted of crime were not considerably high given the concerns circulating that too many criminals were on the street committing violence. According to California state historian, Kevin Starr, Californian's attitudes toward their elected officials and civic organizations "exploded into a supernova of suspicion and distrust."[54] How could killers, rapists and thieves walk the streets after committing heinous crimes against the populous? There had to be something terribly wrong with our courts, our prisons, and our penal code for such things to happen. Californians were not alone in their bewilderment; Americans were registering similar viewpoints. A national survey compiled between 1982-1991 asking: "In general, do you think the courts in this area (poll was administered in cities across the U.S.) deal too harshly or not harshly enough with criminals?" showed an average of 83 percent of respondents answering "not harshly enough." Additionally, a *USA Today* poll in the early 1990s found 86 percent of those surveyed believed that courts were not harsh enough in dealing with criminals.[55]

Public confidence appeared to be decreasing for a few pointed reasons: courts did not seem to exact a meaningful price for criminal behavior, criminal justice workers didn't apprehend, prosecute and jail offenders in a timely manner, and there seemed to be little coordination or planning between the police, the courts and corrections agencies generally.[56] In fact, many saw the courts actually offering incentives for crime as a function of plea-bargaining, long delays between convictions and sentencing and what was perceived as judicial leniency. Viewpoints of California criminal justice professionals demonstrate this view. Probation officers, district attorneys, police chiefs in large cities, public defenders, sheriffs and judges presiding over various levels of California courts were asked about the success of the state's criminal justice system. In answer to a survey, one district attorney wrote: "It is misleading to analyze California's criminal justice system in anything other than the most general manner. No detailed analysis of such a system is likely to be productive because no such system exists. Rather, the agencies that this survey groups together are independent systems themselves and the agencies are not designed to cooperate with the other agencies to reach a common goal..."[57] In essence, the DA argued the criminal justice "system" was really erroneously understood as some coherent or unified set of functions.

Perhaps one example of this fragmentation is the way that law and order legislation in California has been perpetually divorced from budget concerns. Sentencing legislation has not been typically tied to appropriations. Consequently, there has been no reconciliation between the wrath of new sentencing laws entering the books and the inadequate prison facilities that must accommodate the numbers of new inmates. As one criminologist concludes, the system is so disjointed that county court judges actually have a "fiscal incentive" to send felons to state prison. "To the counties it's a free lunch. . . This is the unintended problem of having one level of government sentence people to prison and another level of government responsible for providing the prisons."[58]

In short, there have been—and still are—a good number of problems plaguing the reputation of criminal justice work both federally and in California, many of which have led to the argument that the criminal justice system in the state is simply bankrupt. While that system certainly could not stand in proxy for the entire state government as a whole, the California state government, nonetheless, has been tainted by libertarian arguments that "big government" and bloated bureaucracy undermines a streamlined system of corrections. "Red-tape," union costs and meaningless regulation hurts prison management, as the story goes, and certainly there is ready evidence in reports that the corrections department has been beset by cost over-runs and waste. In contradistinction, the private sector, which relies upon "self-regulation" and the competitive market-place, is understood to be simply less vulnerable to bureaucratic corruption—even if this is untrue. If private companies became responsible for California inmates, according to this reasoning, the logic operating in those companies would demand greater efficiency.

Scandals over the last decade involving the leaders of multi-national corporations, for example Enron, AIG or even a number of the banking institutions involved in the economic financial meltdown of 2008, have soured many toward large corporate entities—especially the executive management of those firms. But the disparagement of U.S. corporations, the flailing U.S. economy, and global economic instability generally have done little to dispel confidence in capitalist arrangements on the whole. As much as the public may loathe and mistrust the greed and dishonesty of individual corporate CEOs and their cohorts, they fail to see them as linked to the healthy functioning, the inherent nature, of capitalist development itself. This purview allows one to trust the impartial laws of supply and demand, and *to believe those laws* can provide superior care for criminal offenders in a qualitatively different way than publicly run institutions. In this context, inmates become simple commodities that must be reproduced—since the logic of running a successful business requires nothing less—and that reproduction, of course, demands that prison commitments increase, or at the very least, remain constant.

As criminology scholars have argued elsewhere, harnessing the profit motive to the prison system (that is, harnessing it to the custodianship of inmates) arranges structural incentives for the growth of incarceration. Those incentives ignore the goals of decreasing state crime rates, shrinking prison populations, and the healthy functioning and/or rehabilitation of current inmates.[59] Furthermore, such a model leaves aside questions of moral responsibility for particular communal functions. For example, is the punishment of our fellow citizens for infractions against the body-politic an act that must be carried out by the people of a given community? Private contracting of prisons allows tax-payers to avoid such issues and simply focus upon cost savings.

Thus, the theme of the superiority of the free-market depends on both a disheartened public that has lost faith in our ability as a collective to govern ourselves, as well a view of incarceration that is removed from any moral writ granted by a community. Committing someone to prison here is not about an act of the state to withhold liberty, to punish a person for transgressing against a commonwealth. It is merely a business arrangement, a managerial challenge, or a science distinct from any normative imperative. Private contracting thus rides upon the rhetorical back of the logics of the political economy of capitalism itself. And given how resilient this discourse is in the U.S., it may be the strongest appeal for transferring prisons into private hands.

Ideological Images of the Offender

There is little question that if the public could find some way to identify with those men and women being imprisoned, it would be more difficult to ignore the manifold conditions associated with mass-incarceration. And if this is true, then it's crucial to pay attention to how criminality is commonly represented—that is, how is the average prisoner imagined? The discourse of criminality seems to typically cut across state lines;

that is, it emerges in what one might call a "national village" whereupon the presentation of crime and those who perpetuate it are typically not just broadcast to isolated local audiences in California (while this is also true), but across the country.

Characteristics ascribed to the offender construct him as an "alien-other," typically male, poor and of color. It would seem little has changed since Frederick Douglas argued so long ago that crime is simply a feature imputed to color.[60] Guy Johnson made the same observation in his work "The Negro & Crime" when he commented that Blackness was so significant to the profile of criminality, it virtually constituted the classification.[61] Perhaps this is why Barry Goldwater's subtle reference so long ago to the threat posed by urban unrest and "violence in the streets" (during his run for president in 1964) never mentioned the dark skin of perpetrators—it wasn't necessary. To many, the panic represented by such a threat already had a color. The appeal managed to simultaneously cultivate a new Republican constituency while legitimating a certain kind of rhetorical strategy dependent upon division and fear.

The marriage of color to crime hasn't changed much over the history of this country. More recently, a study by the University of Chicago found that one out of every two Americans endorsed the claim that Blacks tend to be "violence prone." The endorsement suggests not only that a stubborn prototype for criminal offenders still animates the mind of the average citizen, but also that in accordance with criminological studies, once a frame is adopted to understand criminality, individuals tend to unconsciously select and assimilate facts that continually validate that frame.[62] It's not that "whiteness" (or wealth) bars criminal participation to be sure, but rather that the faces of crime fixed in ideological images of danger and menace are drawn in shades of black and brown. Accordingly, the very discussion of mass incarceration is a discussion of race/ethnicity and its intersection with socio-economic status.

Most often, the descriptions of criminality are peppered with identifiers like the terms *underclass*, *gang-banger*, *superpredator* and more recently the *juvenile psychopath*. What details are wrapped up in such labels? Explaining the likeness of the superpredator, William Bennett and his colleagues note that these creatures are "radically impulsive, brutally remorseless youngsters, including evermore pre-teenage boys, who murder, assault, rape, rob, burglarize, deal deadly drugs, join gun-toting gangs, and create serious communal disorders. They do not fear the stigma of arrest, the pains of imprisonment or the pangs of conscience." In short, they explain, when it comes to identifying this kind of criminal, "race is a proxy" for a kind of "moral poverty" that white children seem to have been able to evade.[63] In reference to the underclass, criminologist James Q. Wilson writes plainly: "The reason we call it an underclass and why we worry about it, is that its members have a bad character: They mug, do drugs, desert children, and scorn education."[64]

Criminality Is a Function of Nature (Not Nurture)

Significantly, the literature describing the superpredator explains his violence as a function of his *nature*, but also often nurtured by a culture of dependency found in the "inner city," or membership of the underclass. In fact, a superpredator is not always understood to be fully human, as Wilson explains, for at his core he is ineluctably a "feral" or "pre-social" being.[65] Even Ronald Reagan borrowed from this grim portrait in his description of the present-day criminal in the 1980s. This individual, he stated, has ". . .a stark staring face—a face that belongs to a frightening reality of our time: the face of the human predator. . .nothing in nature," he cautioned, "is more cruel or dangerous."[66]

The writing of nineteenth century Italian criminologist Cesare Lombroso could easily have served to source these depictions, with the exception that his work never needed to attend to the language and careful politics surrounding twenty-first century discussions of race and class. Putting the case bluntly, he declared, "many of the characteristics found in savages and among the colored races are also to be found in habitual delinquents."[67] Something of a modern scientist at the time, Lombroso's experiments on the physical anthropology of criminal offenders depended squarely upon the theses of eugenics. Offenders, he explained, were born, not made. Such musings allowed his work to become the fodder for criminologists and prison officials in the late 1880s to simply throw their hands up and submit that criminal behavior was irreparably ingrained in the bodies and minds of degenerates. The kindest gesture afforded them, therefore, was incarceration, or perhaps more expedient, forced sterilization. In fact, in the early 1900s, California mandated the sterilization of persons "twice convicted for sexual offenses or three times for other crimes," ultimately sterilizing hundreds of convicts each year in mental health facilities.[68] Before shrinking away from such a propostition, however, it's best we recognize that the suggestion of crime (or poverty for that matter) having its roots in the heredity or the culture of criminals themselves— and needing state intervention—has a particularly long history in the United States. What is most intriguing, if not disturbing, is to recognize how Lombroso's projects and conclusions have morphed into current criminal justice scholarship and public discourse on crime.

Those familiar with such scholarship will remember that James Q. Wilson and Richard Herrnstein, who would later go on to pen the well-known text *The Bell Curve: Intelligence and Class Structure in American Life*, published *Crime and Human Nature* in 1985. Similar to *The Bell Curve*, it argued for the genetic basis for certain behaviors—in this case criminal behaviors—marked by such items as intelligence, race, and body types. Referring to Francis Galton, Charles Darwin's younger cousin who in fact coined the term *eugenics*, Wilson and Herrnstein commend the indexing of intelligence and suggest that such "evolutionary thinking" made possible the correlation of correct answers on intelligence tests to true intelligence the same way "sampling of blood pressure, body temperature, or blood chemistry (refer to) . . . general physiological performance."[69] In other words, intelligence indexes were just as accurate in signaling physiological predilections for criminal tendencies as blood pressure was to indicating general health. By way of concluding their work, the authors ask us to recognize that "constitutional factors" (natural characteristics) arising from racial categories direct the likelihood for criminal behavior. But perhaps realizing this argument would be more likely than either Lombroso's or Galton's work to be contested, the authors declare that there is not anything ethically problematic about revealing the truth about the racial bases for criminality unless one decides the truth is immoral. "Even to allude to the possibility that races may differ in the distribution of those constitutional factors that are associated with criminality will strike some persons as factually, ethically, or prudentially wrong. We disagree. One cannot dismiss such possible connections as factually wrong, without first investigating them. Honest, open scientific inquiry that results in carefully stated findings cannot be ethically wrong, unless one believes that truth itself is wrong."[70]

Crime and Human Nature, as well as texts like it, became a powerful force in American criminological thought. In fact, the book was a best-seller—an uncommon feat for criminal justice scholarship. As the claims of Wilson, Herrnstein, Charles Murray, and other conservative criminologists raised eyebrows, it took very little time for mainstream media to pick up and run with the contentious discourse that made for ratings and sensation. Consequently, such views trickled down to ordinary people, reinvigorating well-worn stereotypes.

The latest iteration of the trope which assigns biological rationales to criminality, however, is the increasingly-common characterization of juvenile offenders as "psychopaths," "budding psychopaths," or individuals with "psychopathic tendencies."[71] In a lecture sponsored by the National Institute of Justice, Laurence Steinberg described the worrisome frequency with which prosecutors, defense attorneys, and judges inquire about psychopathy and its diagnosis among young offenders. To clarify, the clinical construct of psychopathy has been likened to a personality disorder and refers to psychological responses defined primarily by emotional detachment, anti-social tendencies, and chronic instability. But unlike other types of pathologies that might be altered with therapeutic treatments, personality disorders are recognized as "deep-seated" and resistant to therapies—if not all together immutable. In order to ascertain psychopathy, a series of interviews are conducted that typically utilize a revised version of the Psychopathy Checklist for Youth (PCL). The test rates an individual's responses to 20 different dimensions that a trained expert gathers and couples with information taken from a respondent's official file or record.[72] Today, however, the PCL is just one measure being marketed to criminal justice workers as a means to identifying juvenile psychopaths, some of which are being administered to kids as young as ten. It is of note that both today and in the nineteenth and twentieth centuries, theories arguing for a kind of sub-human population—one that could be ascertained by a given "scientific" set of assessments or measures—have been used to justify rationales for differential treatment of particular groups and changes to criminal justice policy. The tests have changed over the generations, but the aims for which the results are to be put seem to remain the same.

These assessments are especially troublesome to concerned practitioners, who like Steinberg, recognize that the accuracy of measures like the PCL are never full-proof. For you see, once an offender's disposition has been rendered, it's definitive. As Steinberg laments: "The fact that assessments of juvenile psychopathy are being used to make decisions about the transfer of young offenders into the adult system—decisions that necessarily imply judgments about the likelihood of individual rehabilitation and that effectively determine whether any attempt will be made to rehabilitate the young offender— makes any false-positive (assessment of the PCL) problem especially worrisome."[73] Whether a "eugenic jurisprudence"[74] attempts to chart "feeblemindedness" (brought to our attention by Harry Olsen, the Chief Justice of Chicago's municipal court), locate "organic brain defects," assess intelligence (as in Herbert Goddard who used the Binet-Simon intelligence test to popular acclaim shortly after WWI) or more recently measure the levels of serotonin in criminal offenders,[75] the consequences have largely remained unchanged. Once a biological and/or cultural basis for the superpredator or the juvenile psychopath has been established, the imperative ascribed them (to commit crime) is understood to be irredeemable, permanent. If this individual's compulsion to offend is not a function of the moral poverty of his culture, nurtured by a "perfect criminogenic environment,"[76] then it is (once again) one of genetics or "prefrontal cortical dysfunction." In any case, the rhetorical construction suggests that nothing can be done for these unfortunate beings, except perhaps isolate them in prisons for their, and our own safety.

As President Reagan explained at the end of the twentieth century, humans are not a product of material conditions or their social environment. That is, criminal behavior does not arise from a set of social circumstances—it's about the inadequacies of specific persons themselves. He argued that "by changing (a given) environment through expensive social programs, this philosophy holds that government can permanently change man and usher in prosperity and virtue." In short, he concluded, "poor socio-economic conditions" or decreased opportunities have nothing to do with crime. Indeed, such a philosophy puts the blame on society when it properly belongs solely on the individual.[77] In these comments, Reagan successfully turns back the clock to embrace a rationale for crime not seen since before the emergence of penal-welfarism. Taken together, his arguments—and those using a eugenic touchstone—unravel a great deal of faith in and indedd, usefulness of rehabilitation or other treatment programs; in effect they become an impractical utopian fantasy. For "social programs" are adopted for those we can alter, those we can help to be better. Perhaps it is Wilson who makes this point exceedingly clear in his claim that we ought to forget about "root causes" when we consider the reasons people commit crime: "[When I hear the phrase] 'Crime and addiction can only be dealt with by attacking their root causes,' I am sometimes inclined, when in a testy mood, to rejoin: 'Stupidity can only be dealt with by attacking its root causes.' I have yet to see a 'root cause' or to encounter a government program that has successfully attacked it. . ."[78]. If we dispel with the notion that people who commit crimes have social, cultural or political backgrounds, or failing that point, that these backgrounds have no impact upon their current life conditions, perhaps Wilson's logic is reaonable. One fact is undeniable: if we abide by a biological rationale for crime, it follows that incapacitation through incarceration becomes the punishment of choice. A look at the statistics on prison commitments in California and across the nation clearly substantiate that this choice *has* been made for over thirty years.

California Prisons: Where Are the Superpredators?

As opposed to the ideological images within the discourses of criminality, the majority of those prisoners convicted of a crime in California are not sentenced for violent offenses that might warrant their identification as some pathological alien-other. They are not inhuman superpredators genetically wired to commit acts of crime. They continue to be, by and large, tried for drug offenses and petty crimes—often as a "third strike." They are typically uneducated, unskilled and unemployed people of color. They have difficulty finding stable work that pays a living wage. Most are men from Los Angeles County, between the ages of 20 and 34, and the majority has a history of drug abuse. The greater number of the men has about an eighth grade education and over half will return to prison for a technical violation of parole.[79] Those from inland and poorer areas of the state make up the greatest numbers of inmates. In fact, the difference in the incarceration rates between poor and wealthy California regions speaks for itself: The northern portion of the state, the San Joaquin Valley and the Inland Empire regions, incarcerate individuals at rates of 792, 785, and 762 per 100,000 residents respectively, while the average rate for the southern California coastal regions and the Bay area is between 336 and 389 per 100,000.[80]

Moreover, while some suggest that crime by people of color or superpredators is increasing, as Michael Tonry makes clear, the proportion of violent crimes committed by Blacks each year, for example, has been stable for more than twenty years. However, the disproportionate incarceration of Blacks *has* increased, especially since the initiation of the war on drugs back in the 1980s.[81] We can see plenty of evidence for this claim in California prisons. The make up of its population is about 69 percent Black and Hispanic and 25 percent white (with the balance identified as "other").[82] When record keeping first began, it was actually Whites that made up the majority of arrestees in the state. That is, in 1978, the present trend was reversed: more Whites were arrested and convicted of drug offenses than any other race.[83] By 1983, the rates for Black, White, and Hispanic arrests became roughly equal. In 1987—which was also the year after coverage of drug-related issues soared in the *New York Times* from 43 stories in 1985 to 220 in 1986—the rates for Blacks and Hispanics began to move nine to ten percentage points above that of Whites and drug law violations became the fastest growing category of convictions in the California criminal justice system.[84] Between 1980 and 1995, the number of African Americans in California prisons increased four-fold—such that by 1996, 1,922 of every 100,000 Black residents of the state were behind bars compared to 236 of every 100,000 White residents.[85] Near the end of the 1990s, Black Californians were being imprisoned under the Three Strikes You're Out measure at 13.3 times the rate of White Californians—not for serious or violent felonies, but rather for petty property crimes or drug possession.

Comparing just the five-year period of 1980-1984 and that of 1995-1999, the drug imprisonment rate grew 914 percent, but the target of these convictions and prison commitments were a pool of marginal drug users found with small amounts of some illegal substance. In contrast to prior decades, the 1990s saw imprisonment for drug possession nearly double while felony drug imprisonment for manufacturing and trafficking remained stable. While in 1980, 379 Californians were sentenced to prison for drug possession offenses, in 1999 that number rose to 12,749. Adjusted for population growth, this is a 2,244 percent increase. At the turn of the millennium, California had the highest imprisonment rate for drug offenders compared to every other state in the nation.[86] In short, drug crimes by Blacks or Hispanics do not outnumber those of Whites. But people of color are arrested and imprisoned at rates vastly disproportionate to both their actual use of drugs or their overall population.[87]

The (Re)Construction of Deviance Through Crime Control

As Emile Durkheim has suggested, law is more than just a means to enforce punishments upon illegal behaviors; in fact, it is a way to define and reinforce particular social norms. Legal sanctions for criminal behavior give us prescriptions for that which is deemed appropriate at a given historical moment. They allow us to draw boundaries around the normative and the deviant. To Durkheim's perspective we might add an argument made by Loic Wacquant. Wacquant claims imprisonment today is both a method to manage individuals' behaviors as well as a means to mark anew ethno-racial identity, thereby reinforcing social hierarchies that have existed for generations. Incarceration serves to hold and control, but also *remake* otherness or deviance. "It has become a substitute apparatus—as opposed to legally sanctioned slavery or Jim Crow laws—for keeping those of color 'in their place.'" That is, he continues, incarceration is the act of keeping prisoners ". . . in a subordinate and confined position in physical, social and symbolic space."[88] Contained within the ideological images of criminality then are the boundaries of privilege and normalcy, of race and pathology—indeed, the very line between an "us" and a "them."

Elsewhere, Wacquant adds to his early argument by suggesting that there exists an immediate and intimate relationship between the signification of ethno-racial identity and the growth of the prison instititution. He contends that ". . .a deep *structural and functional symbiosis has emerged between the collapsing ghetto and the booming prison*. The two institutions interpenetrate and compliment each another in that both ensure the confinement of a population stigmatized by its ethnic origin and deemed superfluous both economically and politically."[emphasis in original][89]

Over the late twentieth and early twenty-first centuries, the appearance of private prisons and the prison industrial complex generally, shifts Wacquant's claims. In the act of sending an individual to prison, he is marked socially and symbolically, to be sure, but now the prisoner is also certainly marked economically. That is, he is not "superfluous economically"—and certainly not politically, as I demonstrate in Chapter 4. On the contrary, as we have seen, the prison population has a very definite capital value assigned to it as a function of the (potential) sale of goods and services within prison industries. This worth is realized as profit to corporate corrections officials as well as to those who supply products and services for the prison institution. It seems that if offenders are not needed as labor in the current political economy or as political constituencies in their communities outside the prison, they are certainly in demand on the inside. We can extend Wacquant's observations to see that prisons mark racial identity, but today they also act to make a profit from that act in so far as without the ideological images which attach themselves to race and class, the public might be less inclined to choose mass incarceration. As I suggested at the start of this work, privatization might be likened to the convict leasing system in the aftermath of slavery, a system whereby inmate labor was purchased by persons outside the prison walls. But today, prison contracting renews, extends and deepens the arrangements of the old leasing system.

Privatization is not just a regression into past social and economic conventions, however. Just as the system of leasing in its own historical time "was in many ways in the vanguard of the region's first tentative, ambivalent steps toward modernity,"[90] according to Alex Lichtenstein, private prisons inhabit a matrix of political economic forces representing the current stage of advanced capitalism. They are powerful in part because they silently reassert the social significance attached to race while turning a profit in the process. The discourse defining criminal images in California provide patterns for making sense out of who is committing crime, why these inmates engage in that crime and what ought to be done about this problem. The tropes aid in the management of the population of offenders and potential offenders because they homogenize, abstract and demonize this population.

When one attempts to make sense of the status of crime and imprisonment in California then, the image of a pathological, culturally-backwards individual who is a member of the underclass stands as a discursive entry point to interpreting these problems. Such an image allows for responses to the trend of mass incarceration that never have to grapple with the structural inequity of political economic conditions within the state, the disproportionate impact of drug law imprisonment on communities of color and the destructive effects of prison itself. In short, like many of the factors we have examined in previous chapters, the images of criminality cannot be understood to be a direct cause for the emergence of private prisons in California. But these images have naturalized the growth of the populations of poor Black and brown men in California state prisons at astonishing numbers—numbers that private contractors have been happy to accommodate.

---

[1] David Garland, *Punishment and Modern Society: A Study in Social Theory* (Oxford: Clarendon Press, 1990) 21.

[2] See: Stuart Hall, Chas Critcher, Tony Jefferson, John Clarke, and Brian Roberts, *Policing The Crisis: Mugging, the State, and Law and Order* (New York: Holmes & Mier Publishers, 1978).

[3] Nandini Jammi, Prevention Works: National Crime Prevention Council, Blog entry. Web. 1 August 2007. Web. 25 June 2011.

[4] Criminal Justice Statistics Center, *Crime In California* (Sacramento: California Department of Justice, 2001) 35.

[5] David F. Greenberg, Valerie West, "The Persistent Significance of Race: Growth in State Prison Populations, 1971-1991," paper presented to Law and Society Association, Aspen, Colorado, June 1998.

[6] Michael A. Fletcher, "Calif. Minority Youth Treated More Harshly, Study Says," *The Washington Post* 3 February 2000: A-16.

[7] William Bennett, John Dilulio, John Walters, *Body Count: Moral Poverty and How to Win America's War Against Crime and Drugs* (New York: Simon & Schuster, 1996) 35.

[8] Julian V. Roberts, Loretta J. Stalens, *Public Opinion, Crime, and Criminal Justice* (New York: Westview Press, 1997) 2.

[9] Kathleen Maguire & Ann L. Pastore, *Sourcebook of Criminal Justice Statistics* (Washington, D.C.: U.S. Bureau of Justice Statistics, 1995).

[10] William J. Chambliss, *Power, Politics, and Crime* (Colorado: Westview Press, 1999) 28.

[11] Barry Glassner, *The Culture of Fear: Why Americans are Afraid of the Wrong Things.* (New York: Basic Books, 1999).

[12] Frank Furedi, *Culture of Fear: Risk Taking and the Morality of Low Expectation* (London: Continuum, 2002) viii; 1.

[13] Cheryl L. Maxson, "Gang Homicide: A Review and Extension of the Literature," eds. M. Dwayne Smith & Margaret A. Zahn, *Homicide: A Sourcebook of Social Research* (Thousand Oaks, CA: Sage, 1999) 239-254. See also: Malcolm W. Klein, *The American Street Gang: Its Nature, Prevalence, and Control* (New York: Oxford University Press, 1995).

[14] K. Horton, "Slaying: Gang Statute Adds Felony Charges in Random Killing Case," *Orange County Register* 7 Aug. 1991: B9.

[15] The language in quotes is from the California Street Terrorism Enforcement and Prevention Act (STEP) which was passed in 1988. I insert it here to illustrate the rhetorically charged discourse used in the text of legislation passed in this period.

[16] Heather MacDonald, "The Illegal Alien Crime Wave," *City Journal* 14. 1 (2004). Web. 21 July 2011.

[17] MacDonald 2011.

[18] Los Angeles Police Department, Home page. "Discipline Report For Quarter 2: 2010," 2010. Web. 25 June 2011.

[19] Lee Brenner, Hajir Ardebili, "To Protect and to Serve: Police Defamation Suits Against California Citizens Who Report Officer Misconduct," *Communications Lawyer* 28.1 (2011) Web. 21 July 2011.

[20] Brenner & Ardebili 3.

[21] Between 2000 and 2005, officials repeatedly found blades in a number of California parks. Mai Tran, "14 Blades Are Found Buried in O.C. Park After Boy's Foot Is Cut," *Los Angeles Times* 2 August 2005: B-3. In addition, freeway shootings in California have become infamous. The crime seems to spike for a while and then decrease for no apparent reason. For example, between March and June of 2005 there were more than a dozen freeway shootings in Los Angeles County. For most of these shootings, there was no identifiable motive. And then, without reason, the shootings ceased for the balance of the summer. In 2010, the shootings began again in Riverside County. This time a "freeway sniper" took aim at an estimated 30 cars along Interstates 15, 10 and 215 in Colton and Riverside. See: Tonya Alanez, "Solutions to Freeway Shootings are Elusive," *Los Angeles Times* 11 June 2005, web. See also: "30 Vehicles Damaged by Freeway Sniper," Reporter Jesse Gary. KTLA, Los Angeles, 21 May 2010. Television.

[22] Furedi 73-74.

[23] Office of the Attorney General, State of California, Department of Justice, "California Gun Sales Up Over 30% During First Six Months of 1999," News Release. 28 Sept. 1999. Web. Michael Riley, "Arizona Shootings Trigger Surge in Glock Sales Amid Fear of Ban," *Bloomberg* 11 Jan. 2011. Web.

[24] David Dillon, "Fortress America: More and More of Us Living Behind Locked Gates," *Planning* 60 (1994): 2-8.

[25] California Department of Justice, *Crime In California* (Sacramento, California, Criminal Justice Statistics Center, 2001) 47.

[26] Michael Hindelang, Michael Gottfredson, James Garofalo, *Victims of Personal Crime: An Empirical Foundation for a Theory of Personal Victimization* (Cambridge, MA: Ballinger, 1978).

[27] California Department of Justice, "Crime" 17.

[28] Christopher D. Condon, "Falling Crime Rates, Rising Caseload Numbers: Using Police-Probation Partnerships," *Corrections Today* Feb. 2003: 44-48.

[29] California Department of Justice, *Crime in California and the United States, 1988-1998* (Sacramento, CA: Criminal Justice Statistics Center, 2000) vi; Joel Rubin & Robert Faturechi, "Killing in L.A. Drops to 1967 Levels," *Los Angeles Times* 27 December 2010: A-1.

[30] Robert Faturechi & Ann Simmons, "Compton's Tide Turns," *Los Angeles Times* 18 Jan. 2011: A-1.

[31] California Department of Justice, "Crime" 12.

[32] Andew Wang, "Feeling Safer? Violent Crime Down Overall," *Los Angeles Times* 9 June 2005: B-2.

[33] Ray Surette, *Media, Crime and Criminal Justice: Images and Realities* (Pacific Grove, CA: Brooks/Cole Publishing Co., 1992).

[34] One of the most well-known theorists proving this point was George Gerbner, a Communication Studies scholar who authored Cultivation Theory. See George Gerbner; Larry Gross, Michael Morgan, Nancy Signorielli, James Shanahan, "Growing Up with Television: Cultivation Processes," in Jennings Bryant & Zillmann, Dolf, Eds. *Media Effects: Advances in Theory and Research* (New Jersey: Lawrence Erlbaum Associates Publishers, 2002) 43-67.

[35] Lori Dorfman & Vincent Shiraldi, *Off Balance: Youth, Crime, and Race in the News.* 1 April 2001. Justice Policy Institute. Web. 30 June 2011.

[36] Dennis Lowry, Tarn Ching, Josephine Nio and Dennis W. Letner, "Setting the Public Fear Agenda: A Longitudinal Analysis of Network TV Crime Reporting, Public Perceptions of Crime, and FBI Crime Statistics," *Journal of Communication* 53.1 (March 2003) 61-72.

[37] Lowry et. al. 67.

[38] Jeffrey Reiman, *The Rich Get Richer and the Poor Get Prison: Ideology, Class, and Criminal Justice* (New York: Pearson, 2004) 61.

[39] Steven Chermak, *Victims in the News: Crime and the American News Media* (Boulder, CO: Westview, 1995); Ted Chiricos, Sarah Eschholz & M. Gertz, "Crime, News, and Fear of Crime," *Social Problems* 44 (1988): 342-357.

[40] Juvenile Crime—Outlook for California: Part IV. May 1995. Legislative Analyst's Office. Web. 1 July 2011.

[41] Katherine Beckett & Theodore Sasson, *The Politics of Injustice: Crime and Punishment in America* (Thousand Oaks, CA: Sage Publications, 2004) 98-99.

[42] Michael W. Flamm, *Law and Order: Street Crime, Civil Unrest, and the Crisis of Liberalism in the 1960s* (New York: Columbia University Press, 2005) 6.

[43] Beckett & Sasson 108. See also, Katherine Beckett, "Setting the Agenda: Street Crime and Drug Use in American Politics," *Social Problems* 41 (1994) : 425-447.

[44] Dan Nimmo, *Newsgathering in Washington: A Study of Political Communication* (New York: Atherton Press, 1964).

[45] Charles Whitney, Marilyn Fritzler, Steen Jones, Sharon Mazzarella & Lana Rakow, "Geographic and Source Bias in Television News 1982-4," *Journal of Electronic Broadcasting and Electronic Media* 33.2 (1989) : 170.

[46] Katherine Taylor Gaubatz, *Crime in the Public Mind* (Ann Arbor: University of Michigan Press, 1995) 3.

[47] Bureau of Justice Statistics, 1986. "Jail Inmates, 1986," Washington D.C.: U.S. Department of Justice; Bureau of Justice Statistics, 1991. "Prisoners in 1990," Washington D.C.: U.S. Department of Justice. Douglas McDonald,

"Private Penal Institutions: Moving the Boundary of Government Authority in Corrections," ed. Michael Tonry, *Crime and Justice: An Annual Review of the Research* (Chicago, University of Chicago Press, 1992) 392.

[48] Bureau of Justice Statistics, "The Number of Adults in Correctional Population Has Been Increasing," Washington D.C.: Department of Justice (2003). Web. 22 July 2011.

[49] Gaubatz 3.

[50] Bureau of Justice Statistics, "Prisoners "Washington D.C.: U.S. Department of Justice (1991) Web. 22 July 2011. Bureau of Justice Statistics, "Jail Inmates, 1990," Washington D.C. : U.S. Department of Justice. Web. 20 July 2011.

[51] Franklin E. Zimring & Gordon Hawkins. "The Growth of Imprisonment in California," *British Journal Of Criminology* 34 (1994): 85-6.

[52] California Department of Justice, "Crime" 45, 43.

[53] California Department of Corrections and Rehabilitation. Corrections: Moving Forward. News Release. Web. Fall 2009. 5 July 2011.

[54] Kevin Starr, "Scorning Public Life Is Shameful," *Los Angeles Times* 21 Sept. 2003: M-2.

[55] Kathleen Maguire, Ann L. Pastore, Timothy J. Flanagan, eds. *Sourcebook of Criminal Justice Statistics-1992.* (U.S. Department of Justice, Bureau of Justice Statisitics. Washington D.C.: U.S. Department of Justice, 1993). See also: USA/CNN/Gallup Poll, "Crime in America," 28 October 1993.

[56] Research & Forecasts, INC., with Ardy Friedberg, *America Afraid: How Fear of Crime Changes the Way we Live* (New York: Nal Books, 1983) 167.

[57] Malcom Davies, "Survey Report: The Expansion of the Criminal Justice System and Penal System in California—Is Greater Coordination Required?" *Bureau of Criminal Statistics Monograph Series* (Sacramento: Office of the Attorney General, California Department of Justice, 2008) 11-12.

[58] Franklin Zimring, Professor of Law, Earl Warren Legal Institute, testimony to the Little Hoover Commission, 26 June 1997, Sacramento, California.

[59] See for example: Nils Christie, *Crime Control as Industry* (New York: Routledge, 1993); Christian Parenti, *Lockdown America: Police and Prisons in the Age of Crisis* (New York: Verso: 1999).

[60] Cited in Mary Ann Curtin, *Black Prisoners and Their World, Alabama, 1865-1900* (Charlottesville and London: University Press of Virginia, 2000) 6.

[61] Guy Johnson, "The Negro & Crime," *Annuls of American Academy of Politics and Social Science* 271 (1941) : 93-104.

[62] Jody David Armour, *Negrophobia and Reasonable Racism: The Hidden Costs of Being Black in America* (New York: New York University Press, 1997) 20. See also: A. Synder, "On the Self-Perpetuating Nature of Social Stereotypes," in D. Hamilton ed. *Cognitive Processes in Stereotyping and Intergroup Behavior* (New Jersey: Lawrence Erlbaum Associates, 1981) 187-190.

[63] William Bennett, John Dilulio, Jr., John Walters, *Body Count: Moral Poverty...and How to Win America's War Against Crime and Drugs* (New York: Simon & Schuster, 1996) 22-23; 27.

[64] James Q. Wilson, "Redefining Equality: The Liberation of Mickey Kaus," *The Public Interest* 109 (1992) : 103.

[65] James Q. Wilson and Richard J. Herrnstein, *Crime and Human Nature* (New York: Simon & Schuster, 1986).

[66] Quoted in Dick Kirschten, "Jungle Warfare," *National Journal* 3 October (1981) 1774.

[67] Cesare Lombroso, "Criminal Man," ed. Sawyer F. Sylvester, Jr. *The Heritage of Modern Criminology* (Cambridge, MA: Schenkman Publishing, 1972) 71. I am indebted to Jerome Miller's work in this section for his clear and cogent discussion of the research used to substantiate the connections between biology, race, and criminality. See Jerome Miller, *Search & Destroy: African American Males in the Criminal Justice System* (Cambridge: Cambridge University press, 1996).

[68] See J. H. Landman, *Human Sterilization: The History of the Sexual Sterilization Movement* (New York: Macmillian, 1932).

[69] Wilson and Herrnstein 151.

[70] Wilson & Hernstein 468. Speaking to the accuracy of the authors' "scientific inquiry," Leon Kamin, who reviewed the work in the *Scientific American*, wrote that the research papers the men used to substantiate their claims simply did not add up to their stated conclusions. "[I]t is hard for me to believe Wilson and Herrnstein have actually read those papers. . .very few of [their] citations are accurate . . .still fewer are adequate." Leon Kamin, "Reply," *Scientific American* May (1986) : 7. As to the "truth" purported to be uncovered in the authors' work, it's worth noting that geneticists have often found more differences between two individuals within the same "race" than those of different "races." In essence, the genetic variance between people is so great as to "render the concept of "race" virtually meaningless." Miller 179.

[71] Laurence Steinberg, "The Juvenile Psychopath: Fads, Fictions, and Fact," *Perspectives on Crime and Justice: 2000-2001 Lecture Series* (March 2002): 35.

[72] Steinberg 38.

[73] Steinberg 41.

[74] See Michael Willrich, "The Two Percent Solution: Eugenic Jurisprudence and the Socialization of American Law, 1900-1930," *Law and History* 16 (1998): 63-111.

[75] W. Wayt Gibbs, "Seeking the Criminal Element," *Scientific American* March (1995): 101-106.

[76] This is the description of space offenders inhabit that Bennett and his colleagues claim is designed to produce "vicious, unrepentant, predatory street criminals." Bennett et al. 14.

[77] Quoted in: Elliott Currie, *Crime and Punishment in America* (New York: Metropolitan Books: 1998) 26.

[78] Miller 138-9.

[79] Criminal Justice Statistics Center, 2001, 37.

[80] Joseph M. Hayes, "California's Changing Prison Population," Public Policy Institute of California. July 2011 web. 27 July 2011.

[81] Michael Tonry, *Malign Neglect—Race, Crime, and Punishment in America* (New York: Oxford University Press, 1995) 4.

[82] Joseph M. Hayes, "California's Changing Prison Population," Public Policy Institute of California. July 2011 web. 27 July 2011.

[83] California Department of Justice, Bureau of Criminal Statistics and Special Services, (Sacramento: Department of Justice, October, 1979) 23.

[84] On the increase of stories in the *New York Times* see: Lucig Danielman and Stephen Reese, "Intermedia Influence and the Drug Issue: Converging on Cocaine," ed. Pamela Shoemaker *Communication Campaigns About Drugs: Government, Media, and the Public* (New Jersey: Lawrence Erlbaum, 1989). On the increase in prisoners see: Daniel Macallair, "Drug Use and Justice: An Examination of California Drug Policy Enforcement," Center on Juvenile and Criminal Justice. 2002. Web. 26 July 2011.

[85] Kathleen Commolly, Lea McDermid, Vincent Schiraldi & Dan Macallair, "From Classrooms to Cell Blocks: How Prison Building Affects Higher Education and African American Enrollment," San Francisco, California: Center on Juvenile & Criminal Justice. 22 Oct. 1996. Print.

[86] Daniel Macallair, "Drug Use and Justice: An Examination of California Drug Policy Enforcement," Center on Juvenile and Criminal Justice. 2002. Web. 26 July 2011.

[87] Tonry 4.

[88] Loic Wacquant, "Deadly Symbiosis: When Ghetto and Prison Meet and Mesh," eds.Tara Herivel and Paul Wright *Prison Nation: The Warehousing of America's Poor* (New York: Routlege, 2003) 83. Angela Davis and Mary Ann Curtin have both, in slightly different ways, suggested a similar thesis. See: Angela Davis, *Are Prisons Obsolete?* (New York: Seven Stories Press, 2003); Mary Ann Curtin, *Black Prisoners and Their World, Alabama, 1865-1900* (Charlottesville and London: University Press of Virginia, 2000).

[89] Loic Wacquant, *Prisons of Poverty* (Minneapolis: University of Minnesota Press, 2009) 157-8. See also: Loic Wacquant, "The New 'Peculiar Institution': On the Prison as Surrogate Ghetto," *Theoretical Criminology* 4.3 (2000) 377-89.

[90] Alex Lichtenstein, *Twice the Work of Free Labor: The Political Economy of Convict Labor in the New South* (London, New York: Verso, 1996).

6

Why Privatization Failed

The preceding chapters have focused upon the structural elements of the state to elucidate the phenomenon of private contracting in California. My claim has been that we mustn't account for the forces giving rise to that phenomenon in isolation from one another. The relations making up the state: those of production, those of legal propriety, those of political efficacy, those of meaning and sense-making, provide a matrix which allowed for an economy to develop in and around private contracts for prison management, as well as around goods and services needed to maintain large prison populations. In California, a set of legal codes and political arrangements complimented the state's unique relations of production. Private, for-profit prisons utilized those politico-legal relations which endowed legislative power and penal authority to allow for a transfer of publicly operated prisons into private hands.

There are an abundance of texts that tell rich stories about the development of the prison industrial complex (PIC) to be sure, but often the problem with examining it as an economic or policy driven phenomenon is that economies do not exist without political frameworks and vice-versa. Here, it is useful to recognize that the hyphen in the hyphenated term *political-economy* is not just a convenient punctuation mark. It symbolizes the symbiosis between the two dimensions of economics and politics that is so thorough, in most cases, the two cannot be truly understood apart.

Privatization and a prison market more generally (for goods or services) developed in a unique system of the above relations. It thrived, for instance, as a function of penal populism wherein a multitude of voices–those of penal scholars, political candidates and heart-broken parents who had lost children—were given influence in penal policy-making. It thrived as those actors utilized ideological constructions of criminality that labeled offenders as *alien-others*. It succeeded as the California economy faltered, social-welfare programs crumbled and social disorganization produced unemployment, familial entropy and instability. And it became possible as "big government" became the antithesis to the free-market and a symbol that promised coherence and efficiency to the practice of incarceration. The relations between these relatively autonomous, but overlapping, dimensions reveal an insight into the character and scope of the criminal justice field in the golden state. They demonstrate not only how various relations of the state intersect, but also the contingent nature of such relations as these offered support for privatization and the prison industrial complex as a whole.

By examining the forces that situate the conditions of existence for California's prison market, my analysis highlights the way that a narrow focus upon formal criminal justice institutions, penal policy, or simple individual actors in the penal field fail to capture the essence of the cultural politics that surround private contracting. Increasingly, criminal justice scholarship has begun to recognize this approach and produce research that builds upon these premises. While some writers, such as Loic Wacquant, label the approach *civic sociology* and suggest it is ". . .an effort to deploy the tools of social science to engage in, and bear upon, a current public debate of frontline significance,"[1] others, cultural studies scholars, for example, simply utilize the integrated focus to produce multi-layered investigations of a research question. The method is important here, however, because it demonstrates how the crime control field is not comprised of single powerful criminal justice agents or penal and/or legal policies and practices that work in isolation. The influence of any of these elements is not simply a function of independent features of a person or law, but rather the result of relationships between each element and with the entire field as a whole. To understand some aspect of the penal field, for instance, the explosion of the California prison population, we must account for it as it produces and is produced by particular conditions and forces that give it its unique character and trajectory. These may be the tendencies to define criminality in certain ways in public discourse, the strength and political potency of surrounding interest groups [eg. crime victims organizations or public employee unions] or the use of tough on crime appeals as a flash-point to rally the state's heterogeneous electorate.

The movement to allow privatization in California can be understood to not only mediate, but also serve as a medium for the relations, as I mention above, of economy, politics, law and public discourse. We cannot ignore the way a contracted prison, for example, is a critical exponent for the production, strategies of representation, and habits of interpreting racial identities as a "new" kind of commodity. The policies regulating incarceration and the politics and discourses surrounding their implementation generate the very space where struggles over the meanings of and uses for race develop. This point can also be understood by recognizing that privatization, with its basic service as the incapacitation of people, provides a vehicle to meet the varied objectives of prison guard unions, crime-victim groups, prisoners'-rights organizations and ambitious legislators. Clearly, private, for-profit prisons have not only been simply businesses, but they have been an object of use; they have constituted what we might designate a "through-put" to the diverse goals of particular social and political actors. If we focus on the scope of the battles within and around incarceration as these are waged by different groups, we can see how they stake out the boundaries of what constitutes criminal behavior, the purposes of punishment and whose power it is to inflict a given penalty. We can also see how a private prison market organizes the transformation of other markets, such as California's withered manufacturing base, its expanding low-paying service-sector, and the informal but high wage drug trade. The present study, in short, has enabled an understanding of the *systematic nature* of privatization and the ways structured organizations and individual actors produce, and at times are produced by, that complicated whole.

The one constant I have returned to in each of the previous chapters has been the way each particular dimension of the state has provided conditions of existence for a prison market, that as I explained in Chapter 1, began in the 1980s, but never fully succeeded.[2] California does not have a booming private prison market—at least not inside the borders of the state (a point I am about to explain in detail). And if I have accounted for how privatization was made possible though a system of cultural poiltics and economic arrangements, the question still stands: what has stood in the way of its development? The issue to consider in this chapter, quite simply is, what happened? Why are private facilities shrinking rather than expanding if so many conditions have been ripe for a private-prison market?

Making Sense of the "Failed" Private Prison Boom in California

Part of the answer to this question lies with the fact that up until the mid-1990s, the California legislature was dominated by the Democratic Party, a party largely supported by state employee unions against private contracting. Not wanting to threaten their own financial backing, Democrats have shied away from aligning with private prison companies. In addition, most of these companies have focused their lobbying power in states that are less resistant to non-unionized labor. In

Florida and Texas, for instance, there are "right-to-work" policies stipulating that employees will not be bound to union membership as a precondition for employment. But perhaps the single most potent reason privatization has not caught hold in the golden state lies with the California Correctional Peace Officers Association (CCPOA), the prison guard union. Their relentless attack against any and all proposals to allow private companies a foothold in the prison business has been the cornerstone to the union's organizing formula and certainly a key to their maintenance of power. The story of the CCPOA's battles to hold back the tide of private contracting—a transfer that many argued was inevitable in the state—is not only telling in terms of understanding the current status of prison privatization, but also instructive for learning about the ways labor organizations can develop into politically potent forces in state power struggles. It demonstrates the developing hegemony of state employee Political Action Committees (PACs), the strategies used in state politics more generally, and how Californians have been affected as a result of those processes. The story of the CCPOA's influence upon the drive toward private contracting is not one that sets the union above the relations of the state, as I have been describing them, but rather is situated within and sometimes at the center of these forces. Thus, this chapter serves to bring California's story of private, for-profit prisons up to date, explain how one player in the state's political field has been able to hold back the movement toward private prisons quite effectively, and what the future may hold for private for-profit companies still looking for a piece of the California penal pie.

The CCPOA: There's Power in Prisons

The California Correctional Officers Association (CCOA), as it was originally known, began rather modestly in 1957 as a way to assuage frustrations of powerlessness and low pay in California prisons, but also as a social club of sorts where men could grab some pizza and beer and fraternize with fellow officers.[3] The group was a set of casual alliances as opposed to a formal, hierarchical organization, but during the 1960s and 70s, the CCOA transformed itself around the tumultuous prisoners' movement for enhanced civil rights. Black Nationalist politics, separatism, and direct demands by inmates for better treatment fueled court battles and legal challenges that changed the practice of corrections irreparably. Prison officers began to feel harassed and collectively threatened by the legal victories against prison protocol and as a result moved to advocate on their own behalf.[4] During the 1980s, the call for "getting tough" on crime ensued and the trend toward hyper-imprisonment spurred growth in both prison facilities and the employment of guards to operate them. California had an especially large prison boom and the state was forced to hire significant numbers of prison officers. Between 1982 and 1992, the union nearly tripled its membership from 5000 to about 15,000. And between 1992 and 2002, another 15,000 members were added to the organization to make the group the second largest state employee union in California. All told, between 1982 and 2001, the union grew an astounding 600 percent.[5] Increases in membership meant increases in dues—in fact today, union members pay in over $25 million a year.[6]

But the union was new to politics in the 1970s and 80s, and they had little experience with how to make the most of their rapidly-expanding funds. They began to work on their image as a beginning step by spending large sums on campaigns to alter their reputation from monstrous thugs to professional public officers charged with the security and safety of California citizens. They also waged an operation to increase their numbers by joining forces with the California State Employees Association (CSEA). As a result, parole agents, prison staff counselors, hybrid guard/medical technicians and others who were working the penal field united with the prison guards to facilitate a new organization: the California Correctional Peace Officers Association (CCPOA).[7] The newly-formed group set their sites on understanding and becoming successful players on the California political field. They quickly learned how to organize, donate, and lobby to gain access to political leaders and power-brokers in Sacramento. According to one member:

> ". . .[W]e started going around and understanding then that there was such things as a political action committee that had funds that donated to races. And this was how you got your foot in the door. It didn't buy you votes, but it bought you access. Where I could walk in or you could walk into a senator's or an assemblyman's office and ask for a meeting and you might get one in about three years. But if you're playing the political game—as they call it—then you have access to these people. And when you have access then you can argue your position. And when you can argue your position you can talk them into voting for your bills. And that's what it amounted to."[8]

From these beginnings, the CCPOA developed an infrastructure, hired its own lobbyists, created coalitions with victims' rights groups among others, established eight PACs, and donated to causes, candidates and ballot initiatives that favored their professional success. By 1987-88, the

CCPOA held the distinction as the largest contributor to state campaigns of all workers' unions in California. By 2010, PACs organized by the CCPOA had spent the previous decade awarding over $30 million to candidates and causes that tended to further a law-and-order agenda.[9]

The passing of the Three Strikes law is one example. At the end of 2004, a little over a quarter of the California prison population was serving time under the Three Strikes You're Out law.[10] Because of the high cost of prison commitments and the increasing number of non-violent offenders accumulating in California prisons, many advocated for restrictions on the law that would assign a third strike solely for a serious or violent crime. A proposition was placed on the 2004 ballot, therefore, to allow the public to weigh in on the issue. But the CCPOA spent heavily to tip the scales. Maintaining the law as it was originally written assured incarceration rates would continue to be high since limiting the law would either mean petty, non-violent offenders would be dealt with using alternative sanctions (like house arrest, community service or half-way houses) or that certain offenses would not qualify as a "third strike" (prohibiting a need for prison sentences to be served by many "third-strike" offenders). In plain terms, altering the law would mean less incarceration and a need for fewer guards to care for state inmates. Given the stakes, the union spent $854,866 to oppose the proposition and triumphed—the polls registering a 52.7 to 47.3 percent defeat. Similarly, two years earlier, the CCPOA spent $1,825,000 to oppose Proposition 5 on the 2008 ballot which sought to limit court authority to incarcerate offenders for specific drug crimes. Once again, the union won the battle: the measure failed 40.5 percent to 59.5 percent. Instead of sending inmates to facilities that might address their drug addiction, they went directly to the California Department of Corrections and Rehabilitation to be guarded by members of the CCPOA.[11]

The CCPOA: Picking Candidates and Attacking Foes

Not only is the union careful in their analysis and support of ballot propositions, they are also careful about which candidates they will support. To make decisions about electoral candidates, the union has developed a sort of "magic bullet" they call the "Magic 13." It consists of a set of thirteen questions administered by way of a face-to-face interview with those who wish the union's endorsement. Tellingly, the first question on the list reads: "What are your thoughts on the utilization of private, for-profit companies to perform prison duties?" Clearly, the prospect of privatization looms large on the union's agenda, and candidates who are open to private contracting are quickly excluded from any aid the union is willing to offer. While the CCPOA has never really explained why private guards are not qualified to adequately supervise state inmates in the same ways unionized prison officers might, we can surmise rather easily that the non-union jobs available in for-profit prisons would redistribute power held by the CCPOA as the resources for and control over California prisoners would have to be shared. Thus, for the sake of simple job security, private contracting in the union's view is a zero-sum game. But perhaps it's also true that if anyone with a bit of training can fulfill the position of "prison guard," then the CCPOA's claim that they "walk the toughest beat in the state" is rather specious. In this sense, private contracts undermine the union's most basic demand that a prison officer deserves a level of respect—and compensation—commensurate with police officers.

Other questions in the "Magic 13" ask about whether the candidate supports legislation that would alter the severity of the Three Strikes law as well as the death penalty in California, two pieces of legislation that have had—and continue to have—a marked effect on the numbers of inmates in state prisons.[12] Candidates or initiatives that expand the use of incarceration have tended to guide the union's choices for sponsorship since they either ensure an increase in the need for prison officers or provide favorable conditions for contract negotiations, which must be ratified by the state legislature.

After decades of charting the union's electoral successes, it is clear their work has paid off. In fact, over the last few years a snapshot of their victories is telling. The CCPOA endorsed 72 candidates for state assembly in the November 7, 2006, California general election. Of those, 71 won office. Of the 20 they endorsed for state senate, 19 were successful and 12 of these candidates received at least 65 percent of the vote tally.[13] More recently, the CCPOA spent $7 million in the state-wide elections in 2010—including $2 million on the governor's race to elect Jerry Brown alone. Of the 107 candidates endorsed by the CCPOA, once again fully 104 won their seats. As one victorious state senator Juan Vargas put it, "I won by 22 votes and without the CCPOA I wouldn't have been close. They literally won this campaign for me."[14]

Along with endorsing candidates and initiatives in state elections, however, the union also spends heavily to attack those it considers foes. Indeed, the CCPOA has developed such a strong reputation for playing political hardball, it has elicited fear mongering in and among political leaders, potential candidates for office and any who might be antagonistic to the union's objectives. As Joshua Page explains, "The specter of the CCPOA affects [political] actors who do and do not have direct contact with the union. Because of that specter, actors consider possible consequences of their actions before taking positions about penal policy and other issues of importance to the CCPOA. They must think about whether their actions will bring the union's wrath. Therefore, the specter of the CCPOA is a *social fact* that has real practical effects in the fields over which it looms [emphasis in original]."[15] This specter, as Page calls it, means that few elected officials or candidates for office risk alienating the union publicly for fear of reprisal. It is common knowledge, as one former state senator Tom Hayden concedes, "they will retaliate."

In the past, CCPOA attacks have amounted to spending five and six-figures on donations to candidates who are running *against* the targeted individual. Additionally, the union has been known to research and publicize information that could undermine their enemies' success.[16] Assemblyman Phil Wyman, for instance, who testified before a senate committee against a bill to limit private prisons, stands as a ready example of the CCPOA's retributive politics. In 2001, Wyman's district included California City. This jurisdiction, as I discussed in Chapter 1, was the location of the Corrections Corporation of America (CCA) prison that the company built on speculation—before it had any formal contracts with the state to house inmates. From Wyman's perspective, the privatization issue was one of providing jobs for his constituents—in this case up to 500 at the CCA facility. But the union's position was absolute. Private for-profit prisons equaled non-union guards, non-union guards equaled sharing the wealth of jobs properly belonging to the CCPOA. Thus, as the *Los Angeles Times* put it, "Whether or not he knew it at the time, Phil Wyman's legislative career ended in 2001 when he testified before [that] senate committee . . . "[17] After Wyman's testimony, the head of the union at the time, Don Novey, walked over to the Assemblyman and told him: "We'll see that you don't get reelected."[18] And according to many, this was exactly what they did. In Wyman's bid for reelection, the CCPOA threw its weight to his opponent, Sharron Runner, and paid for thousands of broadsides against him that tipped the scales. When the election was over, Runner had won handily, but perhaps more importantly, the union's reputation for reprisal had grown exponentially.

While the CCPOA donates to a broad spectrum of politicians both Democrat and Republican, as well as to initiatives which support its platform, most of its focus is staid on legislative branches of government—in particular gubernatorial candidates. It was the 1990 race for governor that delivered the first significant victory for the union, as its investment in one single political leader ultimately paid off in a lesson that later produced the most lucrative contract negotiation in its history. In 1990, the CCPOA endorsed the Republican candidate Pete Wilson instead of his opponent, Democratic mayor of San Francisco, Dianne Feinstein. Shortly after Wilson won office, he began to work to reconcile the meltdown in the state's budget, which in 1991 contained a deficit of a little over $12 billion. To that end, Wilson made a request of all the state employee unions to chip in and slow the rising shortfalls by agreeing to cuts in compensation. Every union refused, with the exception of the CCPOA, which agreed to take a five percent pay cut. To add to this demonstration of loyalty, the union contributed over $400,000 dollars to Wilson's reelection campaign in 1994—at the time, the largest single contribution ever made to a political candidate in California.[19] While it took a full seven years from the time Wilson became governor, a lavish gift was finally awarded union members for their faithful service. On his way out of office, Wilson granted the CCPOA a 12 percent pay raise while simultaneously denying every other state worker's union—with the exception of the firefighters—any increase.[20] By the time the next governor was voted into office, Democrat Gray Davis, the CCPOA had learned how effective it could be to have an ally in the gubernatorial seat. Not only did they spend a hefty $2.3 million directly and indirectly through independent expenditures to get Davis elected in 1998, the union followed up in 2002 (once he was in office), by writing him a check for a little over a quarter of a million dollars—the largest single donation Davis had received upon becoming Governor.[21]

There was quite a bit of blow-back in the press as a result of the guards making the donation. This backlash was because shortly before receiving the lump sum, Davis had decided—during a looming budget-deficit crisis, now reaching upwards of $17 billion—to hike up union members' pay by 33.76 percent over a five-year period.[22] In addition, Davis announced that he would be closing the doors of five of the nine operating Community Correctional Facilities (CCFs) to save the state what he claimed amounted to in excess of $5 million.

The Battles Over the CCFs

As I note in Chapter 1, the first facilities to be contracted to private firms in California were the CCFs, which got their start in 1986. These began because the state was struggling with the increased recidivism of non-violent offenders caught up in the dragnet of toughening parole and probation laws. The California Department of Corrections (CDC) entered into a contract with what is now known as Cornell Corrections to house parole violators at the Hidden Valley Ranch site in La Honda, California. At the time the CDC signed this first contract, the CCPOA had no knowledge of it.[23] In fact, it was not until the facility became operational that the union became aware of its opening. Looking back, the oversight was most likely a matter of the union still attenuating their political prowess and getting up to speed on the legislative process. They simply did not have the network in place to see the development in advance. And, while the CCPOA missed the opportunity to block the first move of these first private facilities in the state, it was a mistake they would not repeat. Their position was clear: private prisons were not acceptable on their watch. The only functions private contractors were to be properly charged with was the lock-up of "illegal aliens awaiting deportation," or the care of "lightweight" juveniles. Otherwise, an official for the union concluded, "for a host of good reasons we are vehemently opposed to turning over the protection of the public to 'business.'"[24]

Even though the CCPOA had managed to stave off medium- and maximum-security private prisons in the state, these private CCFs were still a reminder of its previous failure to protect its own interests. The facilities represented an outsider trespassing on their turf since the private firms were performing a function that, in members' eyes, was solely theirs to dispense. Combined, the CCFs only held about 2,000 prisoners, which was not a large proportion of the total population of a little more than 161,000 housed by the CDC at that time. But, the union wanted the existing nine facilities scuttled, and it wanted Governor Gray Davis to use his executive power to accomplish this aim. The union got its wish. Davis used the budget process to pull funding from the CCFs leaving their contracts to expire. Without a guarantee of state funds, the private facilities would be effectively run out of the state.[25]

But some were not happy with Davis's proposal. The first resistance to Davis' plan came from the Legislative Analyst's Office (LAO) which stated that not only had he over-estimated any cost savings by more than $2 million, but that he had totally dismissed the crisis of prison overcrowding that worsened with every closure of an operational facility. Next, the press ran a series of articles claiming the move was political "pay-back," especially after CCPOA's head lobbyist, Jeff Thompson discussed union raises in a telephone recording meant for the CCPOA. In the recording Thompson professed: "As many of our members are aware, the whole concept of privatization has been a thorn in our side as far as professional development of the correctional peace officer series. . .So the controversial elements are being rejected by

Governor Gray Davis's latest budget. The CCF contracts are gone for the 2002-2003 fiscal year, and that move is much appreciated. It does follow through with promises made by Governor Davis in the past years on this subject matter, and so the governor is a man of his word in that regard."[26] When the press publicized Thompson's message divulging that Davis had made good on his "promises," the link between the two events appeared particularly incriminating.

What was not immediately obvious, however, was that Davis was being targeted. Cornell Corrections, one of the private facilities set to be closed by Davis's budget plan, leaked the hotline message originally meant for the union's rank and file members. Cornell, in addition to the officials of the other private firms that were to be shut down: Wackenhut, Alternative Programs Inc. (API) and Management Training Corp. (MTC), were clearly angry. Why close their doors, they argued, when the prisons they ran were not only helping the state reduce recidivism and rehabilitate inmates with award-winning programs, but also saving the state money in the process?

No matter the advantages of the CCFs, appeals to save them seemed to be falling on deaf ears. Davis was not willing to alter his position and consequently, Cornell elected to challenge Davis head-on. Publicizing what it claimed was a case of quid-pro-quo, the firm accused him of offering favors to the CCPOA in exchange for the union's financial donations. As I note above, the union had given Davis over two-million dollars in campaign contributions and an additional $250,000 check after the announcement of the closures of five CCFs. Cornell followed up by hiring a political consultant and organizing what amounted to a public relations campaign against the governor. Spending $70 thousand, the company produced and aired a half-hour video entitled: *Blood Money: The Killing of Two Award-Winning Programs* which recounted the hotline message left by Thompson and then asked: "Political payoff or a terrible mistake? This is a story about the governor's decision to give the state prison guards a billion dollar pay raise and to kill two award-winning private community correctional programs."[27]

The press covered the battle between Cornell and Davis with keen fascination; and although he tried, the Governor could not get much traction with his own explanations of the events. He was portrayed as Cornell had painted him—a tainted politician who had used his office for his own personal expediency. Moreover, once Cornell obtained a lay analysis of the CCPOA's 2001-2006 contract and forwarded it to the Senate Majority Leader Richard Polanco, Davis had one more strike against him. Polanco convened a public hearing on the contract that further revealed ties between the governor and the guards' union.

At this point Davis began to get weary of these attacks. With more than his fair share of stories in the media accusing him of corruption, ranging from claims that he had punished the teachers' union for failing to donate to his reelection campaign to other suspicious pay-to-play deals with various donors, his political stature was compromised. Worried about his reelection campaign, Davis finally capitulated. He reversed his decision and agreed to return funding to the CCFs as long as Cornell promised to end its negative campaign against him. But it seemed the damage had already been done. Even though the governor did in fact win reelection in November 2002, by February 2003, a campaign had begun to recall him from office. Recall advocates were benefiting from the wrath of the bad press Davis had received dealing not only with the guards' union, but also the the state's spiraling deficits and the perception that Davis was mismanaging state affairs. The public formed a consensus around the desire to punish politicians for what it perceived as corruption plain and simple. Recall officials gathered over 110 percent of the signatures needed to hold a special election by July 2003. And on October 7, 2003, California recalled the first governor ever in the state's history.

The CCPOA Meets "the Governator"

Replacing Davis was actor Arnold Schwarzenegger, perhaps most notorious for his Terminator movies in the 1980s and 90s. Quickly dubbed, "the Governator," Schwarzenegger entered office as a no-nonsense Republican who campaigned on his refusal to take donations from any "special interest." Therefore, according to his own campaign appeals, he would be beholden to no one. The relationship between Schwarzenegger and the CCPOA did not begin with a great deal of mutual affection and rapidly fragmented as the years passed. Once he won the election, the governor ran a relatively independent office; he was moderate on a variety of issues—much to many conservatives' disdain—and with his rather hyper-masculine persona, he seemed unafraid to be linked with the moniker "soft on crime." In May of 2004, the Schwarzenegger administration began what would be the first move in a battle over the control of California's prison system. The first target was the salary increases that had been approved by Davis before he left office. In Schwarzenegger's view, these increases were exorbitant and hardly prudent in light of the state's growing fiscal crises. He requested that the union give back $300 million from the negotiated contract and return to the bargaining table to achieve a more realistic set of benefits and pay. The senate followed suit and vowed not to approve a scheduled 11.3 percent pay raise set to cost California tax-payers $200 million. The CCPOA balked at what they considered stonewalling. Union official Lance Corcoran responded to the opposition by saying that the CCPOA would not be bullied: "In the prison system, if you give in to a bully, you're a punk." The guards' union, he charged, "has never been a punk. I can't say it any more clearly than that."[28] But having little choice without the approval of the legislature, the guards vowed to win back the contract stipulations and agreed to negotiate.

But it was Schwarzenegger that garnered a greater share of political success in this chapter of struggle in that he was able to brand the union as an enemy of reform. His public comments painted the CCPOA as self-interested, political hacks that were in the game of corrections not to increase public safety, but rather to gain power, benefits, and money. State newspapers began to parrot this view; the *Sacramento Bee*, the *Los Angeles Times*, and the *San Francisco Chronicle* ran stories as well as editorials recounting the union's shady tactics that sought to control the prison system and increase their own power through aggressive political strategies. As public disdain toward the CCPOA grew, support for the Davis era contract directives dwindled—if they ever had significant support to begin with.

It is important to consider here that the CCPOA's shrewd contract dealings have been unparalleled. In fact, CCPOA members are *the highest paid prison officers in the nation.* Making an average salary of $73 thousand a year, and often more than $100 thousand with overtime compensation, the guards earn approximately 58 percent more than the national average.[29] As the second largest state employee union in California, their salaries account for 40 percent of the payroll through the state's general fund,[30] and much has been written about California state deficits resting, in no small part, upon the explosion of the corrections budget generally and the union's compensation deals in particular. Part of that compensation includes an impressive benefits package. By the relatively young age of 50, with thirty years of service, CCPOA members can retire with 90 percent of their salary paid to them each year for the rest of their lives. Many teachers in the state, by contrast, may collect a maximum of 75 percent of their salaries upon retirement at age 63. In addition, union members can bank an unlimited number of vacation days, which can be exchanged for cash when they retire. The cash value of these days is calculated at the employee's highest rate of pay while in service. So lucrative are these pay-outs, a number of employees in 2010 actually received checks for amounts greater than their annual salaries. In fact, eighty union members who retired in 2010 received pay-outs of more than $100 thousand each.[31] According to the state's non-partisan Legislative Analyst's Office, the average CCPOA member has accrued about nineteen weeks of leave-time to date—a cash value of approximately $600 million. Guards also have a total of eight weeks off annually in their first year of service and receive an extra $130 a month if they simply visit a doctor for a physical once a year.[32] For an individual who has little more than a GED or a high-school diploma, work as a prison guard might well be the best paying and most secure employment one can aspire to in California. In short, the only state employee union receiving better benefits than the prison officers is the California Highway Patrol.

In the summer of 2004, Schwarzenegger and the union finally renegotiated the contract over which there was so much conflict. The raises promised by Davis would be postponed for a couple of years, not canceled, and in exchange for waiting, the guards would be granted greater control of the day-to-day management of each prison facility and be given the guarantee that no union member would be laid-off for a period of two years.[33] But the relationship between Schwarzenegger and the CCPOA never really warmed after this tussle. The guards resented the Governor's attempt to move the corrections department toward a more pronounced rehabilitative agenda and shortly after the negotiations, the union accused him of reneging on entitlements they claimed he had granted in the negotiations.

Schwarzenegger ignored the union's complaints and without flinching, renamed the California Department of Corrections (CDC), the California Department of Corrections and Rehabilitation (CDCR) to highlight the point that the department had in fact a rehabilitative obligation. He worked on key prison reforms to restructure the system. He called for a new secretary to oversee the control and operations of the state's prison and parole system as a whole. He attempted to reform the parole system such that parole violators would be sent to half-way houses or community centers that would address problems of addiction and re-entry. And he fought against the union members' will to keep guard abuses of prisoners quiet since guards' mistreatment of prisoners was routinely shielded from disciplinary action.

In one instance, a report filed by a federal court investigator offered evidence that guards were shirking their duties and in some cases abusing prisoners outright. In 2004, a Corcoran State Prison inmate who was a dialysis patient bled to death because guards were allegedly too busy watching the Super Bowl game to respond to the man's screams.[34] Guards initially cooperated with the investigation, but then later refused to talk about the details of the case. A "code of silence" among officers made it nearly impossible to discover the truth about why the 58-year old man died from an opening in his medical shunt, even though he apparently yelled and kicked in his cell for hours. At least 40 guards were witnesses to the incident, but according to the report, they kept silent to protect one another. This web of protection practically guaranteed that the use of unauthorized force, or simple neglect, would be almost impossible to detect.[35]

Using tactics from prior campaign battles, the CCPOA confronted Schwarzenegger publicly. They posted a video on their web site declaring: "Everything we've achieved is threatened . . .It's time to fight again," and they began an internal campaign to raise members' dues an extra $33.00 a month to "wage battle against the Schwarzenegger administration."[36] They began to argue loudly against community and prison-based education and job-counseling programs.[37] They teamed with victims' rights groups such as Crime Victims United of California to produce an advertising campaign against the Governor's efforts at prison reform. And they used strategies that sought to shame him before California citizens. In an ad created in conjunction with Crime Victims United, for example, two females who were related to a woman who had been murdered over twenty-five years ago accused Schwarzenegger of "compromising public safety" and turning his back on victims of crime. Somber and emotional, the piece ended with the rebuke: "You promised to stand with victims, Governor. You let us down."[38]

Ending any hope of repairing a relationship between he and the union, Schwarzenegger initiated what would be his final move in 2006. In a public statement, he proposed a plan to double the number of privately-contracted beds in the state, which by that time had grown to 8,500. Over two years, he explained, the state would increase private contracts to house as many as 17,000 inmates.[39] In truth, Schwarzenegger, in conjunction with the CDCR, had already started this process the year prior. The CDCR began to seek out and sign new agreements with CCFs whose contracts had expired; for example, facilities located at the Baker, Mesa Verde, Mc Farland and Leo Chesney sites were all either reopened or re-contracted.[40] In short order, the CCFs were not only *not* being closed-out, as had seemed to be the trend under Davis, but rather experiencing something of a renewal. In addition, the CDCR sent out requests to more than 6,000 public and private entities and law enforcement agencies nationwide to ascertain the plausibility of placing California inmates in institutions outside the state.[41] Schwarzenegger called a special legislative session to deal with the prison crisis that, by this time, had received nationwide press from the Plata v. Davis/ Schwarzenegger court battle.

That case, as I noted in Chapter 3, had resulted in the transfer of the CDCR's medical care system into court-appointed receivership and at this point was still making its way through the appeal process on its way to the Supreme Court. A special three-judge panel at the federal level had ruled that California needed to reduce its prison population by a little over 137 percent of its design capacity, throwing weight to the urgency of the prison reforms Schwarzenegger called for. Among his proposals were building two new prisons, issuing bonds to pay for new prisons, suspending the state construction laws to speed prison building, and housing 4,500 non-violent female inmates in private prisons.[42] On August 30, 2006, the California State Senate passed the prison reform package, moving it to the state Assembly. But the Assembly rejected the legislation, sealing its demise. At this point it was clear: any prison reform that would take place in the state was not going to occur through formal channels. Schwarzenegger, as well as other legislators, had tried time and again to alter the policies, politics and structure of the CDCR. But the legislature seemed unwilling (or unable) to agree to pass any bill that offered real change to the system.

Perhaps realizing as much, less than two months later Schwarzenegger did an end around the entire legislative process as well as the CCPOA. On October 4, 2006, the governor issued Proclamation 4278 declaring a state of emergency. According to the Proclamation:

> " . . .WHEREAS, various trends and factors, including population increases, parole policies, sentencing laws, and recidivism rates have created circumstances in which the CDCR is now required to house a record number of inmates in the CDCR prison system, making the CDCR prison system the largest state correctional system in the United States, with a total inmate population currently at an all-time high of more than 170,000 inmates; and, WHEREAS, due to the record number of inmates currently housed in prison in California, all 33 CDCR prisons are now at or above maximum operational capacity, and 29 of the prisons are so overcrowded that the CDCR is required to house more than 15,000 inmates in conditions that pose substantial safety risks, namely, prison areas never designed or intended for inmate housing, including, but not limited to, common areas such as prison gymnasiums, dayrooms, and program rooms, with approximately 1,500 inmates sleeping in triple-bunks; and WHEREAS, the current severe overcrowding in 29 CDCR prisons has caused substantial risk to the health and safety of the men and women who work inside these prisons and the inmates housed in them ...
> Pursuant to this proclamation: The CDCR shall, consistent with state

law and as deemed appropriate by the CDCR Secretary for the sole purpose of immediately mitigating the severe overcrowding in these 29 prisons and the resulting impacts within California, *immediately contract for out-of-state correctional facilities to effectuate voluntary transfers of California prison inmates to facilities outside of this state* for incarceration consisting of constitutionally adequate housing, care, and programming [italics mine].[43]

In short, "to prevent death and harm," the state had no choice, according to the proclamation, but to unilaterally decrease the number of inmates in its facilities. Ostensibly, the order gave Schwarzenegger the freedom to act in isolation to contract with out-of-state correctional facilities without permission from any other state authority. This is exactly what he did. The CDCR entered into two separate contracts: one with The GEO Group Inc. and one with Correctional Corporation of America (CCA). Each company would provide beds in their facilities in a handful of states across the nation.

The CCPOA, to put it mildly, did not support these contracts. In response, the union filed a lawsuit claiming that the inmate transfers had violated the California Constitution. Along side the Service Employees International Union and a group of inmate advocates, the union attempted to get a temporary restraining order. It claimed that because the state did not follow proper protocol and contracting procedures, the transfers violated state law. But judges in federal and state courts rejected these efforts to block the transfers, and the suit was thrown out. Exactly one month later, eighty California state inmates were on their way to a correctional facility in West Tennessee operated by CCA.[44] The following month, another 150 additional inmates were shipped to Arizona. Over the course of the last five years, California initiated a growing private contracting market for its own state inmates. Today, about 10,000 California inmates are housed in private for-profit correctional facilities in Arizona, Mississippi and Oklahoma. Within three years of Schwarzenegger unilaterally enabling these transfers, CCA has seen the value of its contracts with California grow from $23 million in 2006 to about $700 million in late 2009, a 31-fold increase— and all, according to *Capitol Weekly* (the newspaper serving California legislative politics), without competitive bidding.[45] To put it plainly, although it took a court order mandating a decrease of inmates in the state's prisons and an emergency proclamation by the governor of California, the Golden State finally has an increasingly robust private prison industry—albeit in locations outside of its official borders.

Private Prisons: To Be Continued?

There is genuine reason to believe that these contracts will not only be maintained by the state, but potentially blossom. Because of the ruling by the Supreme Court stipulating that California must transfer 30,000 inmates out of its prisons by 2013, there is still a need for alternative space to house offenders the state must shed. At last count, California's 33 state prisons held approximately 143,000 in space designed for less than 80,000. At about 180 percent of design capacity, the CDCR has its work cut out for it. A proposal dubbed "realignment" was advanced by Governor Jerry Brown to transfer thousands of lower-level inmates to local jails in various California counties, thereby lowering the total numbers in state facilities (and complying with the Court's wishes). These transfers have occurred, but the jury is still out on how effective they actually will be in mitigating the problems they were designed to solve. First, sending the inmates to smaller facilities in these counties would mean state government would need to reimburse local governments for the costs of the service—including medical attention, mental healthcare, rehabilitation services, substance-abuse treatment and counseling etc. While the 2012 election saw the passing of a special proposition (Prop 30) to increase sales-tax to do just that, the most recent prison projections show that the state will *still* be unlikely to adhere to the federal court order mandating the decrease in the prison population. The revised prison population expectations predict that more felons will enter into the system mostly because judges in California are continuing to sentence a number of low-level felons to state prisons rather than county jail. In addition, the Legislative Analyst's Office issued a report suggesting that while the plan to shift offenders to county jails to serve their sentences would help to alleviate some of the overcrowding, "the realignment plan alone," they claimed," [wa]s unlikely to reduce overcrowding sufficiently within the two-year deadline."[46] The report recommended instead that the state continue, "and possibly expand," the out-of-state transfers "at least until such time as [the CDCR] is able to comply with the. . .inmate population reduction targets."[47] As of this writing, the state has decreased its prison population by approximately 27,000 inmates over the past year. But this amount is not nearly enough to comply with the Supreme Court's orders, and no new plan has come forward that might permanently solve this dilemma.

In addition, California's budget crisis has made new prison building on any practical scale needed to house the overflow of prisoners prohibitive. The public does not support bond measures for new prisons and even if this were not so, any new facilities would take years to approve let alone build. It is simply more cost effective to outsource corrections given the high price of incarceration. This fact alone may explain why *half* of new inmates across the nation in 2008-2009 were sent to private facilities to serve their sentences, even though the entire share of U.S. privatized bed stands at less than nine percent.[48] Private contractors, seeing the tide turn in their direction, have publicly celebrated the fact that they occupy a "sweet spot" in the current prison crisis. Essentially, as CCA notes, "states have less money to build" which means "more construction [is getting] outsourced to private companies."[49] As the stakes become higher and the potential for profits rise in California, it not unsurprising that these contractors lobby to improve their opportunities for new or more lucrative state contracts. To that end, CCA's largest single donation in 2010 went to Arnold Schwarzenegger.[50]

Third, private facilities are likely to continue to receive contracts with California since the driving force of its overcrowding problem is a combination of both penal law and public policy. As criminologist Barry Krisberg explains, "It isn't that California has more crime than other places. It's that we have harsher sentences. We keep people longer. We have the highest parole failure rate in the country—meaning we send huge numbers of parolees back to prison for violating rules of parole, not for new crimes. . . California has chosen this unique path of ratcheting up incarceration—way beyond any other state—and it's paying the price."[51] To reverse the state's course, then, is not simply a matter of proposing new laws, but rather passing large-scale sentencing and prison reforms. However, as we have seen, California is invested in mass incarceration. Beyond prison officers who have a stake in the present system, there are legislators, private prison operators, rural communities where prisons are located, vendors who sell products and services, and victims' rights groups whose livelihoods are attached to either large prison populations or tough on crime policies. With so many players satisfied with the status quo, transforming the system seems particularly daunting.

Finally, it is possible that even if for-profit prison companies ceased to provide beds for California inmates, they could still expand their share of contracts with the state by other means. The GEO Group, which recently purchased Cornell Corrections, is beginning to provide alternative sanction services such as supervised release, and treatment programs. To meet what it sees as upcoming trends in punishment, the company is buying smaller firms with contracts in psychiatric care, civil immigration detention and electronic ankle monitoring for low-level, non-serious offenders.[52] And it seems as if their hunch may be right on target. California prison officials are currently discussing a plan that would release thousands of female inmates to serve the remainder of their sentences at home wearing GPS-enabled ankle bracelets. If the plan goes forward, it would likely affect nearly half of all the female inmates held in state facilities and possibly be extended to include some non-violent male inmates as well.[53] This diversification by private companies, therefore, gives us reason to believe we will not be seeing private corporations fade from the "punishment business" anytime soon. The only question seems to be which types of functions they will ultimately serve.

It remains to be seen how the CCPOA will react to such adjuncts to their work. Will they interpret such private services or products such as the GPS monitoring systems as appropriate as long as these are utilized under its control? Or will they decide that such mechanisms render their "beat" less "tough"—that is, they reveal that technology can accomplish a guard's job just as effectively for less—and thus reject the measures? Time will certainly tell. But one fact is certain: because of the astronomical numbers of bodies in custody in California—as well as across the nation—highly paid prison guards are increasingly pricing themselves out of the market. And as we have seen in the case of California, governing officials have little choice but to find cheaper alternatives.

---

[1] Loic Wacquant, *Prisons of Poverty* (Minneapolis: University of Minnesota Press, 2009) 161.

[2] As you will recall, the first private Community Correctional Facility (CCF) opened in 1986 and its start provided an opportunity for private facilities to catch hold and grow in California. These CCFs did grow, and at one point in the 1990s, the California Department of Corrections and Rehabilitation (CDCR) contracted approximately sixteen private facilities. But as of 2011, that number dropped to eight with seven of those contracts set to be terminated. California Department of Corrections and Rehabilitation, "Community Correctional Facilities," 2012. Web. 14 Aug. 2011.

[33] Joshua Page, *The Toughest Beat: Politics, Punishment, and the Prison Officers Union in California* (New York: Oxford Press, 2011) 15. I am indebted to the rich and detailed research on the CCPOA in Page's manuscript. His excellent archival work and in-depth interviews have contributed a great deal to my ability to piece together this comprehensive narrative.

[4] Eric Cummins, *The Rise and Fall of California's Radical Prison Movement* (Palo Alto, CA: Stanford University Press, 1994) 190.

[5] Page 48.

[6] Brian Joseph and Tony Saavedra, "Excess, Deprivation Mark State Prisons," *The Orange County Register* 9 Dec. 2009. Web. 14 Jan. 2010.

[7] Page 43.

 [8] Cited in Page 41-2.

 [9] Stephen Green, "The Changing of the Guard," *Sacramento Bee* 6 Mar. 1989: A1. For the amount of contributions see: California Fair Political Practices Commission, "Big Money Talks: California's Billion Dollar Club." Special Report. 11 March 2010 Web. 15 Aug. 2011.

 [10] Tracey Kaplan, "Group Seeks Initiative to Reform California's Three Strikes Law," *The Mercury News* 14 June 2011. Web. 15 Aug. 2011.

 [11] California Fair Political Practices Commission, 2010.

 [12] Page 55-6.

 [13] California Secretary of State Debra Bowen. November 7, 2006 General Election-Statement of Vote-Contests. 2011. Web. 16 Aug. 2011. California Correctional Peace Officers Association. "Election 2006," *PEACEKeeper* vol 23.5 (2006) : 8-11.

 [14] Steve Lopez, "Donations Create 'Winners,'" *Los Angeles Times* 22 May 2011: A2.

 [15] Page 65. It might be this kind of power that is the most insidious and speaks the loudest of the union's success as a potent political player. One of the clearest examples of this "invisible" power I read while researching the union, is a story told by Joshua Page about how he himself began to recognize the "omnipresence" of the union as he carried out research for his book on their ascendance to power. As he tells it: "I attended a meeting with California Department of Corrections (CDC) officials, staffers, and attorneys who represented prisoners. The subject of the gathering was a "violence control program" that the CDC developed to reduce violence in the state's super-maximum-security prisons. After a couple of hours, the group agreed on changes to the proposed program. But before adjourning, a staffer asked a CDC official if he had discussed the program with the CCPOA. When the official said that he had not, several people dropped their heads to their chests. A few people chuckled to express the apparent futility of the meeting. The official assured the group that he would check with the union immediately. As we left the room, Byrd (a chief consultant who supervised the day-to-day operations of this particular legislative committee's activities) wondered why the CDC wasted our time. Like many others in Sacramento, she believed that the CCPOA had an up or down vote on prison-related policies. Without the union's buy-in, she felt, the violence control program would never see the light of day. This example played out time and time again during my tenure in the legislature" Page, 222.

 [16] Dan Morain, "Potent Prison Guards Union Facing Challenges to Status Quo," *Los Angeles Times* 17 Jan. 2004 : B1.

 [17] Dan Morain, "Guards Union Spreads Its Wealth," *Los Angeles Times* 20 May 2004 : A1; A24-5.

 [18] Morain, "Guards Union. . ." A-24.

 [19] Fox Butterfield, "Political Gains by Prison Guards," *New York Times* 7 Nov. 1995: A1.

 [20] Andy Furillo, "Prison Officers Union on a Roll: Gains Big Raise, Court Victories," *Sacramento Bee* 12 Oct. 1998 : A1.

 [21] Dan Morain, "Davis Gets More Money From Prison Guards," *Los Angeles Times* 30 Mar. 2002 : A1; A13.

 [22] "Prison Guard Clout Endures," editorial, *Los Angeles Times* 1 April 2002 : B10.

 [23] Page 140.

[24] Jeff Thompson, "Prisons for Profit," *Peacekeeper* 5.2 (1987) : 22.

[25] The events surrounding the battle over the CCFs I include here are recorded in Joshua Page's narrative in "Zeroing out the CCFS" in his text *The Toughest Beat* cited above. See: pp. 150-155.

[26] "Prison Guard Clout" B10.

[27] RF Communications, "Blood Money: The Killing of Two Award-Winning Programs." (Sacramento, 2002).

[28] Morain "Guards Union…" A25.

[29] Page 76.

[30] Don Thompson, "Gov's Deal Lifts Vacation Cap for CA Prison Guards," *The Associated Press* 19 April 2011. Web. 20 April 2011.

[31] Jack Dolan, "New Contract for California Prison Guards Lifts Cap on Saved Vacation," *Los Angeles Times* 19 April 2011. Web. 28 April 2011. These large checks are the extreme; the average amount is about $24,000.

[32] Dolan "New Contract" Web.

[33] Institute of Governmental Studies. "California Correctional Peace Officers Association," University of California, Berkeley. 2010. Web. 28 Aug. 2011.

[34] Mark Arax, "Inmate's Open Shunt Led to Bleeding Death," *Los Angeles Times* 7 Feb. 2004. Web. 3 Sept. 2011.

[35] Andy Furillo, "Contract Pits Guards vs. Governor," *Sacramento Bee* 12 June 2005. Web. 28 Aug. 2011. See also on the inmate death at Corcoran: Mark Arax, "Corcoran Guards Mute in Probe of Inmate Death," *Los Angeles Times* 5 March 2004. Web. 30 Aug. 2011.

[36] Furillo, "Contract Pits Guards. . ."

[37] "State Prisons' Revolving Door: Judge's Last-Chance Demand," editorial, *Los Angeles Times* 23 July 2004 : B-12.

[38] Joshua Page, "Victims and Their Guards," *Los Angeles Times* 15 June 2011 : A28.

[39] Andy Furillo, "Prison Budget Shifts Strategy," *Sacramento Bee* 15 Jan. 2006 : A3.

[40] Office of the Secretary, State of California, "Department of Corrections and Rehabilitation Action Taken to Reform California Prison System in Support of the Special Legislative Session," CDCR. Sept. 2005. Web. 20 Aug. 2011.

[41] Office of the Secretary 3.

[42] Rich Pedroncelli, "Schwarzenegger Wants Special Session to Tackle Prison Changes," *USA Today* 26 June 2006. Web. 21 Aug. 2011. Mark Martin, "Prisons in Crisis, Governor Declares," *SFGate.com* 27 June 2006. Web. 22 Aug. 2011.

[43] Office of the Governor. "Prison Overcrowding State of Emergency Proclamation." California.Gov. 2010. Web. 30 Aug. 2011.

[44] Office of the Secretary 7.

[45] John Howard, "Private Prison Company Finds Gold in California," *Capitol Weekly* 28 Jan. 2010 Web. 9 Feb. 2010.

[46] Patrick McGreevy, "California Needs More Time to Fix Prison Overcrowding, Report Says," *Los Angeles Times* 6 Aug. 2011. Web. 1 Sept. 2011.

[47] McGreevy "California Needs More Time. . ."

[48] Kopin Tan, "Private Prison Companies Have a Lock on the Business," *The Wall Street Journal* 25 Oct. 2009. Web. 5 Jan. 2010.

[49] The quote is by the CEO of CCA, Damon Hininger. Daniel Taub, *Bloomberg News* 14 May 2010. Web. 20 May 2010.

[50] "What California's Prison Downsizing Might Represent for Private Detention Contractors," producer. Leslie Berestein Rojas, *Multi-American*, NPR, 89.3, Los Angeles, 23 May 2011.

[51]Cathy Cockrell, "Downsizing the Prison-Industrial Complex," *California Progress Report* 5 May 2010. Web. 20 May 2010.

[52] "What is the GEO Group?" Aarti Shahani prod. *NPR News Investigations*, NPR, 89.3, Los Angeles, 25 March 2011.

[53] Jack Dolan, "Female Inmates' In-Home Custody," *Los Angeles Times* 13 Sept. 201: A-1.

7

The Mythology of Privatization

A recent study published in *Annals of Epidemiology*, an international journal focusing on human illness and disease revealed a rather disturbing fact about the relationship between the African-American population and institutions of correction. While the work had no intention of making an argument about the role of incarceration in the twenty-first century, it suggested a startling conclusion, nonetheless.

According to the research, a black man has a better chance of staying alive in this country if he is confined to a prison or jail. That is, blacks who are incarcerated in a correctional institution (versus blacks who live in the U.S. population at large) are half as likely, at any given age, to be murdered, die from alcohol abuse, drug-addiction, diabetes, or suicide than their white counterparts also imprisoned.[1] In short, for a given sub-set of people in the United States, being sent to jail seems to be the best chance at avoiding premature death. How do we make sense of this finding? How does it situate our understanding of penal practice or the climate of American culture for black men in this era?

The analysis in the previous chapter set out to explain the developments in California's private prison market as a function of the stonewalling and political strategies of the California Correctional Peace Officers Association—the prison guards' union within the state. In this final chapter, I reflect on my analyses as a whole to specify how they comprise a collective rationale for privatization that makes sense of the policies, practices, and transformations I have described over the course of this work. The research addressing the differential peril for white and black prison inmates begins this reflection. When I consider the above questions in light of the immediate concerns of this study, I am obliged to ask about the implications the research might have for the growth and acceptance of private prisons. Does it suggest anything about the potential for privatization to take up a greater role in the corrections field?

One way to interpret the study's implications is to suggest that the prison institution has transformed in ways that give it a qualitatively-different function than it had prior to the last twenty years of the twentieth century. This shift is most noticeable in the additional role the prison plays within the state alongside its function as an instrument of legal punishment. On the one hand, a corrections institution is obviously tasked with penalizing those who commit crime; we send our criminals to prison facilities as a means to serving justice. Offenders are arrested, convicted, sentenced, and expected to learn a lesson that will keep them from committing more crime. But on the other, incarceration has become an institution that offers what might be best described as a type of compromised social welfare. We send our poor, unemployed, uneducated, drug-addicted, and mentally ill to this same facility to be treated (or not) in what many times may be the only available option for those that cannot afford to purchase the help they need—whether that help is drug rehabilitation or mental-healthcare. Here then, incarceration and the services we have historically offered through programs of social service have "come to form a single policy regime," in the words of Katherine Beckett and Bruce Western.[2] The two functions have collapsed into one single institution. If one is unable to get the help needed outside of the prison walls, then there is the chance that the state's punitive apparatus will send this individual into the system of criminal justice to render "treatment" there.

Let me pause here for a moment to suggest that this positioning of the penal function as I am describing it is a component part in what I title, the *mythology of privatization*, and the focus of this final chapter. My primary claim is that around the benefits of adopting privatization in the state of California, a mythology has formed which represents a logic to the movement of private contracting, what one might call an emerging sensibility, and an *economy* that unifies a number of arguments I have made over the course of this analysis. The mythology serves as a way to rationalize and normalize the notion that *prison is the proper response to those who are unable to overcome the challenges of unemployment, illness, psychological trauma or addiction.* The question is no longer: "Why is this citizen unable to cope?" or "What aid can be offered to this individual such that he can function among us?" Rather, the questions posed by many are focused in other ways: "How do we restore order; to what facility can this person be sent such that we can regain control of this social space?"

The mythology of privatization can be understood to work as a set of "truths" that form a narrative naturalizing private contracting, and in so doing, it simultaneously delimits the spectrum of alternative choices that dictate our responses to crime and punishment. It allows society to simply ignore a constructive inquiry into policies that might sidestep incarceration and incapacitation, punishment options that have served as the centerpiece to criminal justice for at least the last three decades.

Mythology Interpreted

But a mythology, as I am making use of the term here, is not altogether false: it is not a moment in the imaginary, as the concept might suggest. It is not a lie. It is something of a parable that serves as an explanation of practice and belief. It is a framework for sense-making about a given intellectual object. Myths do not necessarily prevaricate; instead, they organize. That is, they arrange thought into a coherent unity; they offer meaning to attitudes, values, beliefs, and knowledge. They construct information into identifiable, normative, and seemingly universal truths. They weave a familiar story out of oftentimes disparate and messy bits of data and detail.

Throughout this work, I have claimed that rather than being a simple event of market capitalism or correctional policy, privatization ought to be interpreted as a matrix of social relations that integrate economic, political, and rhetorical forces. Organizing the interpretation of these forces, then, is the mythology of privatization. It serves to account for the material and discursive conditions surrounding the drive to privatize California state prisons by providing a story that links financial logic, political disputes, and ideological perspectives. In all, the mythology allows us to see that which is taken for granted in the assent to privatization and the ways that assent restricts the scope of responses to crime on the whole. This chapter is therefore focused upon unpacking the mythology and answering at least three questions: What 'truths' provide practical meaning for adopting private contracting in the Golden State? What is the contour or shape of such 'truths'? And, how do these provide sense or logic to the prospect of private for-profit prisons as a solution to economic challenges, policy ills or rhetorical problems?

Returning to the finding that black men live longer behind bars (as opposed to white men) than they do on the street, we see that the mythology of privatization works to *define incarceration as the fitting response to social welfare ills.* Or rather, the criminal justice system in California makes no real differentiation between the two needs: one for the punishment of offenders acting against the state, the other for the lack of resources to address issues of health and financial need, for example. And this collapse seems perfectly unremarkable—if noticed at all. Those who relied upon education or apprentice programs, medical services, mental-health assistance, or drug and alcohol treatment are now often finding "treatment" in the only program tax-payers are seemingly willing to or able to support—incarceration.

As California imprisons more and more citizens, privately-contracted prisons become one solution to the urgent set of problems this collapse has wrought, one that presents prison as the suitable means to govern classes of "socially marginal" or "socially disabled" individuals. The political-economic blooming of global capitalism, as it has transferred jobs out of the country, concentrated poverty in specific geographical pockets, compounded structural unemployment, and encouraged social dislocation, has eaten away at social safety-nets and widened the gap between the very wealthy and the severely impoverished. Part of this phenomenon is because the economy of the U.S. has transformed to favor the transient multinational, or perhaps more accurately, the transnational corporation. These corporations, by way of advanced technologies and the collapse of isolated economic systems, roam all over the globe in search of cheap production and flexible labor markets. Whereas the accumulation of capital at one time in California operated through a myriad of industries serving the state, the nation, and indeed, worldwide, today those markets have either dried up or transformed to serve the concentrated interests of fewer and fewer individuals and organizations. It is from this purview then that we are able to see that the extraction of wealth in capitalist social systems is an incredibly creative process. Indeed, through the madness of the exponential growth of the California prison system, capital has come to feed upon a pool of profit often produced by *raced social-entropy* and discrimination; which is to say, the disintegration of the social safety net has become a market investment.

To make this claim is also to recognize that the integration of the prison and the manifold services of social-welfare depend upon a different imagining of the delinquent today. In the era of penal-welfarism, our obligation was to cure the offender, to enable him to enter society as a full-fledged member restored of his ability to live an ordered and productive life. While the actual results of imprisoning inmates might not have always materialized such a "cure" over the years for which this working ideal held sway, the philosophy was no less revered. Today, this logic has been turned on its head. On the whole, the societal perception is that convicts are not worthy of treatment; they are understood to be ill suited for rehabilitation. Part of the explanation for this shift can be attributed to a change in how we frame rationales for crime. That is, once we decided that offenders could not be cured or restored to a status of functioning citizen, efforts and resources directed toward rehabilitation as a means to accomplish such a transformation evaporated. But the shift also lies in our altered perception of the poor over the last two generations. David Garland writes that today, the poor are seen to be the cause of their own lack of effort and bad choices:

> In the increasingly prosperous world of the 1990s and since, these persistently poor populations are easily viewed as 'different' and not merely 'disadvantaged. Like persistent criminals and career criminals, they are conveniently regarded as an alien culture, a class apart, a residuum left behind by the fast-paced, high-tech processes of the globalized economy and the information society. The themes that continue to dominate crime policy—rational choice and the structures of control, deterrents, and disincentives, the normality of crime, the responsibilization of individuals, the threatening underclass, the failing, overly lenient system—have come to organize the politics of poverty as well.[3]

We might observe that once those living in poverty ceased to be identified as "white and rural (in the imagery of the Great Depression and the War on Poverty)" and began to be viewed as "black and urban (in the iconography of the wars on crime and drugs)," they were unworthy of sympathy and help; they were caught up in a kind of politics of poverty, as Garland suggests, wherein their conditions were simply their own fault.[4] Whereas earlier communities found it possible to identify with these individuals, today, they tend to see them as threatening and alien.

A snapshot: California's Gross State Product surpassed the trillion-dollar mark in 1997—this is the amount equal to the Gross Domestic Product of the U.S. as a whole back in 1970. At the same time, the rate of family poverty in the state more than doubled.[5] The state prison population was being held in facilities at 206 percent of their design capacity that same year and the prison population had risen some 300 percent from what it was in 1980.[6] The growth in the penal population has coincided—literally—with a rise in poor families and a decline in welfare recipients. The welfare agencies and programs meant to aid in the event of downward economic cycles have seemed to all but disappear, but profits produced from the custodianship of poor, black, brown, under-educated offenders has risen—and with little public notice. The mythology of privatization naturalizes private contracting (and the prison industrial complex) as a service that works to "clean up social junk." And as that "junk" continues to expand, private hands have become both wealthy and indispensable.

Imprisonment Is Our Best Option

A second assumption supporting the mythology of privatization is the notion that *imprisonment is the best and most effective response to crime*. There are two points to consider here. First is the perception of inevitability of crime in the twenty-first century; today it is understood to be a commonplace occurrence that cannot be stopped. That is, it is not a solvable problem—crime is something we simply have to deal with on a moment-to-moment basis. Chapter 2 suggested this view has not always been commonly held. The eradication of crime was believed to be possible in the early years of the progressive era. But now we accept the idea that illegality is a perennial challenge that we have no choice but to constantly battle. Prisons, therefore, serve the community much like cemeteries might be said to serve the terminally ill. They are an insurance policy for at-risk populations that must be regulated. They are places to house individuals who cannot be helped in any other way. Californians make room in these facilities for the unavoidable delinquency that crime control workers are charged with controlling. By using advanced recording technologies, systematized computer software, and offender management systems, criminal justice officials measure criminal tendencies and the successes of given patrolling plans. The criminal justice apparatus manages what cannot be made obsolete. Prisons are just one more tool in the arsenal to fight this war; they are not about a psychology of treatment, but rather a system of containment.

Second, while the state has the occasional mental-health, job-training or welfare treatment for a lucky few, it is clearly not committed to the use of these programs as a large-scale solution to issues of crime and delinquency. Even though such reentry or inmate welfare programs are offered, on the whole they are reserved for a small sub-set of those in need because by and large offenders are constituted as intractable, as unable to be transformed—and so the next best thing seems to simply be to isolate them from the rest of society. Rehabilitation never fully recovered from the attacks it endured over three decades ago both in California and across the nation; treatment is therefore suspect, a gamble, an investment that may render little pay-off in the end.

Still, the rehabilitation of incarcerated offenders is caught up in a web of contradiction. California went as far as to rename the Department of Corrections the California Department of Corrections and Rehabilitation (CDCR) in 2005 and often touts its "Adult Programs" as the heart of its pledge to inmate treatment. At least some portion of the California public seems ready to hear the arguments for rehabilitation today—even if this willingness is couched in the self-interested discourse of saving tax-dollars. Furthermore, in 2012, Californians finally agreed to amend the state's Three Strikes law, passing Proposition 36 with 69 percentof the vote. The change, which many would say was a long time in coming, means that offenders who are sentenced to 25 years to life in prison (for a "third strike") must commit a serious or violent crime as opposed to simply stealing a slice of pizza or posessing marijuana. The law stands, perhaps, as a gesture towards "racheting down" tough on crime legislation. In the same election, Californians also voted on abolishing the death penalty (Proposition 34). The proposition lost, but by the smallest margin in recent history: 47 percent to 53 percent of all votes cast. It may be too soon to interpret these results as meaningful or a mark of some shift in the electorate towards crime and criminals. We will have to wait and see. But what has not changed, of course, is the reliance upon incarceration as the seemingly most appropriate response to crime.

The privatization of prison facilities is quite sensible given this premise. If the crime problem cannot be solved, and the reduction of crime has little to do with reorienting a broken inmate back into civic life, then it makes sense to simply incapacitate criminals. And by extension, it makes little difference if a public or private entity carries out this task. In fact, the regulation of populations that are likely to cause community problems, if nothing else, ought to be economically prudent. Taxpayer dollars are scarce, so why not meet the crime problem head-on with the competition of the free market? In this way the mythology of privatization harnesses the engine of capitalist ingenuity and utilizes the appeals capitalist market economies share more generally.

Market Capitalism Will Solve State Problems

A third mode through which the mythology of privatization becomes tenable is, therefore, the notion that *the market is a fair and neutral mechanism to control expenditures of state services.* Thus, private for-profit prisons are a far better investment for cash-strapped states. Within this narrative framework, the opposite of a self-regulating system is the state institution of government. Large governments imply bloated bureaucracy, corruption and unhealthy, burdensome functioning. It stands to reason that private companies are better suited to simple custodial care motivated as they are by self-interest and a desire for continued contracts. Public corrections departments like the CDCR cannot be counted upon to hold down costs given that as a department, it is not accountable, like a private company is, to its shareholders or a definitive bottom-line. The obvious formulation becomes, and we see this model across a spectrum of public services transferred into private hands, business is not only qualitatively-different from public provision, but it is also less apt to be exploited by those charged with its control. The mythology sets forth, in fact, the principle that privatization is both sensible and superior *precisely because* it is not subject to government control. It conceptualizes the "public" provision of corrections to be altogether different from "private" for-profit companies that provide the same service. But the work in this analysis seems to demonstrate that such a framework may be misleading, however, and misleading in a way that emboldens the mythology of privatization in a fourth way.

Public Provision Is Not Private Provision (With One Exception)

The assertion advanced in this case follows: *public and private organizations are distinct and oppose one another in formula and function.* As the examination of the California Corrections and Peace Officers Association (CCPOA) illustrates, however, this perspective seems suspect in more ways than one. The captive and seemingly inexhaustible incarcerated population serves as a mechanism to produce profit for the CCPOA in the form of salaries, benefits, and even political capital. The service the union produces, much like any private company, pays a wage—to be sure. But in the process of providing that service we also see the union lobbying to increase its productive power, limit competition, conquer new markets (in the form of custodianship of low-level, parolee violators, for example) and promote ideological discourse that positions and normalizes a law and order perspective of crime and criminality. The CCPOA, for example, works to ensure harsher punishments for convicted offenders as well as policies that keep prisoners incarcerated for longer periods of time. They might be said to be ambassadors for "tough on crime" discourse and committed to candidates for office with a similar pledge. In short, the union utilizes diverse tactics and strategies to maintain its market share. It sets out to protect its capital (those subject to legal punishment) and cast out potential competitors.

Given such features, is the state employee workers' union that controls California's prison facilities so qualitatively different from a private business? Are the interests of a for-profit company so distinct? If this analysis is accurate, the state—its officials and/or representatives—might be better understood as every bit as invested as the private sector in the extraction of profit from the very people it has been charged to care for and reform—little different from a corporation like Corrections Corporation of America or the GEO Group. There is reason to believe, as Ambalavaner Sivanandan argues, that in the final calculation businesses are, at bottom, essentially in the business of government while governments, similarly, are in the business of businesses."[7] Which is to say, public officials of California are in fact one of the most potent forces of capital in the Golden State. As the CCPOA sits in congressional committee meetings, advises members of congress and political officials on prison policy, as the union constitutes an influence upon government decisions and penal law—even in the absence of its immediate material presence—the union certainly comprises state action from a practical standpoint. From one purview then, the prison population in California serves as a kind of profitable "trough of resources" from which to draw—even as it is loathed and resented for its criminaliy. But distinctions between "public" entities and "private" entities that feed from this supply may in many ways not make much difference. Both have their own interests in mind and can be seen to use a group of individuals few seem to champion. The benefit of seeing the state and private business as opposing systems, however, is really the capacity to construct private business as a panacea, as an antidote to all the complaints we have about "bloated government" and bureacracy. Market functions may therefore be mystified, and appear as the final remedy to a complex and fitful problem. Once we posit public and private as opposites, we are invited to interpret the business of private contractors as relatively neutral, to see in them the savvy of a free-flowing commercial enterprise and to view the market as the fair and balanced arbiter of a simple service. After all, the market does not take sides: it allows competition to iron out all dysfunction and conflict that might lurk in the bowels of an entrepreneurial pursuit.

While the mythology posits public provision of corrections and private provision as separate, it can't help but contain contradictions. One of these is that while state control and private control are understood as vastly different, the function of caring for prisoners by either is understood as the same. The practical delivery of care for prison inmates doesn't change according to the mythology—there is no specific skill or symbolic legitimacy or meaning attached to being punished by a representative of the state. Thus, ironically, the mythology *of privatization* suggests a fifth *truth* that might be stated as such: *private companies and state agencies are no different in cases where the propriety of delivering punishment is questioned.*

In this case, the mythology declares that the variance between the two entities has no impact upon ethical concerns one might have with a private for-profit company punishing a citizen for a crime committed against the public. Or, to put it another way, to withhold a citizen's freedom, to administer punishment, is not an act that must necessarily be carried out by an official of the state who stands in proxy for a community that has been wronged. On the contrary, punishing an individual who has transgressed against the communal body is a responsibility divorced from any such wrong; it makes little difference which person wears the prison guard uniform—a privately-paid employee or a state-appointed official. So when the question arises: "[should] private for-profit companies, their administrators and line employees . . .be involved in handling the two most precious possessions of every citizen—their liberty and their life[?]" the answer offered by way of the logic of the mythology of privatization is, "Of course."[8] To many, there is no difference between public and private seizure of freedom in the circumstance of punishing offenders who have transgressed against the state. At least none that would affect a private company's moral status to accomplish this function.

In fact, many who argue for private-contracting of corrections suggest that the individuals who *sentence* and *seize* criminals are those who handle the "life and liberty" of any given inmate, not those who confine them. Why is this so? Because there is supposedly a distinction between those who allocate punishment and those who deliver it. Conceivably, a society bound by the rule of law requires both private contractors and government representatives to abide by that law. And it is this law, as Charles Logan puts it, not the civil standing of the actor, that ascertains the legitimacy of incarceration. As long as a private company is within the bounds of the rule of law, that is, they obtain custodianship of offenders by those who work as legal officials of the California Penal Code, there are no other ethical concerns to take into account. To decide who ought to incarcerate law-breakers then, we must simply look at which agencies are doing the better job.[9] In this way, performance becomes the primary criterion to evaluate the appropriateness of privatization; if private prisons run more smoothly, *ipso facto* they are superior to publicly run institutions—regardless of ethical issues. It's clear then that by this logic, the moral responsibility for punishing can be passed to private hands as long as that function can be better accomplished by those to whom we assign the job.

Against this view, John Dilulio suggests that the message to those who abuse liberty is: because of your transgression, you have lost your right to the benefits of freedom. "[This] is the philosophical brick and mortar of every correctional facility," he argues,"—a message that ought to be conveyed by the offended community of law abiding citizens, through its public agents, to the incarcerated individual." Without "the moral writ of the community" which exists in the symbol of "the arresting officer, the robes of the judge, and the state patch of the corrections officer," incarceration is no more legitimate than if one private citizen imprisoned another.[10]

Here then, distinguishing between allocating punishment and delivering punishment seems to be the key to allowing private contractors to sidestep the charge that they have no right to withhold liberty from a private citizen. Divorcing these two functions strategically shifts the basis upon which one might judge a moral component of punishment. A sharp distinction between sentencing one to punishment and delivering that punishment functions as a rhetorical insulator; it serves to present the act of sentencing as a special judicial event separate or severed from punishing an inmate.[11] As Richard Sparks argues, incarceration is then understood to be a mere business arrangement, a managerial challenge, or a science emptied of any normative concerns. And of course we see this is precisely how the mythology works to legitimize the standing of for-profit prisons—as a simple object of market investment, devoid of any ideological position. In sum, the mythology of privatization is content to situate public and private agencies as opposites, except when taking that position undermines its own ends. It is unsurprising that an ideological system should contain contradictions, for quite often, a contradiction is the very ground upon which such systems rely. In fact, we might say that the primary premise of ideological discourse itself is the covering over, the obscuring of flaws in reasoning. In this case, the mythology deflects recognition of the inherent moral component in the act of inflicting punishment; it allows performance to be the measure of propriety enabling privatization to appear quite natural.

Safety at Any Cost

Turning to a sixth and final rationale for the mythology of privatization, we find that *as crime continues to increase, safety and protection are the most important values of California citizens.* Even though state residents are safer than they have been in decades, the perception that the world is increasingly more risky and worrisome prevails. Fear is, consequently, a central preoccupation for Californians; it enables them to believe a violent crime is just around the corner. To this end, residents continue to invest in products like security cameras and services that protect their homes and families. They buy guns and pepper spray; they take self-defense courses and memorize emergency numbers. They are prompted to be evermore "vigilant" and watch others around them. And they are able to imagine themselves as victims and utilize that conceptual potential as a means to link to one another as a community. As noted in Chapter 5, violent crime in California decreased 70 percent over the last decade—and this plunge in the state was greater than it was across the U.S. as a whole. So why the fear and dread? How does the mythology of privatization benefit from the misconception that crime is increasing? How does it use the fearfulness that accompanies this belief?

First, the misconception directs social actors to propose harsh penalties for would-be criminals. A culture of fear and "tough on crime" penal policies make use of one another as part of a cycle. The first step in justifying punitive measures is declaring that there is no other way to gain control over an overwhelming and intimidating enemy. Enemies breed terror and alarm; they summon dread and anxiety. Zero tolerance policies are techniques of regaining authority, of squelching an adversary who is unable to be controlled in any other fashion. As the antagonism between fear and punitive penal policy has progressed in California, incarceration has expanded. On the whole, residents seem unwilling to soften harsh disciplinary controls or rethink mandatory sentencing. Thus, prison populations have grown—even in the wake of less crime—and the winners have been private companies eager to invest in the growing ranks of prison inmates. If residents believed they were fundamentally safe, if they felt less threatened, the amount of resources spent upon corrections would be allocated differently and perhaps decreased altogether. The fact that just 21 percent of parolees in California complete parole (half the number of the national average), for example, would be pause for rethinking the way those resources are spent. And fears over becoming victimized could be translated into inquiries into the troubles of the current system which seems unable to restore prisoners' abilities to re-enter society. When 80 percent of California's inmates who recidivate have a mental illness, it's clear that there is a very different problem at hand than one wherein vicious thugs enjoy terrorizing the public.[12] It is not necessarily a problem that demands an iron fist, but one that calls for reasoned planning around the challenges presented by mental health. But when the discourse surrounding penal sentencing focuses on anxiety, panic and reactionary authoritarianism, social focus takes up a very different target. It fails to account for the fact that the prison problem today is partly an issue of conceptualizing that problem—wrongly. The mythology of privatization cannot afford to examine this conceptualization; it cannot afford to lose support for incapacitation, for mere holding tanks. As long as private companies are unprepared (and unneeded) to offer for-profit services that might address this different issue, they, and other supporters of prolonged incarceration, will frame California cities as risk-filled zones of combat—places that must lock up thousands of delinquents who might otherwise threaten citizen safety.

Second, if we are fighting against an ever-present danger represented by the typical superpredator who delights in victimizing us, the mechanism that joins us together becomes perpetual risk; it serves as perhaps one of the few means to unify communities that seemingly have little in common. As cities across the state continue to diversify demographically, as illegal immigration pits the haves against the have-nots, as political divergence between progressives and conservatives expands, social homogeneity in the Golden State is becoming more and more a relic of the past. How do Californians elicit social solidarity? The threat and apprehension of becoming victimized, as I have already argued, is one very powerful key. Yet when unity is built on moral outrage and fearfulness, it entrenches the division between those who are marked as criminals or would be criminals and those who fear that they will become victims of crime.

The mythology of privatization supports this division. It cannot afford to allow citizens to see themselves in offenders; it will not enable the recognition of our common humanity. If citizens identify with prisoners, simple incapacitation ceases to be the single answer for issues of crime and delinquency. We would have a need to look deeper into these issues; we would have to consider the complexity of the challenge of crime with greater care. My analysis is not attempting to claim that individuals who steal, who injure others, or do harm to communities do not exist, only that the manifold responses to these individuals lacks foresight and cannot succeed in genuinely decreasing crime. Persons who engage in acts harmful to society exist, yes, but it is the meanings we construct of these acts and of these persons that serve as the platform for designing penal policy. Within the angry image of the career criminal lies the revulsion that turns citizens toward one another. It endows the mythology of privatization with powerful representations of the vicious predator, the psychopath, and the culturally-crazed offender as the culprit in each illegality committed. It disables tolerance and institutionalizes distrust. The tropes provide a shortsighted imperative: lock 'em up and throw away the key; incapacitate, regulate, control these populations. In this way, concern over crime is not nasty bigotry or discrimination: it's just simple good sense.

The Logic of Privatization

This book has been about the expansion of private for-profit prisons as an indispensable part of the prison industrial complex (PIC) in the twenty-first century. I have argued that one can understand the support for private contracting in California through the prism of the mythology of privatization. I have tried to show how the forces of economics have adapted to shifts in the market brought about by high penal populations and distrust in state government. I have described the political responses to problems of fearfulness and anxiety linked to crime and social disintegration. And I have attempted to explain how the desire for security and control has hastened the discourses of exclusion which imagine the socially marginal as caricatures of alien-others. As the formulation of mythology of privatization illustrates, when we look at why this penal trend has become an integral element of our responses to the crises in corrections today—by this, I mean crises in perpetually expanding prison populations, problems with a lack of funds to adequately house these offenders and a lack of understanding and/or cultural commitment that might predispose us to rethink the cycle of incarceration—we see that it is not simply because private companies stand to make sizeable profits. It is not just because the PIC creates wealth for private company owners, shareholders, or executives. It is not because the state seems unable to solve problems of illegality, of security, of order. And it is certainly not because those who break laws are unable to be integrated into community. Privatization has emerged because it meets a number of disparate needs which appear in advanced capitalist societies today, needs that crystallize around the penal sanction of incapacitation, the political ascendance of moral individualism, and our seemingly insatiable global economy. It has emerged because the public currently sees those who are arrested as people who make "rational choices" to harm others out of their inherent psychological, biological or cultural pathologies. And thus, the logical response to these individuals is incarceration.

Incarceration is streamlined and made "smarter" by privatization; it is buoyed by the rhetoric of market idealism and capitalist superiority. Gone is the middle ground of the penal-welfarist logic that recognizes a space, as David Garland notes, between crimes committed in either "complete freedom" or at the opposing end of the spectrum, as a function of "irresistible compulsion." We have given up on the notion that offenders engage in illegality upon a field wherein their actions are always already socially situated and constrained, alongside the opportunities for realizing those acts.[13] Prison privatization is relatively easy to adopt in the abstract, as it circumvents most, if not all, social critique of public policy. It directs attention away from the conditions offenders combat such as structural sources of unemployment, a lack of healthcare—particularly mental-healthcare—and substance abuse; its appeal never grapples with systematic poverty or the social disincentives to solve any of these problems. Privatization elides questions of race and class in the demographics of prison populations. It is not concerned with the commodification of specific populations understood to be in need of regulation, segregation. Its highest ideals are consumerist freedoms, an ethics born of individualism, efficient and unrestrained capitalist functioning and retribution for those who would stand in the way of its unfettered growth. There is no accident in the current rise of the private for-profit prison (or, I would argue, the privatization of many other traditionally state-managed services). The only question is whether or not private prisons can be recognized as an equation that (re)produces a cycle of exclusion that appears to benefit a select few.

If we return to Michel Foucault's observation that the failure of the prison to produce orderly societies, to turn out restored citizens, may in fact be a logical output of the present system, and if we then realize that the structure of capitalism expands the competition to produce that which it treats, we are obliged to recognize that private prisons cultivate more of what the failing prison system has to offer. They produce in a mechanized fashion the ails of the present arrangement. It may be time to reckon with the fact that if the capitalist market is to be truly useful, it must serve human interests. That is, it must be harnessed to the value of communal solidarity and linked to projects that will encourage the emancipation of the human spirit. As it stands today, the privatization of our states' public prisons cannot hope to accomplish any of these ideals.

---

[1] David Rosen, David Wohl, and Victor Schoenbach, "All-Cause and Cause-Specific Mortality Among Black and White North Carolina State Prisoners, 1995-2005," *Annals of Epidemiology* 21 (2011) : 719-726.
[2] Katherine Beckett & Bruce Western, "Governing Social Marginality," *Punishment & Society* 3 : 1 (2001) : 43-59. For more research substantiating this argument see: Rusch and Kircheimer 1939; Garland 1985, 1990; Parenti 2000.
[3] David Garland, *The Culture of Control: Crime and Social Order in Contemporary Society* (Chicago: University of Chicago Press, 2001) 196.
[4] Katherine Beckett & Theodore Sasson, "The War on Crime as Hegemonic Strategy: A Neo-Marxian Theory of the New Punitiveness in U.S. Criminal Justice Policy," *Of Crime and Criminality: The Use of Theory in Everyday Life*, ed. S. Simpson (Boston: Pine Forge Press, 2000) 68.
[5] Between 1969 and 1995, it grew from 8.4 percent to 17.9 percent. Ruth Wilson Gilmore, "Globalization and U.S. Prison Growth: From Military Keynesianism to Post-Keynesianism," *Race & Class* 40-2/3 (1998/99): 179.
[6] Theodore Caplow & Jonathon Simon, "Understanding Prison Policy and Population Trends," *Prisons*, eds. Michael Tonry and Joan Petersilia (Chicago: University of Chicago Press, 1999) 63-120.
[7] Ambalavaner Sivanandan, "Globalism and the Left," *Race & Class* 40-2/3 (1998/99) : 5-19.

[8] David Shichor, *Punishment for Profit: Private Prisons/Public Concerns* (London, Sage, 1995) 54.

[9] Charles Logan, *Private Prisons: Cons and Pros* (Oxford, Oxford University Press, 1990) 5. See also Logan's "The Proprietary of Proprietary Prisons," *Federal Probation* 51 (1987) 35-40 and Logan's views in "Objections and Refutations" ed. Stephen Easton *Privatizing Correctional Services* (Vancouver: British Columbia: The Fraser Institute, 1998).

[10] John DiIulio, *No Escape: The Future of American Corrections* (NY: Basic Books, 1991) 197.

[11] Richard Sparks, "Can Prisons Be Legitimate?: Penal Politics, Privatization, and the Timelessness of an Old Idea," *British Journal of Criminology* 34 (1994) 24; See also Nicola Lacey, *State Punishment* (London: Routledge, 1988) 14.

[12] SpearIt, "Mental Illness in Prison: Inmate Rehabilitation & Correctional Officers in Crisis," *Berkeley Journal of Criminal Law* 14 (2009) : 227-302.

[13] Garland 198.

Bibliography

Alanez, Tonia. "Solutions to Freeway Shootings are Elusive." *Los Angeles Times* 11 June 2005, Web. 13 Nov. 2012.

Althusser, Louis. *Lenin and Philosophy and Other Essays.* Trans. B. Brewster. New York: Monthy Review, 1971.

American Friends Service Committee. *Struggle For Justice: A Report on Crime and Punishment in America.* New York: Hill & Wang, 1971.

Anderson, David C. *Crime and the Politics of Hysteria.* New York: Random House, 1995.

Arax, Mark. "Corcoran Guards Mute in Probe of Inmate Death." *Los Angeles Times* 5 March 2004. Web. 30 Aug. 2011.

---. "Inmate's Open Shunt Led to Bleeding Death." *Los Angeles Times* 7 Feb. 2004. Web. 3 Sept. 2011.

Armour, Jody David. *Negrophobia and Reasonable Racism: The Hidden Costs of Being Black in America.* New York: New York University Press, 1997.

Armstrong, Philip, Andrew Glyn & John Harrison. *Capitalism Since 1945.* Oxford, Basil Blackwell, 1991.

Badie, Bertrand and Pierre Birnbaum. *The Sociology of the State.* Trans. Arthur Goldhammer. Chicago: The University of Chicago Press, 1983.

Bailey, Walter. "Correctional Outcome: An Examination of 100 Reports." *Journal of Criminal Law, Criminology and Police Science* 57 (1966): 153-160.

Bates, Eric. "Private Prisons." *The Nation* 5 Jan. 1998: 11-18.

Baudrillard, Jean. *The System of Objects.* Trans. James Benedict. New York: Verso, 1996.

Beckett, Kathrine. *Making Crime Pay: Law and Order in Contemporary American Politics.* New York: Oxford University Press, 1997.

---. "Setting the Agenda: Street Crime and Drug Use in American Politics." *Social Problems* 41 (1994) : 425-447.

Beckett, Kathrine & Theodore Sasson. *The Politics of Injustice: Crime and Punishment in America.* Thousand Oaks: Pine Forge Press, 2000.

Beckett, Katherine & Theodore Sasson. "The War on Crime as Hegemonic Strategy: A Neo-Marxian Theory of the New Punitiveness in U.S. Criminal Justice Policy." *Of Crime and Criminality: The Use of Theory in Everyday Life.* Ed. S. Simpson Boston: Pine Forge Press, 2000.

Beckett, K. & B. Western. "Governing Social Marginality: Welfare, Incarceration and the Transformation of State Policy." *Punishment and Society* 3 (2001): 43-59.

Bell, Charles G. & Charles M. Price. *California Government Today: Politics of Reform.* Homewood, Illinois: The Dorsey Press, 1980.

Bellon, Bertrand & Jorge Niosi. *The Decline of the American Economy.* New York, Black Rose Books: 1988.

Bennett, William, John Dilulio, & John Walters. *Body Count: Moral Poverty and How to Win America's War Against Crime and Drugs.* New York: Simon & Schuster, 1996.

Best, Joel. *Random Violence: How we Talk about New Crimes and New Victims.* Berkeley, CA: University of California Press, 1999.

Blomberg, Thomas G. & Karol Lucken. *American Penology: A History of Control.* New York: Aldine De Gruyter, 2000.

Bluestone, Barry & Harrison, Bennett. *The Great U-Turn: Corporate Restructuring and the Polarizing of America.* New York, Basic Books: 1988.

Blume, Howard. "Charters Get a Chance to Grow, But How Big." *Los Angeles Times* 2 Sept. 2009 A1/A10.

Bottoms, Anthony. "The Philosophy and Politics of Punishment and Sentencing." *The Politics of Sentencing Reform.* Eds. Chris Clarkson & Rod Morgan. Oxford: Clarendon, 1995.

Boutellier, Hans. *Crime and Morality: The Significance of Criminal Justice in Post-modern Culture.* Boston: Kluwer Academic Publishers, 2000.

Boyarsky, Bill. *The Rise of Ronald Reagan.* New York: Random House, 1968.

Bratton, William J. "How to Win the War Against Crime." *New York Times* 5 April 1996:   A-17.

Burby, Jack. "Governor Pat Brown, A Personal Memoir." *California Journal* (April 1996) : 47-8.

Butterfield, Fox. "Political Gains by Prison Guards." *New York Times* 7 Nov. 1995: A1

Breckinridge, Sophonisba & Edith Abbott. *The Delinquent Child and the Home.* New York : Charities Publication Committee, 1912.

Brenner, Lee, Hajir Ardebili. "To Protect and to Serve: Police Defamation Suits Against California Citizens Who Report Officer Misconduct." *Communications Lawyer* 28.1 (2011) Web. 21 July 2011.

Brenner, Robert. *The Boom and the Bubble: The U.S. in the World Economy.* New York: Verso, 2002.

Brown, Edmund G. Address. "On Human Rights." To the Joint Session of the Legislature: Sacramento. California. 14 Feb. 1963.

---. *Economic Report of the Governor: 1965.* Sacramento, California: California Office of State printing, 1965.

---. *Economic Report of the Governor: 1980.* Sacramento, California Office of State printing: 1980.

---. *Economic Report of the Governor: 1980 Statistical Appendix.* Sacramento, California Office of State printing: 1980.

Bureau of Justice Statistics. "Jail Inmates, 1986." Washington D.C.: U.S. Department of Justice; Bureau of Justice Statistics, 1991. "Prisoners in 1990," Washington D.C. : U.S. Department of Justice.

Bureau of Justice Statistics. "The Number of Adults in Correctional Population Has Been Increasing." Washington D.C.: Department of Justice (2003). Web. 22 July 2011.

Cahn, Mathew Alan, H. Eric Schockman, & David M. Shafie. *Rethinking California: Politics and Policies in the Golden State.* New Jersey: Prentice Hall, 2001.

California Budget Project. *A Growing Divide: The State of Working California 2005.* Sacramento, California: California Budget Project, Sept. 2005.

California Citizens Budget Commissioner. *A 21ˢᵗ Century Budget Process for California.* Sacramento, CA: Center for Governmental Studies, 1998.

California County Fact Book. California: County Supervisors Association of California. 1968. Print.

California Correctional Peace Officers Association. "Election 2006," *PEACEKeeper* vol 23.5 (2006) : 8-11.

California Department of Corrections and Rehabilitation. "Community Correctional Facilities." 2010. Web. 14 Aug. 2011.

California Department of Corrections and Rehabilitation. Corrections: "Moving Forward." News Release. Fall 2009. Web. 5 July 2011.

California Department of Finance, Demographic Research Unit. 1995 Population Projection Series, *Total Population by County, By Year, By Race and Ethnicity.* Sacramento: California, 1996.

California Department of Justice. *Crime In California.* Sacramento, California, Criminal Justice Statistics Center, 2001.

California Department of Justice. *Crime in California and the United States, 1988-1998.* Sacramento, CA: Criminal Justice Statistics Center, 2000.

California Department of Justice. Bureau of Criminal Statistics and Special Services. *Adult Felony Arrest Dispositions in California.* Sacramento: California Department of Justice, 1979.

California Economic Growth: Short Term Uncertainties, Long Term Trends. Palo Alto: Center for Continuing Study of the California Economy. 1991. Key-3.

California Fair Political Practices Commission. "Big Money Talks: California's Billion Dollar Club." Special Report. 11 March 2010 Web. 15 Aug. 2011.

California Healthcare Services. "Fast Facts." California.Gov Homepage. 4 Jan. 2011. Web. 3 Feb. 2011.

California Legislature Senate Committee on Governmental Efficiency. "Welfare in California: Report to the State Senate." Sacramento, 1970.

California Secretary of State, Debra Bowen. November 7, 2006 General Election-Statement of Vote-Contests. 2011. Web. 16 Aug. 2011.

California: Department of Finance of the State of California. *California Statistical Abstract.* Sacramento Printing Office. 1970. Print.

California: Department of Finance of the State of California. *California Statistical Abstract.* Sacramento Printing Office. 1981. Print.

Campagna, Anthony S. *The Economy in the Reagan Years: The Economic Consequences of the Reagan Administrations.* London: Greenwood Press, 1994.

Cannon, Lou. *Governor Reagan: His Rise to Power.* New York: Public Affairs, 2003.

Caplow, Theodore & Jonathon Simon. "Understanding Prison Policy and Population Trends." *Prisons: Crime and Justice-26.* Eds. Michael Tonry & Joan Petersilia. Chicago: University of Chicago Press, 1999. 63-120.

Casstevens, Thomas W. *Politics, Housing, and Race Relations: California's Rumford Act and Proposition 14.* Berkeley: Institute of Governmental Studies, University of California, Berkeley, 1964. 19-20.

Center on Juvenile and Criminal Justice. "Race and the Juvenile Justice System: Disproportionate Minority Confinement." 2003. Web. 26 August 2005.

Central Intelligence Agency. "The World Fact Book: United States." Nov. 2010. Web. 7 Nov. 2010.

Chambliss, William J. *Power, Politics, and Crime.* Colorado: Westview Press, 1999.

Chen, Stephanie. "Pennsylvania Rocked by 'Jailing Kids for Cash' Scandal." CNN Justice Page. 23 Feb. 2009 Web. 2 Aug. 2011

Chermak, Steven. *Victims in the News: Crime and the American News Media.* Boulder, CO: Westview, 1995.

Chiricos, Ted, Sarah Eschholz & M. Gertz. "Crime, News, and Fear of Crime." *Social Problems* 44 (1988): 342-357.

Chomsky, Noam. "Drug Policy as Social Control." *Prison Nation: The Warehousing of America's Poor.* Eds.Tara Herivel and Paul Wright. New York: Routlege, 2003.

Christie, Nils. *Crime Control as Industry.* New York: Routlege, 1993.

Clark, R. "Situational Crime Prevention." *British Journal of Criminology* 20: 2 (1980) : 136-147.

Cleeland, Nancy. "Low-Pay Sectors Dominate U.S. and State Job Growth." *Los Angeles Times* 22 Jan. 2004: A-1, A-22.

---. "Unions Gain Ground in Golden State." *Los Angeles Times* 31 Aug. 2003: C-1; C4.

Cloward, Richard & Lloyd E. Ohlin. *Delinquency and Opportunity: A Theory of Delinquent Gangs.* New York: Free Press, 1960.

Cockrell, Cathy. "Downsizing the Prison-Industrial Complex." *California Progress Report* 5 May 2010. Web. 20 May 2010.

Commolly, Kathleen, Lea McDermid, Vincent Schiraldi & Dan Macallair. "From Classrooms to Cell Blocks: How Prison Building Affects Higher Education and African American Enrollment." San Francisco, California: Center on Juvenile & Criminal Justice. 22 Oct. 1996. Print.

Condon, Christopher D. "Falling Crime Rates, Rising Caseload Numbers: Using Police-Probation Partnerships." *Corrections Today* (Feb. 2003) : 44-48.

Croly, Herbert. *The Promise of American Life.* New York: Capricorn, 1909.

Cummins, Eric. *The Rise and Fall of California's Radical Prison Movement.* Palo Alto, CA: Stanford University Press1994.

Currie, Elliott. *Crime and Punishment in America.* New York: Metropolitan Books: 1998.

---. "Crime and Market Society: Lessons from the United States." *The New Criminology Revisited.* Eds. Paul Walton & Jock Young. New York: St. Martins, 1998. 130-142.

Curtin, Mary Ann. *Black Prisoners and Their World, Alabama, 1865-1900.* Charlottesville and London: University Press of Virginia, 2000.

Danielman, Lucig & Stephen Reese. "Intermedia Influence and the Drug Issue: Converging on Cocaine." *Communication Campaigns About Drugs: Government, Media, and the Public.* Ed. Pamela Shoemaker. New Jersey: Lawrence Erlbaum, 1989.

Davis, Angela. *Are Prisons Obsolete?* New York: Seven Stories Press, 2003.

Davis, Gray. *Economic Report of the Governor: 2000.* Sacramento, California: State Capitol, 2000.

Davies, Malcolm. *Punishing Criminals: Developing Community-Based Intermediate Sanctions.* Westport: Greenwood Press, 1993.

---. *Survey Report: The Expansion of the Criminal Justice System and Penal System in California—Is Greater Coordination Required?* Bureau of Criminal Statistics Monograph Series. Sacramento: Office of the Attorney General, California Department of Justice, 1988.

Department of Health and Human Services. *Social Security Bulletin, Annual Statistical Supplement, 1986.* Washington D.C.: The Brookings Institution, 1986.

Deukmejian, George. *Economic Report of the Governor: 1985.* Sacramento, California Office of State printing: 1985.

Dillon, David. "Fortress America: More and More of Us Living Behind Locked Gates." *Planning* 60 (1994): 2-8.

Dolan, Jack. "New Contract for California Prison Guards Lifts Cap on Saved Vacation." *Los Angeles Times* 19 April 2011. Web. 28 April 2011.

---. "Female Inmates' In-Home Custody." *Los Angeles Times* 13 Sept. 2011: A-1.

---."Sick Inmates a Threat Only to State's Budget." *Los Angeles Times* 2 March 2011 : A1.

Domanick, Joe. *Cruel Justice: Three Strikes and the Politics of Crime in America's Golden State.* Berkeley: University of California Press, 2004.

Donziger, Steven R., ed. *The Real War on Crime: The Report of the National Criminal Justice Commission.* New York: Harper Perennial, 1996.

Dorfman, Lori & Vincent Shiraldi. *Off Balance: Youth, Crime, and Race in the News.* 1 April 2001. Justice Policy Institute. Web. 30 June 2011.

Duster, Tony. "Crime, Youth Unemployment and the Black Urban Underclass." *Crime and Delinquency* 33: 2 (April 1987) : 300-316.

Eagleton, Terry. *Ideology: An Introduction.* New York: Verso, 1991.

Earnest, Leslie. "Job Losses Working Their Way Into More Sectors in California." *Los Angeles Times* 17 June, 2003: C-01; C-7.

Edsall, Thomas B. & Mary D. Edsall. *Chain Reaction: The Impact of Race, Rights, and Taxes on American Politics.* New York: W.W. Norton & Company, 1991.

Emmelman, Debra S. "Defending the Poor: Commonsense 'Classism' in the Adjudication of Criminal Cases." Browning *For the Common Good: A Critical Examination of Law and Social Control.* Eds. Robin Miller & Sandra Lee. Durham: Carolina Academic Press, 2004.

Engels, Fredrich. *Anti-Dühring.* Chicago: Charles H. Kerr & Co., 1935.

---. *Socialism: Utopian and Scientific.* Trans. Edward Aveling. New York: International Publishers, 1935.

Faturechi, Robert & Ann Simmons. "Compton's Tide Turns." *Los Angeles Times* 18 Jan. 2011: A-1.

Fausset, Richard. "Inmates Losing Space as Prisons Add Bunks." *Los Angeles Times* 28 July 2004: B-1, B-8.

Feeley, Malcom & Jonathon Simon. "Actuarial Justice: The Emerging New Criminal Law." *The Futures of Criminology.* Ed. David Nelken. New York: Sage: 1994. 173-201.

Feeley, Malcom & Jonathon Simon. "The New Penology: Reformulating Penal Objectives and Implications For Penal Growth." Proceedings of: *Growth and Its Influence on Correctional Policy-Perspectives on the Report of the Blue Ribbon Commission.* Berkeley, CA, July 1991.

Field Research Corporation. "Tabulations From a Survey of California Registered Voters about the U.S. Supreme Court Ruling Mandating that California Reduce its Prison Population and the Governor's Proposals to Comply with the Ruling." Prepared for Capitol Alert and the *Sacramento Bee*. 16 June 2011. Web. 12 July 2011.

Fierce, Milton. *Slavery Revisited: Blacks and the Southern Convict Lease System, 1865-1933*. New York: African Studies Research Center, Brooklyn College, City University of New York, 1994.

Fine, Sidney. *Laissaz Faire and the General-Welfare State: A Study of Conflict in American Thought 1865-1901*. Ann Arbor: The University of Michigan Press, 1956.

Flamm, Michael W. *Law and Order: Street Crime, Civil Unrest, and the Crisis of Liberalism in the 1960s*. New York: Columbia University Press, 2005.

Fletcher, Michael R. "Calif. Minority Youth Treated More Harshly, Study Says." *The Washington Post* 3 February 2000:A16.

Foucault, Michel. *Discipline and Punish: The Birth of the Prison*. New York: Vintage, 1977.

---. *Madness and Civilization: A History of Insanity in the Age of Reason*. New York: Vintage Books, 1965.

---. "On Attica." *Foucault Live: Collected Interviews, 1961-1984*. Ed. Sylvére Lotringer, Trans. Lysa Hochroth & John Johnston. New York: Semiotext(e), 1996. 113-121.

---. "The Punitive Society." Trans. Robert Hurley. *Michel Foucault: Ethics—Subjectivity and Truth (The Essential Works of Michel Foucault, 1954-1984 Vol. 1)*. Ed. Paul Rabinow. New York: New Press: 1997. 26-38.

Fox, Sue. "Inmates Forced to Sleep on Floor." *Los Angels Times* 15 Aug. 2004: B-1, B-8.

Frankel, Marvin. *Criminal Sentences: Law Without Order*. New York: Hill and Wang, 1973.

Friedman, Lawrence. "The Crime Movement at its First Decade." *Public Administration Review* 45 (1986) : 790-794.

Furedi, Frank. *Culture of Fear: Risk Taking and the Morality of Low Expectation*. London: Continuum, 2002.

Furillo, Andy. "Contract Pits Guards vs. Governor." *Sacramento Bee* 12 June 2005. Web. 28 Aug. 2011.

---. "Prison Budget Shifts Strategy; Govenor Looks to Rely on County Jails, Private Prisons to Ease Overcrowding." *Sacramento Bee* 15 Jan. 2006: A-3.

---. "Prison Officers Union on a Roll: Gains Big Raise, Court Victories." *Sacramento Bee* 12 Oct. 1998 : A1.

Garland, David. *The Culture of Control: Crime and Social Order in Contemporary Society*. Chicago: The University of Chicago Press, 2001.

---. *Punishment and Modern Society: A Study in Social Theory*. Chicago: University of Chicago Press, 1990.

Gaubatz, Kathyn. *Crime in the Public Mind*. Ann Arbor: University of Michigan Press, 1995.

Gerber, Rudolf J. & Patrick D. McAnany, eds. *Contemporary Punishment; Views, Explanations, and Justifications*. Notre Dame: University of Notre Dame Press, 1972.

Gerbner, George, Larry Gross, Michael Morgan, Nancy Signorielli, James Shanahan. "Growing Up with Television: Cultivation Processes."*Media Ef-*

fects: Advances in Theory and Research. Eds. Jennings Bryant & Dolf Zillmann. New Jersey: Lawrence Erlbaum Associates Publishers, 2002. 43-67.

Gest, Ted. *Crime & Politics : Big Government's Erratic Campaign for Law and Order.* New York : Oxford University Press, 2001.

Gibbs, W. Wayt. "Seeking the Criminal Element," *Scientific American March* (1995): 101-106.

Gilmore, Ruth Wilson. "Globalization and US Prison Growth: From Military Keynesianism to Post-Keynesian Militarism." *Race & Class* 40: 2-3 (1998/99) 171-188.

Glassner, Barry. *The Culture of Fear: Why Americans are Afraid of the Wrong Things.* New York: Basic Books, 1999.

Goldfarb, Ronald. "Prisons: The National Poorhouse." *The New Republic* 1 Nov (1969): 15-17.

Gordon, Avery F. "Globalism and the Prison Industrial Complex: An Interview with Angela Davis." *Race & Class* 40 (1998-1999): 145-157.

Gordon, Tracy. *Fiscal Realities: Budget Tradeoffs in California Government.* San Francisco, CA: Public Policy Institute of California, 2007.

Gosselin, Peter G. "If America is Richer, Why Are Its Families So Much Less Secure." *Los Angeles Times* 10 October 2004: A-1; A-26, A-27.

Greenberg, David F. & Valerie West. "The Persistent Significance of Race: Growth in State prison Populations, 1971-1991." Law and Society Association. Aspen, Colorado, June 1998.

Green, Lee. "Infinite Ingress." *Los Angeles Times Magazine* 25 Jan. 2004. Web. 15 Nov. 2012.

Green, Stephen. "The Changing of the Guard." *Sacramento Bee* 6 Mar. 1989: A1.

Grupp, Stanley E. ed. *Theories of Punishment.* Bloomington: University of Indiana Press, 1971.

Guccione, Jean. "2,600 Jail Inmates to be Released to Cut Costs." *Los Angeles Times* 9 March 2003: B1, B-10.

Gunnison, Robert. "Privately Run Prison Planned for Mojave." *San Francisco Chronicle* 1 August 1997: A22.

Haas, Lucien C. *California State Archives State Government Oral History Program.* Ed. Carlos Vasquez. Department of Special Collections Oral History Program. University of California, Los Angeles, 1989.

Hall, Stuart. *The Hard Road to Renewal: Thatcherism and the Crisis on the Left.* New York: Verso, 1988.

Hall, Stuart, Chas Critcher, Tony Jefferson, John Clarke, and Brian Roberts. *Policing The Crisis: Mugging, the State, and Law and Order.* New York: Holmes & Mier Publishers, 1978.

Halper, Evan. "Inmates' Medical Tab Nears $1 Billion." *Los Angeles Times* 2 June 2004: B-1.

Halper Evan & Jenifer Warren. "State Senators Take on Guards." *Los Angeles Times* 19 May 2004: A-1; A-21.

Hamptom, Jean. "The Moral Education Theory of Punishment." *Philosophy and Public Affairs* 13 (1999): 211-240.

Harding, Richard. *Private Prisons and Public Accountability.* Buckingham: Open University Press, 1997.

---. "Private Prisons." *The Handbook of Crime and Punishment.* Ed. Michael Tonry. New York: Oxford University Press, 1998. 626-658.

Harry, Jennifer. "California Ditches Plans for Privatized Prisons." *Corrections Today* 62 (2000): 20.

Harvey, David. *The Condition of Postmodernity: An Enquiry into the Origins of Cultural Change.* Cambridge, Blackwell, 1990.

Hawley, Ellis W. "Challenges to the Mixed Economy: The State and Private Enterprise." *American Choices: Social Dilemmas and Public Policy Since 1960.* Eds. Robert H. Bremner, Gary W. Reichard & Richard J. Hopkins. Columbus: Ohio State University Press, 1986.

Hayes, Joseph M. "California's Changing Prison Population." Public Policy Institute of California. July 2011 Web. 27 July 2011.

Hegel, G. W. *The Philosophy of the Right.* Trans. T. M. Knox. Oxford: Oxford University Press, 1967.

Hindelang, Michael, Michael Gottfredson, James Garofalo. *Victims of Personal Crime: An Empirical Foundation for a Theory of Personal Victimization.* Cambridge, MA: Ballinger, 1978.

Homan, Paul T. "The Pattern of the New Deal." *Political Science Quarterly* 51 (June 1936): 161-184.

Horton, K. "Slaying: Gang Statute Adds Felony Charges in Random Killing Case." *The Orange County Register* 7 Aug. 1991: B9.

Howard, John. "Private Prison Company Finds Gold in California." *Capitol Weekly* 28 Jan. 2010 Web. 9 Feb. 2010

Hunter, Robert. *Poverty.* New York : The Macmillan Company, 1904.

Institute of Governmental Studies. "California Correctional Peace Officers Association." University of California, Berkeley. 2010. Web. 28 Aug. 2011.

Jacobs, D. & R. Helms. "Toward a Political Model of Incarceration: A Time Series Examination of Multitude Explanations for Prison Admission Rates." *American Journal of Sociology* 102 (1996): 323-357.

Jammi, Nandini. Prevention Works: National Crime Prevention Council. Blog Entry. Web. 1 August 2007. Web. 25 June 2011.

Johnson, Guy. "The Negro & Crime." *Annuls of American Academy of Politics and Social Science* 271 (1941) : 93-104.

Johnson, Hans. "Illegal Immigrants," Public Policy Institute of California. Dec. 2010. Web. 23 Dec. 2010.

Joseph, Brian & Tony Saavedra. "Excess, Deprivation Mark State Prisons." *The Orange County Register* 9 Dec. 2009. Web. 14 Jan. 2010.

Kaminer, Wendy. "Federal Offense: the Politics of Crime Control." *Atlantic* June 1994: 102.

---. *It's All the Rage: Crime and Culture.* New York: Addison-Wesley Publishing, 1995.

Kaplan, Tracey. "Group Seeks Initiative to Reform California's Three Strikes Law." *The Mercury News* 14 June 2011. Web. 15 Aug. 2011.

Kappeler,Victor, Mark Blumberg, & Gary Potter. *The Mythology of Crime and Criminal Justice.* Illinois: Waveland Press, 1993.

Karmen, Andrew. "The Situation of Crime Victims in the Early Decades of the Twenty-First Century." *Visions For Change: Crime and Justice in the*

Twenty-First Century. Eds. Roslyn Muraskin and Albert R. Roberts. New Jersey: Prentice Hall, 2002, 39-51.

King, Roger. *The State in Modern Society: New Directions in Political Sociology*. London: Macmillan, 1986.

Kirschten, Dick. "Jungle Warfare." *National Journal* 3 October (1981): 1774-1786.

Klein, Malcolm W. *The American Street Gang: Its Nature, Prevalence, and Control*. New York: Oxford University Press, 1995.

Krikorian, Greg. "Three-Strike Law Has Little Effect, Study Says." *Los Angeles Times* 5 March 2004: B-1, B-10.

Krislov, Daniel. "Ideology and American Crime Policy, 1966-1996: An Exploratory Essay." *The Crime Conundrum: Essays on Criminal Justice*. Eds. Lawrence M. Friedman & George Fisher. Boulder: Westview, 1997. 107-116.

Kvaraceus, W. & W. Miller. *Delinquent Behavior: Culture and the Individual*. Washington D.C.: National Education Association, 1959.

Landman, J. H. *Human Sterilization: The History of the Sexual Sterilization Movement*. New York: Macmillian, 1932.

Lawrence, Steve. "Prison Building Boom Grows Amid Questions." *Daily News* 30 September 2004: A-1.

Lessan, G. "Macro-economic Determinants of Penal Policy: Estimating the Unemployment and Inflation Influences on Imprisonment Rate Changes in the United States, 1948-1985." *Crime, Law and Social Change* 16 (1991): 177-198.

Levy, Stephen. *California Economic Growth: Regional Market Update & Projections 1988*. Palo Alto CA, Center for the Continuing Study of the California Economy, 1988.

Levy, Stephen & Robert K. Arnold. *Special Report: The Outlook for the California Economy*. Palo Alto, California: Center For Continuing Study of the California Economy,1991.

Lewin, Tamar. "Discrepancy By Race Found in Trying Of Youths." *The New York Times* 3 February 2000: A-21

Lewis, Charlton. "The Indeterminate Sentence." *National Prison Association Proceedings*. 1900.

Lewis, Oscar. "The Culture of Poverty." *Scientific American* 215 (1966): 1-16.

Lichtenstein, Alex. *Twice the Work of Free Labor: The Political Economy of Convict Labor in the New South*. London, New York: Verso, 1996.

Lichter, Robert and Linda Lichter. *1993—The Year in Review: TV's Leading News Topics, Reporters and Political Jokes*. Washington, D.C .:Media Monitor, 1994.

Lichter, Robert and Linda Lichter. *1999—The Year in Review: TV's Leading News Topics, Reporters and Political Jokes*. Washington, D.C.:Media Monitor, 2000.

Lifsher, Marc. "Busting Into the Prison Business—Corrections Corp. of America Casts Longing Eyes on California." *The Wall Street Journal* 27 May 1998: 1.

Lilly J. R. & P. Knepper. "The Corrections-Commercial Complex." *Crime and Delinquency* 39 (1993): 150-66.

Liptak, Adam. "Supreme Court Hears Arguments on California Prison Crowding." *The New York Times* 30 Nov. 2010.

Logan, Charles. "Evaluation Research in Crime and Delinquency: A Reappraisal." *Journal of Criminal Law, Criminology and Police Science* 63 (1972): 378-387.

Lombroso, Cesare. *Crime: Its Causes and Remedies.* London: W. Heinemann,1911.

---. "Criminal Man." *The Heritage of Modern Criminology.* Ed. Sawyer F. Sylvester, Jr. Cambridge, MA: Schenkman Publishing, 1972.

Lopez, Steve. "Donations Create 'Winners.'" *Los Angeles Times* 22 May 2011: A2.

The Los Angeles Police Department. "COMPSTAT" Official Website of the Los Angeles Police Department. 2008. Web. 4 Feb. 2011.

Los Angeles Police Department.. "Discipline Report For Quarter 2: 2010." Official Website of the Los Angeles Police Department. 2010. Web. 25 June 2011.

Lowry, Dennis, Tarn Ching, Josephine Nio and Dennis W. Letner. "Setting the Public Fear Agenda: A Longitudinal Analysis of Network TV Crime Reporting, Public Perceptions of Crime, and FBI Crime Statistics." *Journal of Communication* 53.1 (March 2003) : 61-72.

Lungren, Dan. "Our Tough Law Works." *USA Today* 24 Feb. 1997: A-10.

Lustig, Jeffrey R. "The War at Home: California's Struggle to Stop the Vietnam War." *What's Going On: California and the Vietnam Era.* Eds. Eymann, Marcia A. and Charles Wollenberg. Berkeley: University of California Press, 2004. 59-82.

Macallair, Daniel. "Drug Use and Justice: An Examination of California Drug Policy Enforcement." Center on Juvenile and Criminal Justice. 2002. Web. 26 July 2011.

MacDonald, Heather. "The Illegal Alien Crime Wave." *City Journal* 14.1 (2004). Web. 21 July 2011.

Maguire, Kathleen, Ann L. Pastore, & Timothy J. Flanagan, Eds. *Sourcebook of Criminal Justice Statistics-1992.* U.S. Department of Justice, Bureau of Justice Statisitics. Washington D.C. : U.S. Department of Justice, 1993.

Mandel, Ernest. *From Class Society to Communism: An Introduction to Marxism.* Trans. Louisa Sadler. London: Billing & Sons Ltd., 1977.

Martin, Mark. "Prisons in Crisis, Governor Declares." *SFGate.com* 27 June 2006. Web. 22 Aug. 2011.

Martinson, Robert. "What Works?—Questions and Answers about Prison Reform." *The Public Interest* 35 (1974) : 22-54.

Marx, Karl. *Capital Volume I.* New York: International Publishers, 1967.

---. *The Eighteenth Brumaire of Louis Bonaparte.* New York: International Publishers, 1963.

Marx, Karl & Fredrich Engels. *The Communist Manifesto.* New York: Bantam, 1992.

---. "The German Ideology." *Marx-Engels Reader.* Ed. Robert Tucker. New York: W. W. Norton & Co., 1978.

Mathiesen Thomas. "Television, Public Space and Prison Population." *Punishment & Society* 3-1 (2001): 35-42.

Matusow, Allen J. *The Unraveling of America: A History of Liberalism in the 1960s.* New York: Harper and Row 1984.

Mauer, Marc. *Race to Incarcerate.* New York: The New Press, 1999.

Maxson, Cheryl L. "Gang Homicide: A Review and Extension of the Literature." *Homicide: A Sourcebook of Social Research.* Eds. M. Dwayne Smith & Margaret A. Zahn. Thousand Oaks, CA: Sage, 1999. 239-254.

McDonald, Douglas. "Private Penal Institutions: Moving the Boundary of Government Authority in Corrections." *Crime and Justice: An Annual Review of the Research.* Ed. Michael Tonry. Chicago: University of Chicago Press, 1992.

---. "The Costs of Operating Public and Private Correctional Facilities." *Private Prisons and the Public Interest.* Ed. D. C. McDonald. New Brunswick, NJ: Rutgers University Press, 1990. 92-106.

---. "Public Imprisonment By Private Means: The Re-emergence of Private Prisons and Jails in the United States, The United Kingdom, and Australia." *British Journal of Criminology* 34 (1994): 29-43.

McDonnell, Patrick. "Union Membership Increases in the State." *Los Angeles Times* 8 Sept. 2009: A-9.

McGee, Michael Calvin. "The 'Ideograph': A Link Between Rhetoric and Ideology." *Quarterly Journal of Speech* 66 (1980) : 335-347.

McGirr, Lisa. *Suburban Warriors: The Origins of the New American Right.* Princeton: Princeton University Press, 2001.

McGreevy, Patrick. "California Needs More Time to Fix Prison Overcrowding, Report Says." *Los Angeles Times* 6 Aug. 2011. Web. 1 Sept. 2011.

Mehta, Seema. "California Briefing: Dropouts Cost the State $1.1 billion, Study Finds." *Los Angeles Times* 24 Sept. 2009: A-14.

Miller, Jerome. *Search & Destroy: African American Males in the Criminal Justice System.* Cambridge: Cambridge University Press, 1996.

Menninger, Karl. *The Crime of Punishment.* New York: Viking Press, 1968.

Merl, Jean. "Study Finds Rampant Illiteracy in L.A. County." *Los Angeles Times* 9 September 2004: B-1; B-8.

Messinger, Sheldon, John E. Berecochea, David Rauma, Richard A. Berk. "The Foundations of Parole in California." *Law and Society Review* 19-1 (1985) : 69-106.

Meyerson, Harold. "Striking Home." *Los Angeles Times* 7 Dec. 2003: M-1; M-3.

Mitford, Jessica. *Kind and Usual Punishment: The Prison Business.* New York: Random House, 1973.

Mohan, Geoffrey & Ann Simmons. "Diversity Spoken in 39 Languages." *Los Angeles Times* 16 June 2004,: A1, A24.

Morris, Norval. *The Future of Imprisonment.* Chicago: University of Chicago Press, 1974.

Morris, Terrence. "Social Values and the Criminal Act." *The Nation* 4 July 1959.

Morain, Dan. "Davis Gets More Money From Prison Guards." *Los Angeles Times* 30 Mar. 2002 : A1; A13.

---. "Guards Union Spreads Its Wealth." *Los Angeles Times* 20 May 2004: A1; A24-5.

---. "Guards' Raises Could be Higher Than Expected." *Los Angeles Times* 4 March 2004: B-6.

---. "Potent Prison Guards Union Facing Challenges to Status Quo." *Los Angeles Times* 17 Jan. 2004: B-1.

---. "Prison Budget Comes Up $544 Million Short." *Los Angeles Times* 1 Nov. 2003: B-8.

---. "Private Prison Deal Voided." *Los Angeles Times* 4 Feb. 2005: B-3.

---."Private Prisons? A Sweet Deal For Some." *Sacramento Bee* 7 Jan. 2010 Web. 26 Jan. 2010.

Morgan-Besecker, Terri. "Crime of Punishment?" *The Times Leader* 1 March 2009 Web. 2 August 2011.

Moynihan, Patrick. "The Negro Family: The Case For National Action." *The Moynihan Report & the Politics of Controversy*. Eds. Lee Rainwater & William Yancy. Cambridge: MIT Press, 1967.

Munson, Wayne. *All Talk: The Talkshow in Media Culture*. Philadelphia: Temple University Press, 1993.

Murray, Charles. *Losing Ground: American Social Policy, 1950-1980*. New York: Basic Books, 1984.

Nimmo, Dan. *Newsgathering in Washington: A Study of Political Communication*. New York: Atherton Press, 1964.

Offe, Claus. *Contradictions of the Welfare State*. Cambridge: MIT Press, 1984.

Office of the Attorney General, State of California, Department of Justice. "California Gun Sales Up Over 30% During First Six Months of 1999." News Release. Web. 28 Sept. 1999.

Office of the Governor. "Prison Overcrowding State of Emergency Proclamation." California.gov. 2010. Web. 30 Aug. 2011.

Office of the Governor. "Prison Populations & Recidivism." Dec. 2010. Web. 20 Dec. 2010.

Office of the Secretary, State of California. "Department of Corrections and Rehabilitation Action Taken to Reform California Prison System & in Support of the Special Legislative Session." California Dpartment of Corrections & Rehabilitation. Sept. 2005. Web. 20 Aug. 2011.

Owens, John R., Edmond Costantini, & Louis F. Weschler. *California Politics and Parties*. London: The Macmillan Company, 1970.

Own, Henry & Charles L. Schultze, Eds. *Setting National Priorities: The Next Ten Years*. Washington D.C.: The Brookings Institution, 1976.

Packard, Vance. *The Waste Makers*. New York: Pocket Books, 1969.

Page, Joshua. *The Toughest Beat; Politics, Punishment, and the Prison Officers Union in California*. New York: Oxford Press, 2011.

Page, Joshua. "Victims and Their Guards." *Los Angeles Times* 15 June 2011 : A28.

Parenti, Michael. *Lockdown America: Police and Prisons in the Age of Crisis*. New York: Verso, 1999.

Pedroncelli, Rich. "Schwarzenegger Wants Special Session to Tackle Prison Changes." *USA Today* 26 June 2006. Web. 21 Aug. 2011.

Pens, Dan. "The California Prison Guards' Union." *The Celling of America: An Inside Look at the U.S. Prison Industry*. Eds. Daniel Burton-Rose, Dan Pens & Paul Wright. Monroe, Maine: Common Courage Press, 1998. 134-139.

Pillsbury, Samuel. "Why Are We Ignored? The Peculiar Place of Experts in the Current Debate About Crime and Justice." *Criminal Law Bulletin* 31:4 (1995): 306-336.

Pittman, Genevra. "Black Men Survive Longer in Prison Than Out: Study." *Reuters* 14 July 2011. Web. 4 Sept. 2011.

Polsky, Andrew J. *The Rise of the Therapeutic State.* Princeton: Princeton University Press, 1991.
Pooley, Eric. "Frontier Justice: Fed up New Yorkers Are Taking the Law Into Their Own Hands." *New York* July 1990: 32-40.
Pratt, John. *Penal Populism.* New York, Routledge: 2007.
"Prison Guard Clout Endures." Editorial. *Los Angeles Times* 1 April 2002: B10.
Public Policy Institute of California, "Poverty in California." March 2009. Web. 23 Dec. 2010.
Radzinowicz, Sir Leon. "Penal Regressions." *Cambridge Law Journal* 50 (1991) : 422-444.
Ronald Reagan. Address. Meeting of the National Sheriffs Association, Las Vegas, Nevada, 19 June, 1967.
---. Address. Inaugural Message of Ronald Reagan, Governor. Sacramento, California: Jan. 1967.
---. *Economic Report of the Governor: 1968.* Sacramento, California: State Capitol, 1968.
Reed, Deborah. *California's Rising Income Inequality: Causes and Concerns.* San Francisco: Public Policy Institute of California, 1999.
Reeves, Jimmie L. & Richard Campbell. *Cracked Coverage: Television News and the Anticocaine Crusade, and the Reagan Legacy.* Durham, NC: Duke University Press, 1994.
Reiman, Jeffrey H. *The Rich Get Richer and the Poor Get Prison: Ideology, Class, and Criminal Justice.* New York: John Wiley & Sons, 1998.
Reiterman, Tim. "Scathing Report on Prison Doctors." *Los Angeles Times* 11 Aug. 2004: B-1, B-7.
Reith, John W. "The Mineral Fuels." *California and the Southwest.* Ed. Clifford M. Zierer New York: John Wiley & Sons, 1956.
Research & Forecasts, INC., with Ardy Friedberg. *America Afraid: How Fear of Crime Changes the Way We Live.* New York: Nal Books, 1983.
Michael Riley. "Arizona Shootings Trigger Surge in Glock Sales Amid Fear of Ban." *Bloomberg* 11 Jan. 2011. Web.
Riveland, Chase. "Prison Management Trends, 1975-2025." *Prisons: Crime and Justice.* Eds. Michael Tonry & Joan Petersilia. Chicago: University of Chicago Press, 1999. 163-203.
RF Communications. *Blood Money: The Killing of Two Award-Winning Programs.* Videotape. Sacramento, 2002.
Roberts, Julian V. & Loretta J. Stalens. *Public Opinion, Crime, and Criminal Justice.* New York: Westview Press, 1997.
Rodriguez, Gregory. "Will White Influx Put Down Roots in L.A. Core?" *Los Angeles Times* 19 July 2004 : B-11.
Rosen, David, David Wohl, and Victor Schoenbach. "All-Cause and Cause-Specific Mortality Among Black and White North Carolina State Prisoners, 1995-2005." *Annals of Epidemiology* 21 (2011) : 719-726
Rothman, David J. *Conscience and Convenience: The Asylum and its Alternatives in Progressive America.* Boston: Little, Brown and Company, 1980.
---. *The Discovery of the Aylum: Social Order and Disorder in the New Republic.* Boston: Little Brown & Co., 1990.
---. "Prisons: The Failure Model." *The Nation* Dec. 1974: 656-7.

Rubin, Joel, Andrew Blankstein, Scott Gold. "LAPD's Change in Focus: The King Video Ushered Police int a YouTube World." *Los Angeles Times* 3 March 2011:A-1; A-10.

Rubin, Joel & Robert Faturechi. "Killing in L.A. Drops to 1967 Levels." *Los Angeles Times* 27 December 2010: A-1.

Schlosser, Eric. "The Prison-Industrial Complex." *The Atlantic Monthly* 282:6 (1998) : 51-77.

Schneider, Gregory L. *Conservative Century: From Reaction to Revolution.* Maryland: Rowan & Littlefield, 2009.

Schrag, Peter. *Paradise Lost: California's Experience, America's Future.* New York: New Press, 1998.

Scott, James C. *Seeing the Like the State: How Certain Schemes to Improve the Human Condition Have Failed.* New Haven: Yale University Press, 1998.

Silberman, Charles E. *Criminal Violence, Criminal Justice.* New York: Random House, 1978.

Simon, Jonathon. "Governing Through Crime." *The Crime Conundrum: Essays on Criminal Justice.* Eds. George Fisher & Lawrence Friedman. New York: Westview Press, 1997. 171-190.

Sivanandan, Ambalavaner. "Globalism and the Left." *Race & Class* 40-2/3 (1998/99) : 5-19.

Skelton, George. "Surrogates Just Won't Do; In Budget Crisis, the State Needs Davis to Lead." *Los Angeles Times* 12 June 2003: B-10.

Smith, Paul. *Millennial Dreams.* New York: Verso, 1997.

Snyder, A.,"On the Self-Perpetuating Nature of Social Stereotypes." *Cognitive Processes in Stereotyping and Intergroup Behavior.* Ed. D. Hamilton. New Jersey: Lawrence Erlbaum Associates, 1981.

Southern California Library. "Fear of a Gang Planet: An Interview with Mike Davis." *Without Fear. . .Claiming Safe Communities Without Sacrificing Ourselves* 26 April 2007 : 44-53.

Sparks, Richard. "Can Prisons be Legitimate?: Penal Politics, Privatization, and the Timelessness of an Old Idea." *British Journal of Criminology* 34 (1994) : 14-29.

SpearIt. "Mental Illness in Prison: Inmate Rehabilitation & Correctional Officers in Crisis." *Berkeley Journal of Criminal Law* 14 (2009) : 227-302.

Spiro, Shimon E. & Ephraim Yuchtman-Yaar. *Evaluating the Welfare State: Social and Political Perspectives.* New York: Academic Press, 1983.

Spitzer, Steven. "Toward a Marxian Theory of Deviance." *Social Problems* 22 (1975): 638-651.

Staff. "Big Pay-Back: Davis Makes SOP to Prison Guards' Union." *The San Diego Union-Tribune* 19 March 2002: B-8.

Staff. "Davis Proposes to Cut Five Prisons in State Budget." *Associated Press State & Local Wire* 15 March 2002. A-1.

Staff. "Pound Foolish: Prison System in State of Emergency." *The San Diego Union Tribune* 3 May 2004, B-6.

Staff. "Prisons Are Not Enough." *Los Angeles Times* 7 July 1999: B-6.

Staff. "Prison Guards' Clout Difficult to Challenge." *San Francisco Chronicle* 2 Feb. 2004: A-1

Staff. "Writing Bad Law." *American Lawyer Media, L.P.* 31 (May 1994) : 7.

Stanford Research Institute. *The California Economy, 1947-1980.* Menlo Park, California: Stanford Research Institute, 1960.

Starr, Kevin. "Scorning Public Life Is Shameful." *Los Angeles Times* 21 Sept. 2003: M-2.

State of California. *Economic Report of the Governor: 1990*. Sacramento, California: Office of the State of California,1990.

State of California. *Economic Report of the Governor: 1995*. Sacramento, California: Office of the State of California, 1995.

State of California, Little Hoover Commission. *Beyond Bars Correctional Reforms to Lower Prison Costs and Reduce Crime*. Sacramento, California 1998.

"State Prisons' Revolving Door: Judge's Last-Chance Demand." Editorial, *Los Angeles Times* 23 July 2004 : B-12.

Steinburg, Laurence. "The Juvenile Psychopath: Fads, Fictions, and Fact." *Perspectives on Crime and Justice: 2000-2001 Lecture Series*. Mar. (2002): 35-64.

Steinberg, Stephen. *The Ethnic Myth: Race, Ethnicity, and Class in America*. Boston: Beacon Press, 1989.

Stenmetz, George. *Regulating the Social: The Welfare State and Local Politics in Imperial Germany*. Princeton: Princeton University Press, 1993.

Stone, Randolf N. "The Criminal Justice System: Unfair and Ineffective." Chicago Assembly on Crime and Community Safety. Nov. 19-20, Chicago, 1992.

Street, Paul. "Color Blind: Prisons and the New American Racism." *Prison Nation: The Warehousing of America's Poor*. Eds. Tara Herivel & Paul Wright. New York: Routlege, 2003.

Summer, Lawrence H. "The U.S. Current Account Deficit and the Global Economy." The 2004 Per Jacobsson Lecture. Washington D.C., 3 Oct. 2004.

Surette, Ray. *Media, Crime and Criminal Justice: Images and Realities*. Pacific Grove, CA: Brooks/Cole Publishing Co., 1992.

Sutherland, E. H. *Principles of Criminology*. Philadelphia: Lippincott, 1939.

Talbot, Emily. "Social Science Instruction in Colleges." *American Social Science Journal* 22 (1887) : 12-14.

Tan, Kopin. "Private Prison Companies Have a Lock on the Business." *The Wall Street Journal* 25 Oct. 2009. Web. 5 Jan. 2010.

Tannenbaum, Frank. *Crime and the Community*. New York: Columbia University Press, 1938.

"The Indeterminate Sentence." *Atlantic Monthly* 108 (1911) : 330-331.

Therlault, Denis C. "California Finds That Prisons Aren't So Easy To Cut." *San Jose Mercury News* 23 March 2010.

Thomas, Charles. *Correctional Privatization: The Issues and the Evidence*. Proc. of a Conference on the Privatization of Correctional Services. July 1996. Toronto Canada.

Thomas, Charles & Charles Logan. "The Development, Present Status and Future Potential of Correctional Privatization in America." *Privatizing Correctional Institutions*. Eds. Gary Bowman, Simon Hakim, and Paul Seidenstat. N.J.: Transaction, 1993. 219-21.

Thompson, Don. "Gov's Deal Lifts Vacation Cap for CA Prison Guards." *Associated Press* 19 April 2011. Web. 20 April 2011.

Thompson, Jeff. "Prisons for Profit." *Peacekeeper* 5.2 (1987) : 22.

Tonry, Michael. *Sentencing Matters*. New York: Oxford University Press, 1996.

---. *Malign Neglect—Race, Crime, and Punishment in America.* New York: Oxford University Press, 1995.

"Total Population Estimates in California." CARAND.org RAND California: California Statistics. RAND Corporation, n.d. Web 13 May 2010

Tran, Mai. "14 Blades Are Found Buried in O.C. Park After Boy's Foot Is Cut." *Los Angeles Times* 2 August 2005: B-3.

United States. Attorney General. *Survey of Release Procedures: Vol 2 Probation.* Washington, D. C. 1939.

United States. Bureau of the Census. *Historical Statistics of the United States, Colonial Times to 1970.* Washington, D.C.: Government Printing Office, 1975.

United States. Department of Health and Human Services. *Social Security Bulletin, Annual Statistical Supplement, 1986.* Washington D.C.: The Brookings Institution, 1986.

United States, President's Task Force. *Victims of Crime.* Washington D.C., 1982.

United States. *The Challenge of Crime in a Free Society: A Report by the President's Commission on Law Enforcement and Administration of Justice.* Washington D.C.: U.S. Government Printing Office, February 1967.

United Way. *Population Estimates and Components of Change: Los Angeles County Race and Ethnic Groups.* Los Angeles: California, 1998.

United Way. *Population Estimates and Components of Change: Los Angeles County Language Spoken at Home and Ability to Speak English.* Los Angeles: California, 1998.

U.S. Attorney General. *Survey of Release Procedures. Vol. 2: Probation.* Washington, D.C., 1939.

U.S. Bureau of the Census. *Historical Statistics of the United States, Colonial Times to 1970.* Washington, D.C.: Government Printing Office, 1975.

U.S. Bureau of Justice Statistics, "The Number of Adults in Correctional Population has Been Increasing." Washington D.C.: Department of Justice. 2003. Web. 22 July 2011.

U.S. President's Task Force. *Victims of Crime.* Washington D.C., 1982.

USA/CNN/Gallup Poll. "Crime in America." 28 October 1993.

Villmoare, Edwin & Virginia V. Neto, *Victim Appearances at Sentencing Hearings Under the California Victims' Bill of Rights*, U.S. Department of Justice: National Institute of Justice. Washington, D. C.: U.S. Government Printing Office, 1987.

Wacquant, Loic. "Deadly Symbiosis: When Ghetto and Prison Meet and Mesh." *Mass Imprisonment: Social Causes and Consequences.* Ed. David Garland. London: Sage, 2001. 82-120.

---. "The New 'Peculiar Institution': On the Prison as Surrogate Ghetto." *Theoretical Criminology* 4.3 (2000): 377-89.

---. *Prisons of Poverty.* Minneapolis: University of Minnesota Press, 2001.

Walmsley, Roy. "World Prison Population List: Sixth Edition." *International Centre for Prison Studies.* Kings College London. 2005. Web. 12 July 2006.

Walters, Dan. *The New California: Facing the 21st Century.* Sacramento: California Journal Press, 1992.

---. "Prisons Still Eat Into California Budget." *Sacramento Bee* 11 Jan 2010.

Walton, Isis N. "The Prison Industrial Complex: Contributing Mechanisms and Collateral Consequences of Disproportionality on African American Communities." *Disproportionate Minority Contact: Current Issues and Policies.* Ed. Nicolle Parsons-Pollard. Durham, NC: Carolina Academic Press, 2011.

Walton, Paul & Jock Young. *The New Criminology Revisited.* New York: St. Martin's Press, 1998.

Wang, Andrew. "Feeling Safer? Violent Crime Down Overall." *Los Angeles Times* 9 June 2005: B-2.

Warren, Jenifer. "Relatives of Dead Inmate to Sue State." *Los Angeles Times* 30 Sept. 2004: B-5.

---. "Takeover of State Prisons is Threatened." *Los Angeles Times* 21 July 2004: A-1, 21.

---. "Panel Calls Prison Policies Costly Failure." *Los Angeles Times* 14 Nov. 2003: B-1.

Welch, Michael. *Corrections: A Critical Approach.* New York: McGraw-Hill, 2004.

"What California's Prison Downsizing Might Represent for Private Detention Contractors," Prod. Leslie Berestein-Rojas. *Multi-American*, NPR. 89.3, Los Angeles. 23 May 2011.

"What is the GEO Group?" Prod. Aarti Shahani. *NPR News Investigations*, NPR. 89.3, Los Angeles. 25 March 2011.

Whitney, Charles, Marilyn Fritzler, Steen Jones, Sharon Mazzarella & Lana Rakow. "Geographic and Source Bias in Television News 1982-4." *Journal of Electronic Broadcasting and Electronic Media* 33.2 (1989): 159-174.

Weiss, R. "Repatriating Low-Wage Work: The Political Economy of Prison Labor Reprivatization in the Postindustrial United States." *Criminology* 39 (2001): 253-291.

Wells, David. *Marxism and the Modern State: An Analysis of Fetishism in Capitalist Society.* New Jersey: Humanities Press, 1981.

Wilkins, Leslie T. *Evaluation of Penal Measures.* New York: Random House, 1969.

Williams, Carol J. "State Gets Two Years to Cut 43,000 From Prisons." *Los Angeles Times* 5 Aug. 2009 A-1, A-19.

Willrich, Michael. "The Two Percent Solution: Eugenic Jurisprudence and the Socialization of American Law, 1900-1930." *Law and History* 16 (1998): 63-111.

Wison, James, Q. "Redefining Equality: The Liberation of Mickey Kaus." *The Public Interest* 109 (1992) : 101-108.

---. *Thinking About Crime.* New York: Basic Books, 1975.

Wilson, James Q. & R.J. Herrnstein. *Crime and Human Nature.* New York: Simon & Schuster, 1986.

Wines, Frederick. *Punishment and Reformation: A Study of the Penitentiary System.* New York : T. Y. Crowell, 1919.

Wilson, Pete. "'Three Strikes' Law Truly Makes California Safer." *Los Angeles Daily News* 9 Mar. 1997: V-3.

Wright, Paul. "Slaves of the State." *The Celling of America: An Inside look at the U.S. Prison Industry.* Eds. Daniel Burton-Rose, Dan Pens & Paul Wright. Monroe, Maine: Common Courage Press, 1998.

Wright, William & Michael Dixon. "Community Prevention and Treatment of Juvinile Delinquency: A Review of Evaluation Studies." *Journal of Research in Crime and Delinquency* 14 (1977): 35-67.

Zarembo, Alan. "Prisoners Face High Death Rate After Release." *Los Angeles Times* 11 Jan. 2007: A-19.

Zimring, Franklin. "The New Politics of Criminal Justice: Of 'Three Strikes,' Truth-in-Sentencing, and Megan's Laws." *Perspectives on Crime and Justice: 1999-2000 Lecture Series*. 4 (2001).

---. "Populism, Democratic Government, and the Decline of Expert Authority: Some Reflections on 'Three Strikes' in California." *Pacific Law Journal* 28 (1996).

---. Professor of Law, Earl Warren Legal Institute, Testimony to the Little Hoover Commission, 26 June 1997, Sacramento, California.

---. "Three Strikes, You're Out: Crime in California." *The Economist* 15 Jan. (1994): 30.

Zimring, Franklin E. & Gordon Hawkins. "The Growth of Imprisonment in California." *British Journal of Criminology* 34 (1994): 83-96.

Zimring, Franklin E. & Gordon Hawkins. *Incapacitation: Penal Confinement and the Restraint of Crime*. New York: Oxford University Press, 1995.

Zimring, Franklin E., Sam Kamin & Gordon Hawkins, *Crime & Punishment in California: The Impact of Three Strikes and You're Out*. Berkeley: Institute of Governmental Studies Press, University of California, Berkeley, 1999.

Index

About the Book

What explains the boom in private prisons—especially since the record of privatization for rehabilitating prisoners and saving taxpayer dollars is, at best, mixed? Karyl Kicenski examines the privatization of California state prisons to illuminate the forces that shape and distort our criminal justice policies.

Tracing the growth of private prisons from 1980 to the current day, Kicenski explores the role of political and economic factors, as well as the impact of changing public attitudes toward crime and governance. The result is a clear set of lessons for the uneasy partnership between public safety and for-profit enterprise.

Karyl Kicenski is professor of communication studies at College of the Canyons.